Black America Series

Natchitoches Parish

Cane River National Heritage Area

This project was funded by the Cane River National Heritage Area Commission.

On the Front Cover: Farm Security Administration photographer Marion Post shot this image of farm laborers. Taken in 1942 somewhere in the Cane River region, this photograph represents a typical sight seen throughout the parish. (Courtesy of the Library of Congress.)

On the Back Cover: Local photographer John Thomas Guillet captured this image of members of the African American community as they marched through Jackson Square. The area that defined "the Square" once included much of the northwestern portion of the city. Today this area represents the heart of the black community. (Courtesy of John Thomas Guillet.)

BLACK AMERICA SERIES

NATCHITOCHES PARISH

Rolonda D. Teal

ARCADIA PUBLISHING

ISBN 978-0-7385-5269-9

Published by Arcadia Publishing
Charleston, South Carolina

Printed in the United States of America

Library of Congress Catalog Card Number: 2007927469

For all general information contact Arcadia Publishing at:
Telephone 843-853-2070
Fax 843-853-0044
E-mail sales@arcadiapublishing.com
For customer service and orders:
Toll-Free 1-888-313-2665

Visit us on the Internet at www.arcadiapublishing.com

This book is dedicated to the memory of all the descendants of the African diaspora whose feet touched the soil of Louisiana, particularly in Natchitoches Parish.

A special dedication goes to Shelia Richmond, who first introduced me to the community of Jackson Square.

Contents

Acknowledgments

There are numerous people who contributed invaluable time, research, and local historical knowledge toward the completion of this book; I apologize now if I have left anyone out.

I wish to thank Dr. Nancy Morgan and the Cane River National Heritage Area Commission and superintendent Laura Gates with the Cane River Creole National Historical Park for providing the essential support needed to make this vision a reality. To Carla Cowles-Whitfield, I say thanks for having the vision to initiate the collection of more than 100 interviews of African Americans in Natchitoches Parish. Many of the quotes and background information accompanying the photographs come directly from those interviews.

The African American Oral History Project began in 2001 and combined forces with the Ben D. Johnson Foundation in a grassroots effort to document the lives of African Americans. This project was funded by the Cane River Creole National Historical Park, the Cane River National Heritage Area Commission, and the National Park Service's Lower Mississippi Delta Regional Initiatives.

I would also like to acknowledge Dr. Janis Hutchinson, who served as the principal investigator in providing a synopsis of the entire collection. The resulting manuscript, *African Americans in Natchitoches, Louisiana: An Oral Remembrance*, is expected to be completed by the end of 2007.

I am extremely grateful to the Prints and Photographs Division of the Library of Congress, whose professionalism is much appreciated.

Many local citizens and organizations enthusiastically provided images and stories to go along with them. Specifically, I wish to thank Mary Linn Wernet and Sonny Carter from the Cammie Henry Research Center located on the campus of Northwestern State University. Their familiarity with the historical collections made my job much easier.

To all the community members who shared with me telephone numbers, old memories, and their time, I say thanks. Special thanks goes to Erdis Beaudion, Albert Coles, Robert "Bobby" DeBlieux, Terrel Delphin, John Thomas Guillet, Ida Ruth Mitchell-Hamilton, Ambrose Hertzog, Patricia Ward-Hoover, Alma Johnson, Billye Sue Johnson, Councilwoman Sylvia Morrow, Edward Ward, Marvin and Clara Toussaint, Burton and Dr. Sue Weaver, and the descendants of John Lewis Sr.

Finally, to all the Natchitoches history enthusiasts who have provided previous research and added to the collection of information available on African Americans in the region: I wish to thank Patricia Antley, Caroline Breedlove, Dr. Susan Dollar, Sandra Prud'homme Haynie, Dr. Bennie Keel, Dr. Dayna Lee, Dr. Ann Patton Malone, Dr. Christina Miller, and Carol Petravage.

Introduction

Natchitoches is one of the longest-settled areas in Louisiana. Founded in 1713 by French Canadian Louis Juchereau de St. Denis, Natchitoches served as a French military site and trading post and also provided a way to block Spain's eastward expansion. Red River, later known as the Cane River, passed through Natchitoches, providing a water route for trade. Fort St. Jean Baptiste des Natchitoches was established here in 1716 to secure trade with the Natchitoches tribe, a branch of the Caddo Nation. It is at this Colonial fort that we find the earliest records of enslaved Africans in the parish.

The 1722 census of the fort clearly illustrates the diversity of the colony in its formative years. The census lists 20 black slaves and 8 Native American slaves among a total population of 54 people. By 1766, about 40 percent of the non–Native American population of Natchitoches was African or Franco-African slaves, making almost half of the adult population in Natchitoches African in origin.

Following the 1803 Louisiana Purchase, when the Colonial territory was acquired by the United States, the Cane River region became even more ethnically diverse. During the period 1815–1835, the region experienced an influx of thousands of Americans from the poorly developed lands of the lower South. They moved into the Mississippi and Red River Valleys in search of new lands for cotton production, often bringing their slaves with them. These migrant slaves had been raised in an English environment, which was quite different from the French and Spanish cultures common in Louisiana. It is with this influx that the local enslaved population became exposed to the religious concepts of Protestantism and the Baptist Church. Several of the regional plantations had brush arbors where the enslaved population could worship. Later, church structures were built on-site so that laborers would not have to leave the plantation to attend services.

The early 18th century brought changes in plantation living with the invention of mechanized spinning and weaving machinery in England. This new equipment led to an increase in demand for cotton, which was primarily grown and exported to Europe from the southern United States. Plantations increased their slave holdings, and African Americans flooded the state of Louisiana from places like Georgia, Alabama, Mississippi, and North Carolina. By the onset of the Civil War, cotton produced with slave labor comprised 60 percent of all goods exported from America. This period of mass production is commonly called the era of "King Cotton."

During the post-emancipation era, there was no redistribution of land or wealth to former slaves. New labor regulations were enacted before the end of the Civil War requiring free blacks to work. They were free to choose their employers but had to complete one-year contracts.

While the labor contracts were initially negotiated by the Freedmen's Bureau, by 1867, two-thirds of freedmen did not want assistance from the bureau in negotiating contracts. Under the contract system, overseers closely supervised freedmen, and the plantation continued to be the basic unit of production. Many freedmen found themselves working for their prior owners and living in the quarters they had lived in while enslaved.

African Americans took this time in the late 19th century to build churches and educational institutions that were often placed on or near the plantations on which they had worked while enslaved. In the early 20th century, schools and churches were located on plantations throughout the parish. For example, St. Savior Baptist Church was both a school and church from the 1920s to the 1950s and was connected with Future Plantation. St. Andrew and St. Mary Baptist Churches were associated with Melrose Plantation, and St. Paul and Morning Star Baptist Churches were connected to Oakland Plantation.

During and after the Reconstruction era (1865–1877), black churches were often used to house schools for African Americans until separate buildings could be constructed, usually on donated church land. St. Matthew Baptist Church offered classes to students in the early 1900s, while St. Andrew Church opened its doors for the education of local children in the 1940s.

The Natchitoches Parish School Board collaborated with several churches and private landowners who donated or sold land, at a small fee, for the development of public schools. In 1939, according to Natchitoches Parish School Board records, St. Matthew Baptist Church donated land for the construction of St. Matthew Public School. Eight years later, the three-room schoolhouse became St. Matthew Senior High. After the 1964 Civil Rights Act and court-ordered school integration in 1968, educational systems in the parish were gradually culturally diversified. According to Lawrence Vaughn, "Some plantation community schools closed because of integration."

The civil rights movement of the 1960s produced local African American community leaders, such as Ben Johnson and Dr. Edward Johnson, who helped organize a local chapter of the National Association for the Advancement of Colored People (NAACP). Most of the men's work was done in secrecy since the NAACP was outlawed in Louisiana. Other community leaders like Sylvia Morrow and Robert Jackson helped create the Voters and Civic League, which was organized to protect voter registration participants. These types of organizations were instrumental in facilitating a peaceful transition from segregation to integration in this region.

Enslaved Africans constituted some of the earliest settlers of the area, and since that time, their descendants have made significant contributions to the economic and social development of the region. Thousands of African Americans have been involved in agricultural production in the parish. Service in all branches of the armed forces illuminates the military contributions Natchitoches' African Americans have made toward protecting the freedoms of our country. The artistic contributions of folk painter Clementine Hunter, especially her documentation of plantation culture in Louisiana, exposed Natchitoches to worldwide attention. What has resulted is a present-day Natchitoches that is fast becoming a tourism mecca because of the nexus of rich cultural heritages that form the character of the region.

One

From Sun Up 'til Sun Down

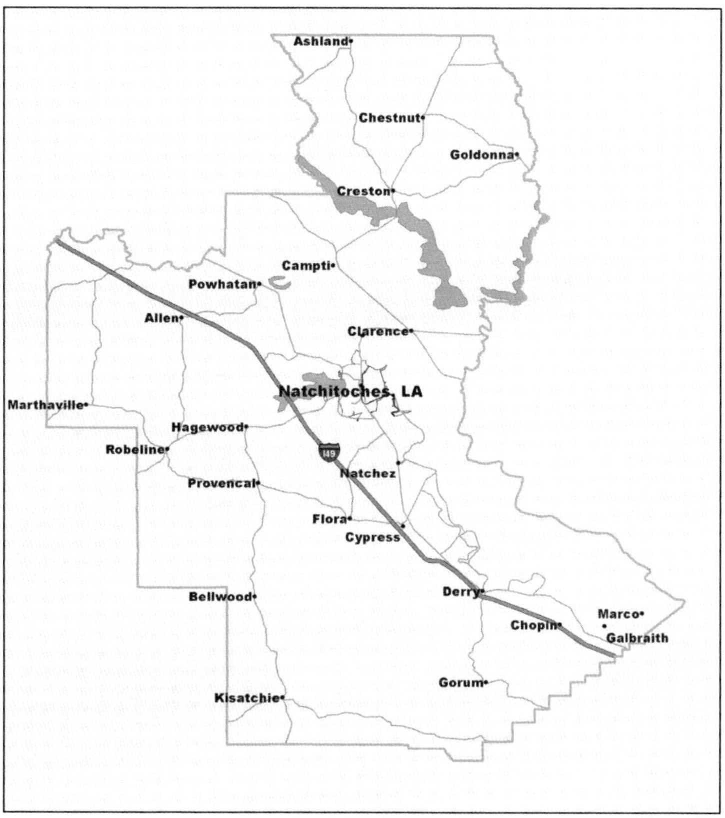

Natchitoches Parish, historically home to many small and large plantations, is today a quaint region nestled in the northwestern portion of Louisiana. Popular with tourists, the parish encompasses approximately 2,000 square miles and has a population of about 39,000 residents. This map illustrates the location of some of the plantations, rivers, and other sites that are discussed in this manuscript. (Courtesy of Michael Fontenot, Louisiana Regional Folklife Program.)

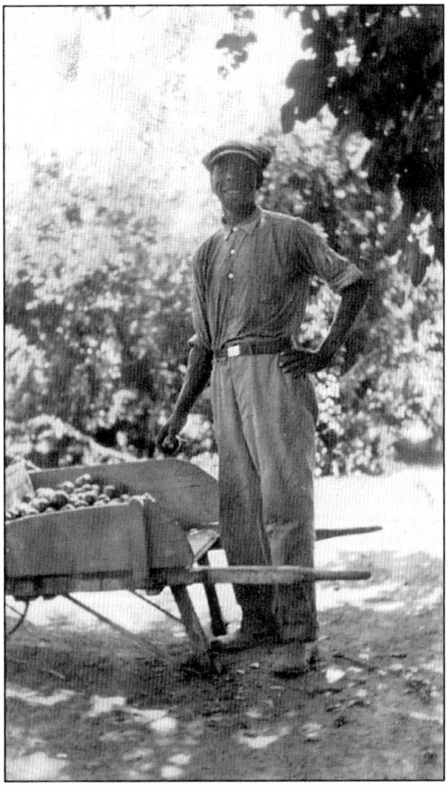

Vegetable harvesting occurred during spring and fall months. Potatoes were often stored in "potato houses" so that they were available year-round. A young man from Melrose Plantation gathers potatoes for a meal that day or for storage until the lean winter months. (Courtesy of Cammie Henry Research Center, Northwestern State University.)

Two young boys perform some chores on Melrose Plantation. Baskets such as the one shown were used for carrying fruit, flowers, and other small items. (Courtesy of Cammie Henry Research Center, Northwestern State University.)

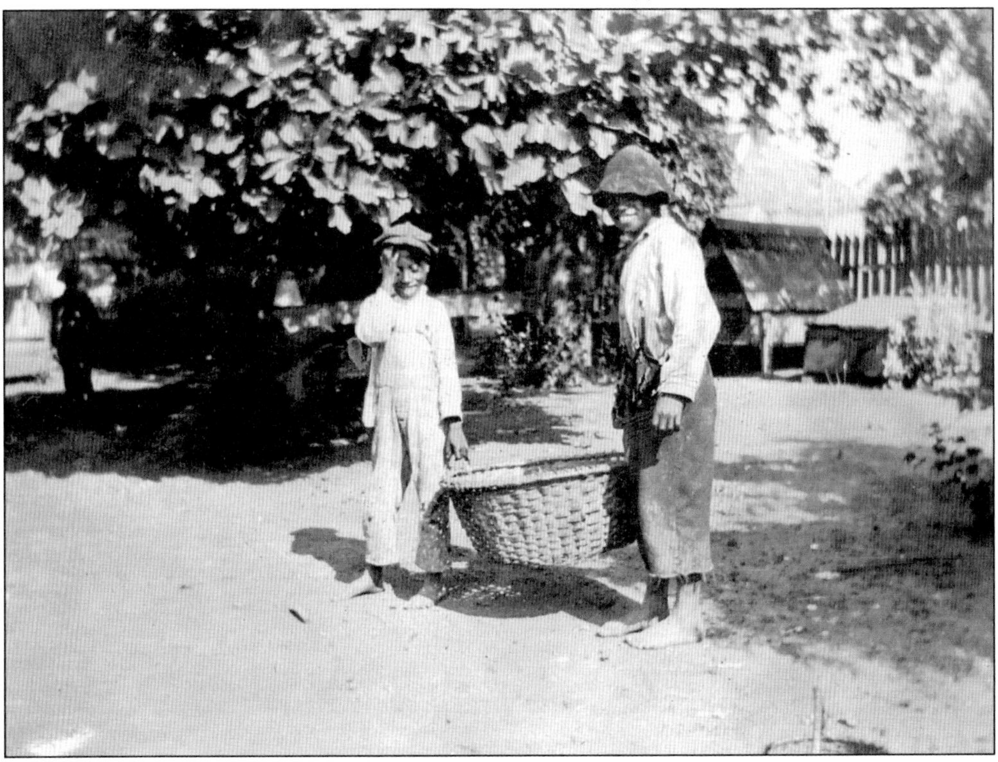

After picking apples from the orchard, Henry Tylon's son carries the load back to the main house at Melrose Plantation. Note the traditional African way of transporting heavy objects on top of the head. (Courtesy of Cammie Henry Research Center, Northwestern State University.)

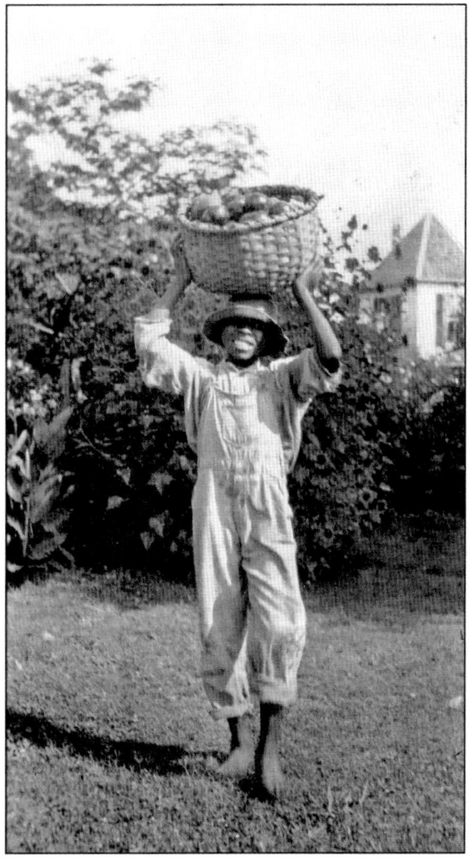

Female children often had the responsibility of providing primary care for younger siblings while their parents were away at work. This sense of responsibility sometimes extended into adulthood. John Winston credits his older sisters for affording several of their younger siblings a chance to further their educations. (Courtesy of Ambrose Hertzog Jr.)

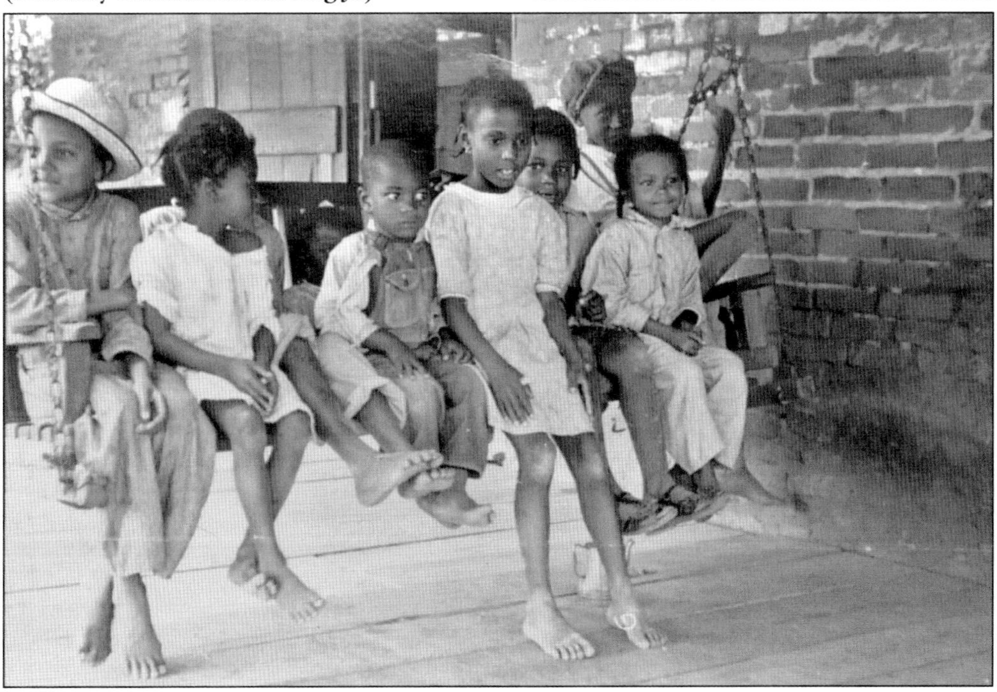

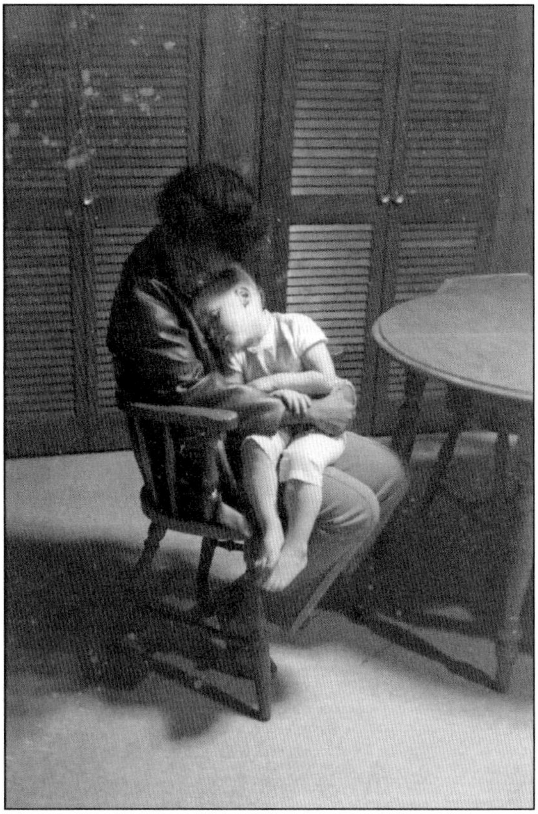

This casual photograph captured Ruby Ann Page seated with Burton D. Weaver III in her lap, both asleep. Young African American females also helped care for and became the playmates of white children. As youths, they were allowed to develop mutually caring relationships, yet these relationships often changed as they grew older and adapted to the social norms. (Courtesy of the Weaver family.)

By the time youths reached adulthood, they were ready to enter the fields with mule labor. Farming continued to be the main profession of many rural residents in the region during the first decades of the 20th century. (Courtesy of Cammie Henry Research Center, Northwestern State University.)

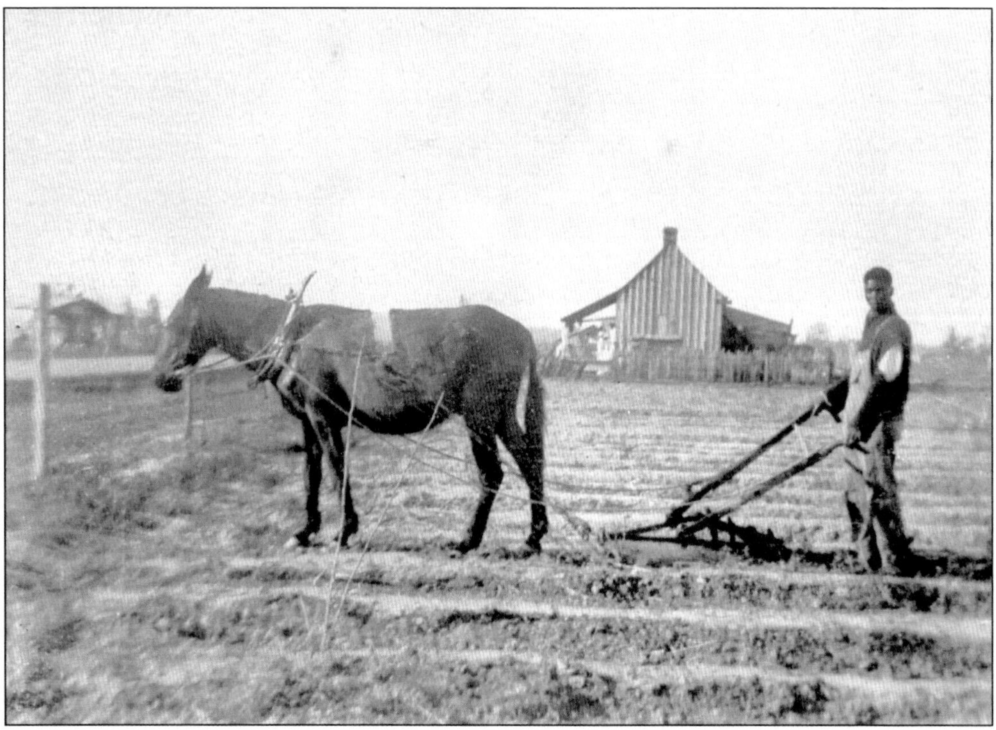

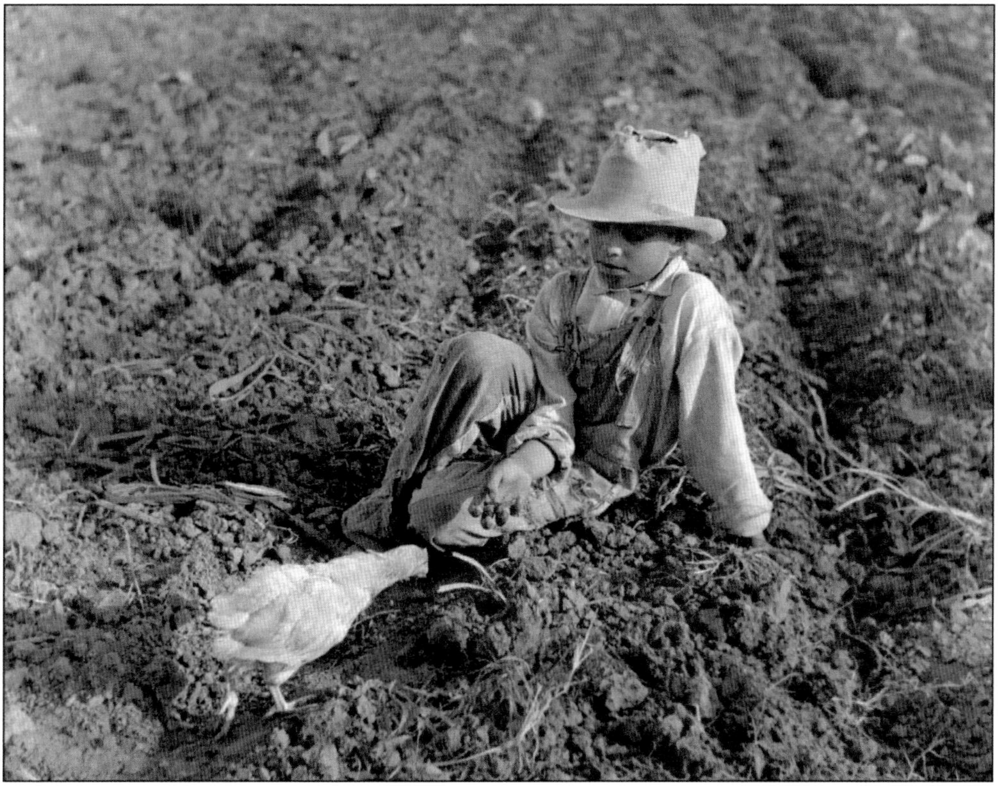

Although this is probably a staged photograph, it was not uncommon for a boy this young to work in the fields. This one probably played in the field after it had been harvested. (Courtesy of the Library of Congress.)

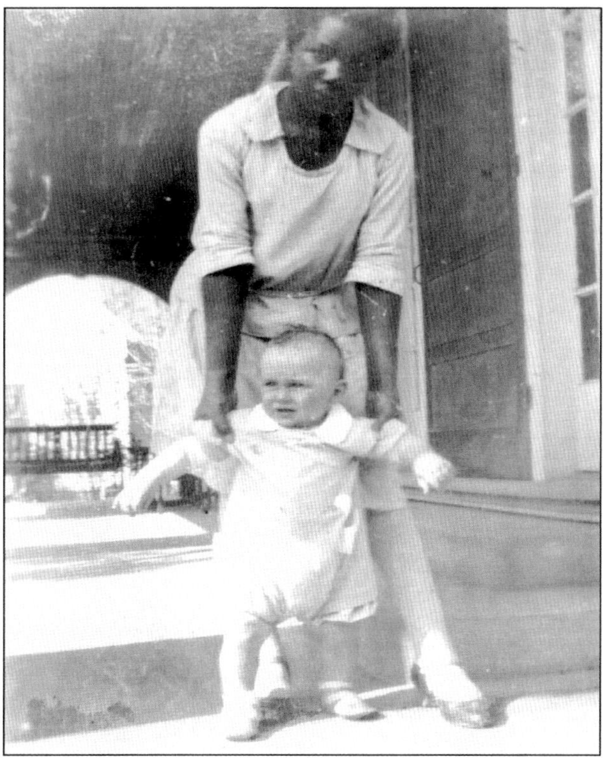

One of the better jobs was that of a house servant or nanny. Just as boys helped with chores outdoors, young girls were trained in the care of children and the home. (Courtesy of Cammie Henry Research Center, Northwestern State University.)

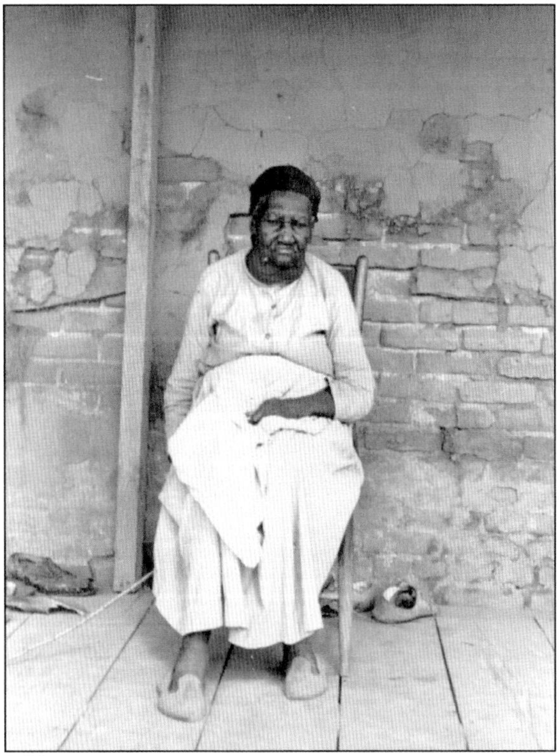

This woman's name is no longer remembered by members of the Hertzog family; however, they do recall that she was a midwife in her younger years. (Courtesy of Ambrose Hertzog Jr.)

Rosa Rachal, a cook at Magnolia Plantation, on average provided three meals a day for the plantation owners and other house staff. When the Hertzogs had company during the holidays or at other special occasions, Rosa received help in the kitchen from other staff members. On occasion, Rosa sat at the end of the table with the family for meals. (Courtesy of Ambrose Hertzog Jr.)

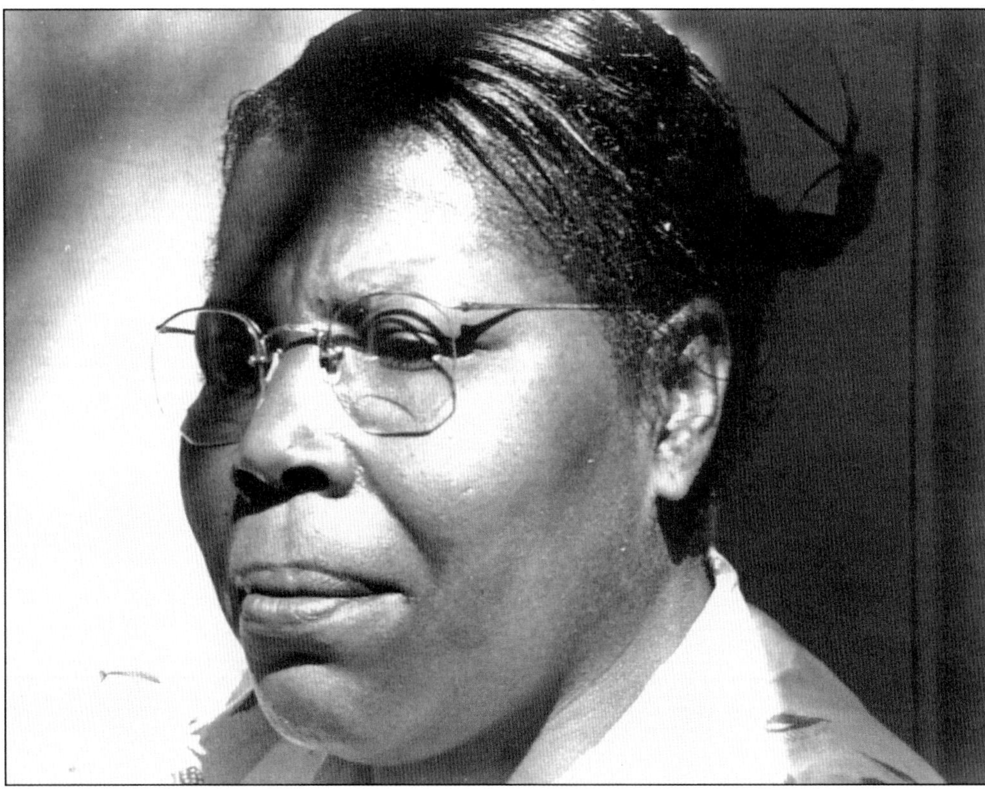

Walter Telphin sometimes cooked for the Hertzogs at picnics. Southern cuisine, especially that of Louisiana with its gumbos and jambalayas, has its reputation steeped in the imaginative spices used by African American cooks. (Courtesy of Ambrose Hertzog Jr.)

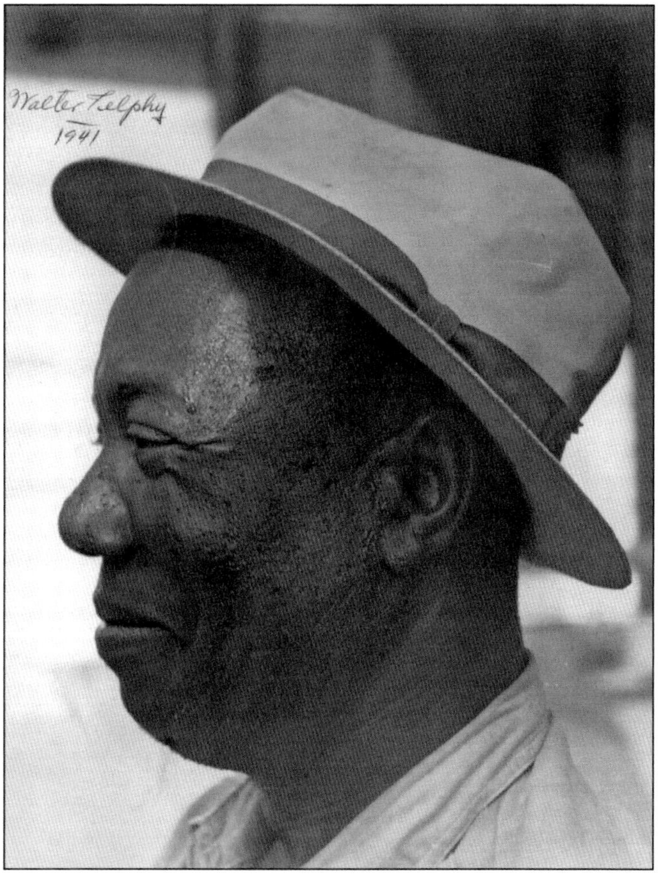

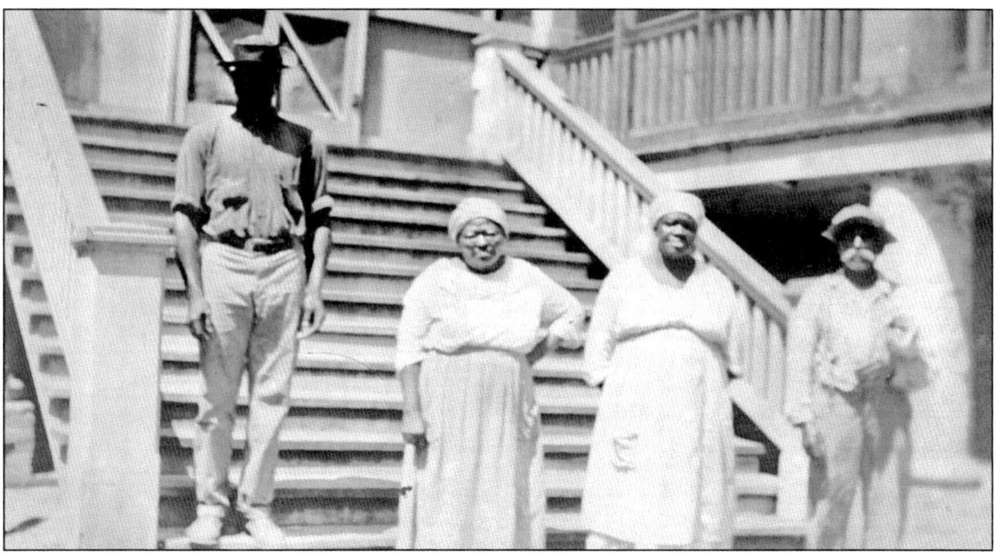

For every 50 to 100 people who worked in the fields, there were 6 to 12 individuals who worked as servants. In this image are the servants at Magnolia Plantation who worked during the 1940s and 1950s. (Courtesy of Cammie Henry Research Center, Northwestern State University.)

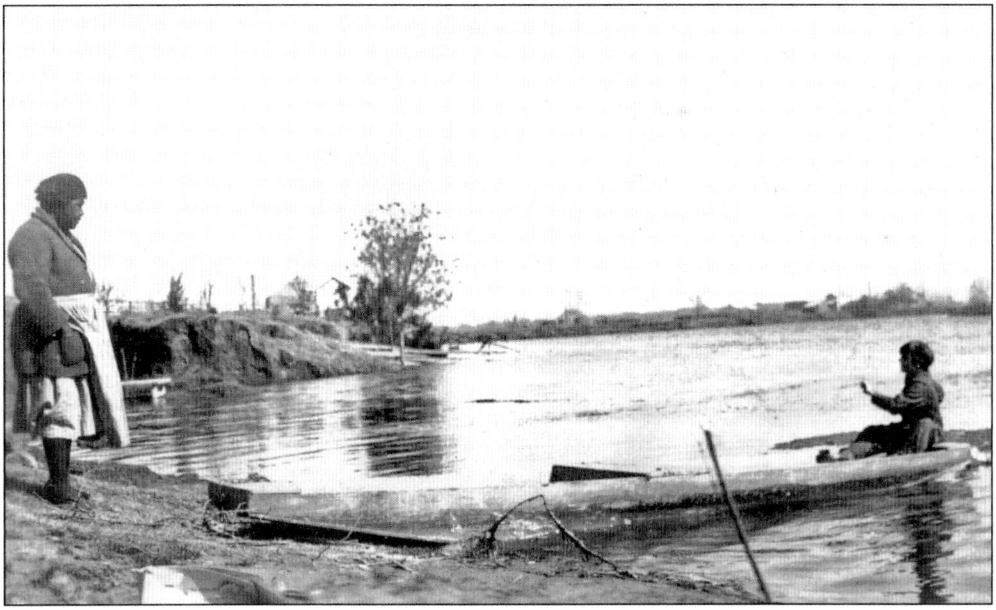

The responsibilities of servants extended beyond the boundaries of the house. Oftentimes house servants escorted the plantation family on private picnics and outings. (Courtesy of Cammie Henry Research Center, Northwestern State University.)

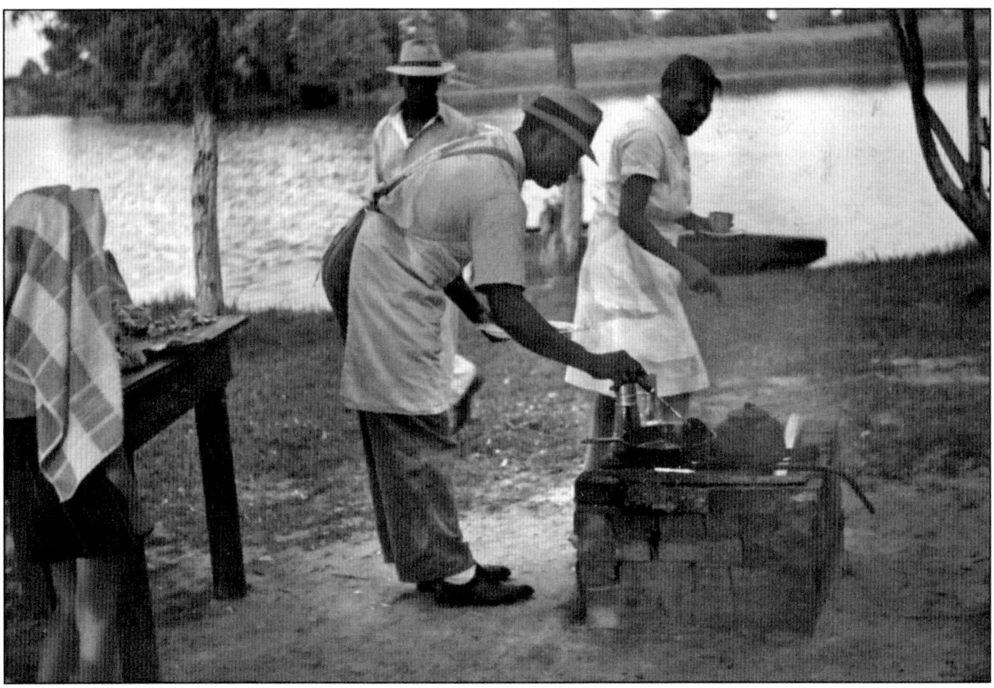

Rosa Rachal and Walter Telphin prepare food along the banks of the Cane River as John Vercher looks on. The Hertzog family, owners of Magnolia Plantation, often fished and picnicked on the river. The staff was brought along to prepare that day's catch. (Courtesy of Ambrose Hertzog Jr.)

John Vercher is remembered as a jack-of-all-trades. According to Ambrose Hertzog Jr., "He could do almost anything, repaired stuff, and worked with horses." Next to John is Mary Jane Cheatam, who worked as a cook for the Hertzogs sometime in the early 1940s. (Courtesy of Ambrose Hertzog Jr.)

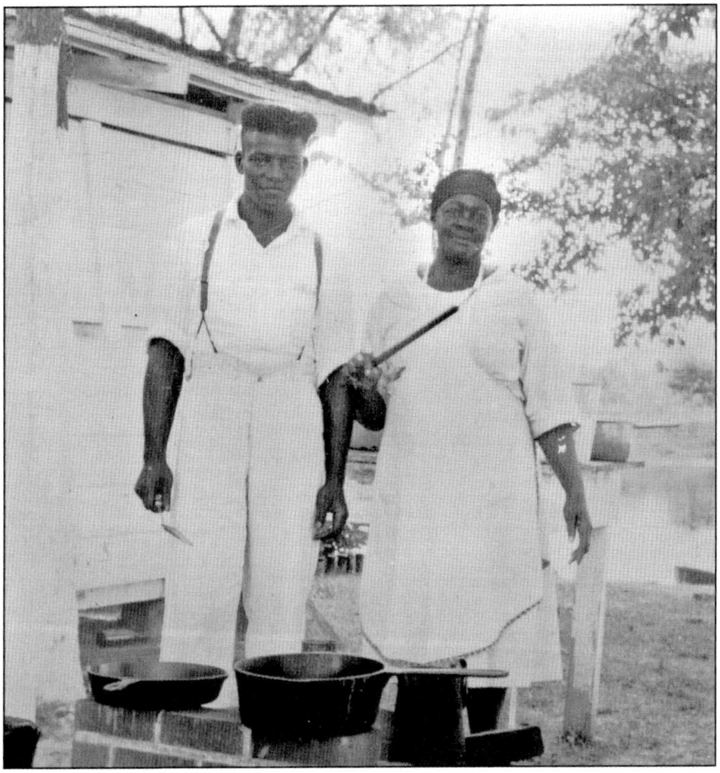

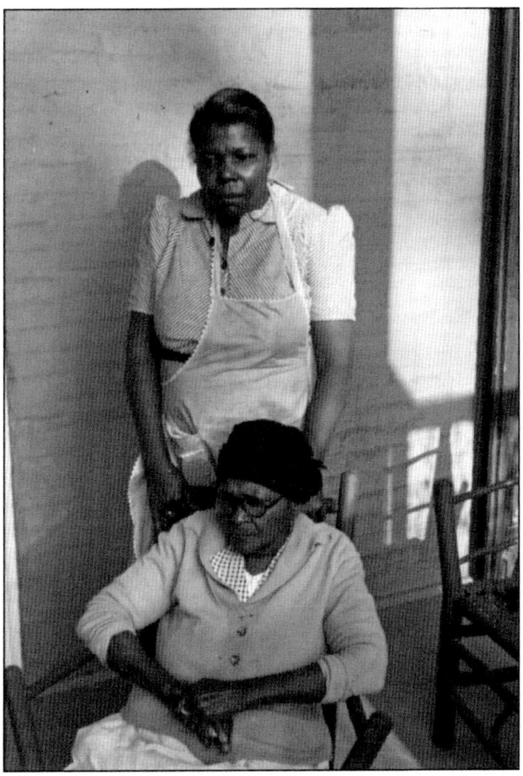

Rosa Rachal, a cook for Magnolia Plantation, stands behind her mother, Martha Littleton, who was also known as "Aunt Martha." Martha, too, was a cook at Magnolia for many years. Oftentimes the role of cook spanned several generations of women. (Courtesy of Ambrose Hertzog Jr.)

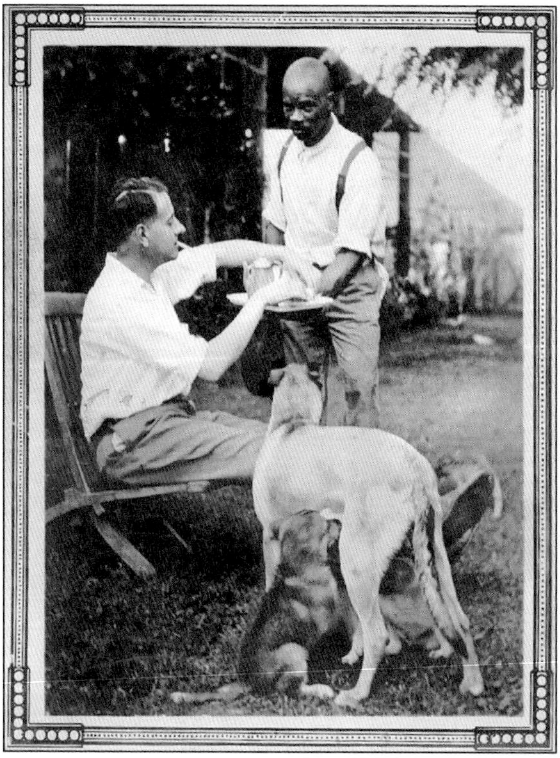

Francois Mingnon came from New York to visit Natchitoches and decided to stay at Melrose Plantation. While there, he became Clementine Hunter's unofficial agent and is credited with inspiring her to paint the African House murals. During a break from work, Francois (seated) receives refreshments from an attendant. (Courtesy of Cammie Henry Research Center, Northwestern State University.)

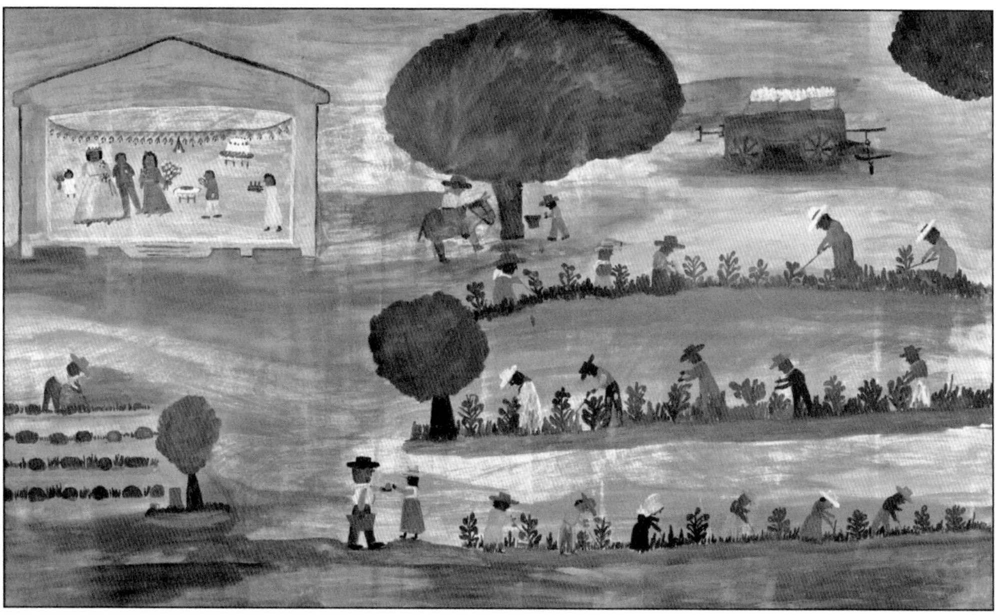

Clementine Hunter began painting the African House murals on June 8, 1955. When she finished less than two months later, there were a total of nine panels with varying themes. Each panel successfully documented some facet of African American life in the parish. In this panel, titled "The Spring Planting and Wedding," Clementine celebrates new life through marriage and crops. (Courtesy of the Historic American Buildings Survey, photographer James Rosenthal.)

White shirts, black pants, and dress shoes are indicative of the type of attire worn by house servants. This same outfit, when complemented with a tie, could easily be worn to church services. (Courtesy of Cammie Henry Research Center, Northwestern State University.)

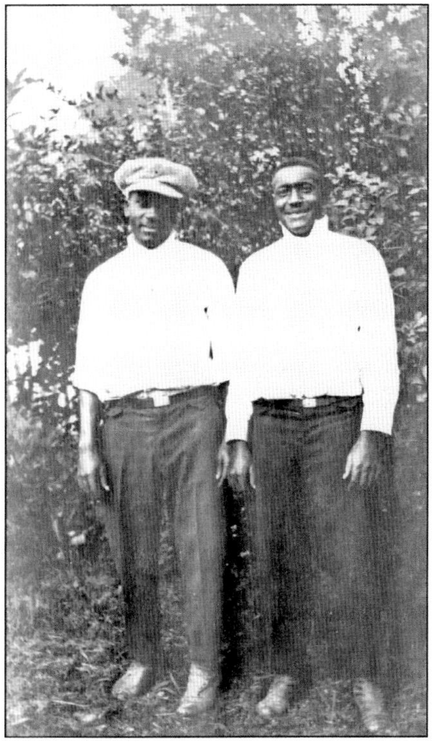

Christmas was always one of the happiest times on the plantation. Many African American children received apples, oranges, and candy as presents. The wrapped packages being carried by the men likely belonged to people who lived in the main house at Melrose Plantation. (Courtesy of Cammie Henry Research Center, Northwestern State University.)

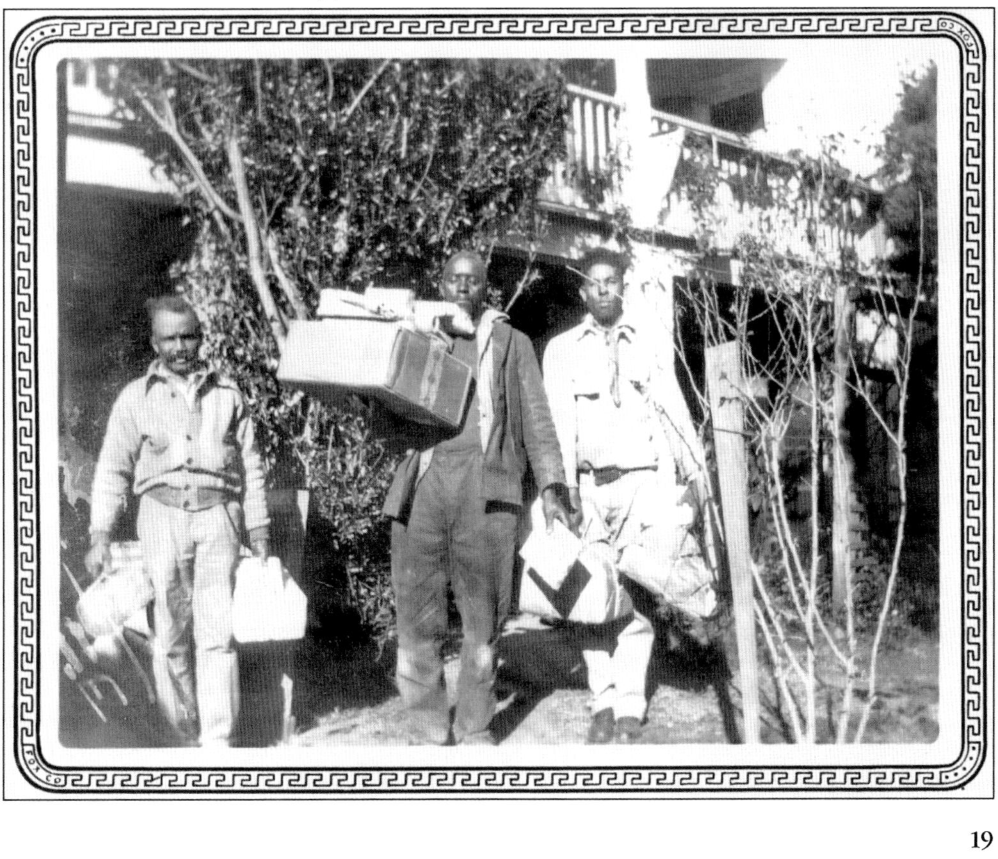

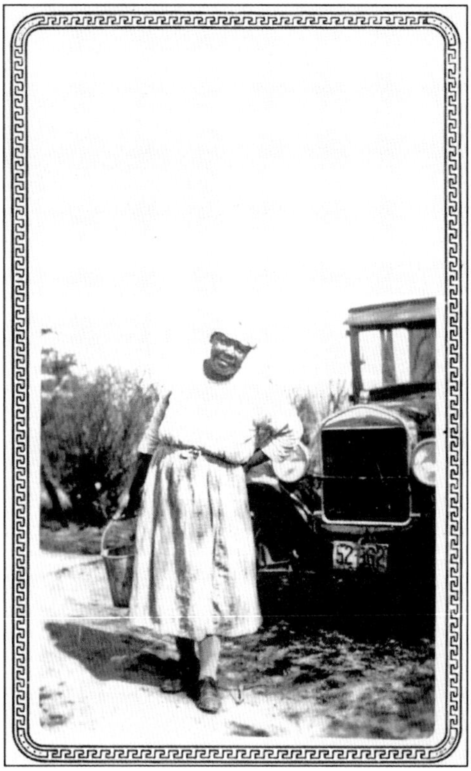

Sometimes the work of servants included washing the automobiles on the plantation. Note that even while working outside, house servants dressed in better clothing than most other workers. (Courtesy of Cammie Henry Research Center, Northwestern State University.)

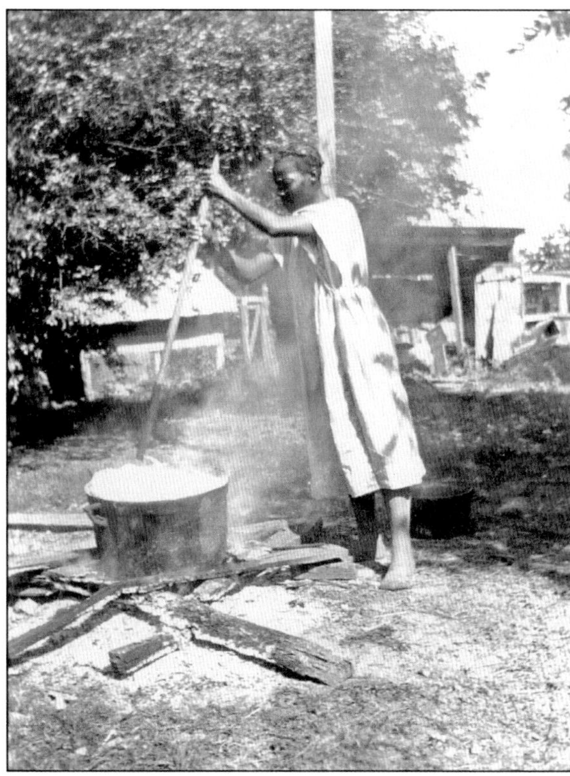

Local resident Willie Mae Tennarse described the process of washing on laundry day: "You had to boil [the clothes] in the wash pot. You boil it in that wash pot with soap. They would make their lye soap and all. You take [the clothes] out the wash pot and put them back over in the tub and put more water on them. You would rub them out. Then you got to pass them through more water and rinse them. Then you put them in more water with bluing in them. You then rinse [the clothes] and hang them up." Susie ?, shown washing clothes, is quite adept at this process, which was difficult work to perform in the summer because of excessive heat. (Courtesy of Cammie Henry Research Center, Northwestern State University.)

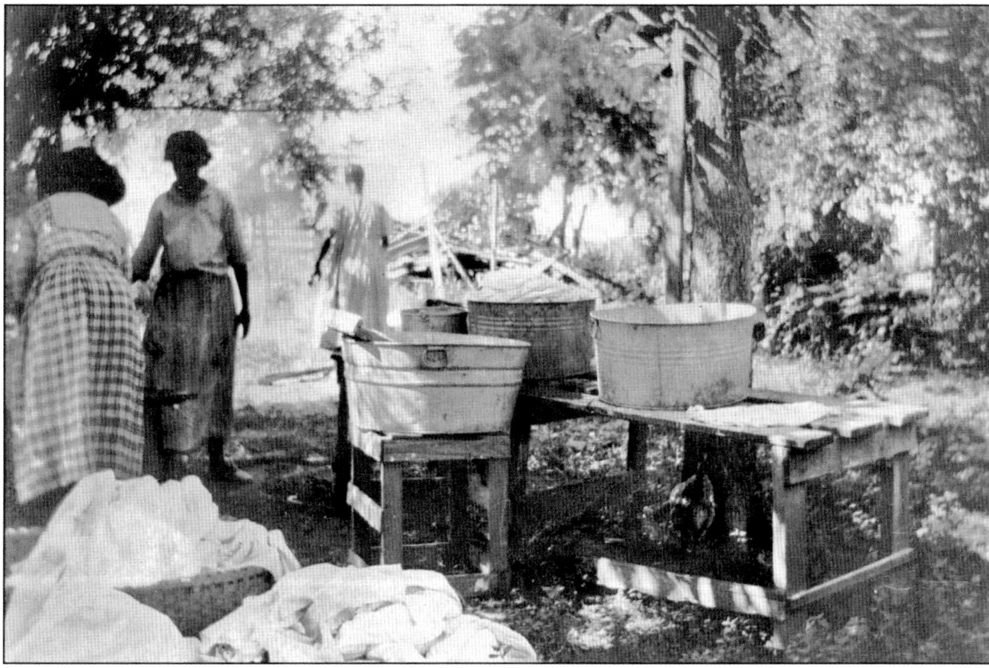

It took several women most of the day to finish the laundry for residents at the main house. Wash-day meant cleaning the linens from several beds, as well as clothing and curtains. Women sometimes used an assembly-line technique to better handle the large volume of laundry. (Courtesy of Cammie Henry Research Center, Northwestern State University.)

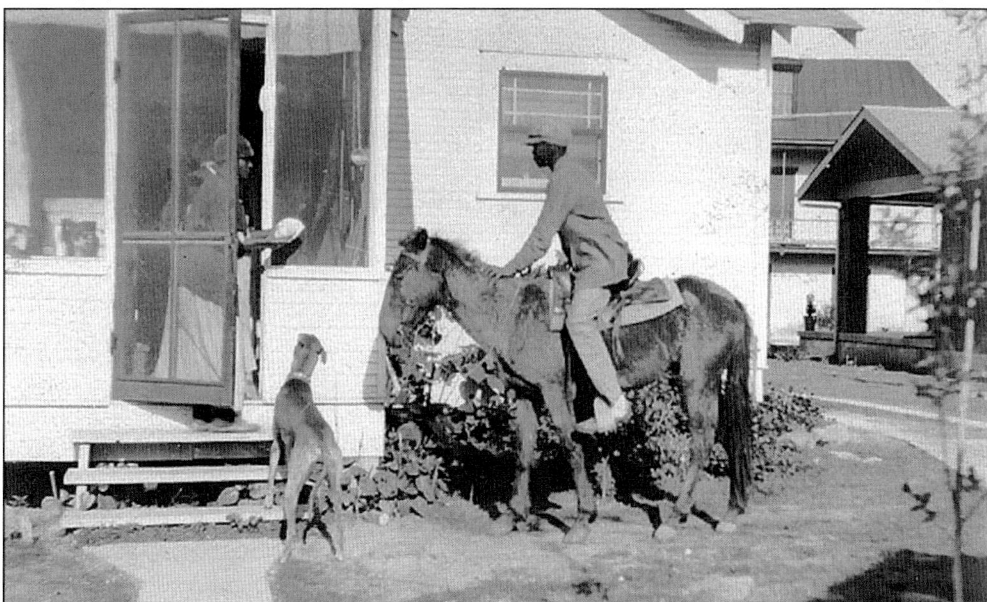

Horses continued to be a major source of transportation for many residents well into the 1960s. This gentleman appears to be providing a type of courier service or perhaps is simply showing an act of kindness towards an elder. (Courtesy of Cammie Henry Research Center, Northwestern State University.)

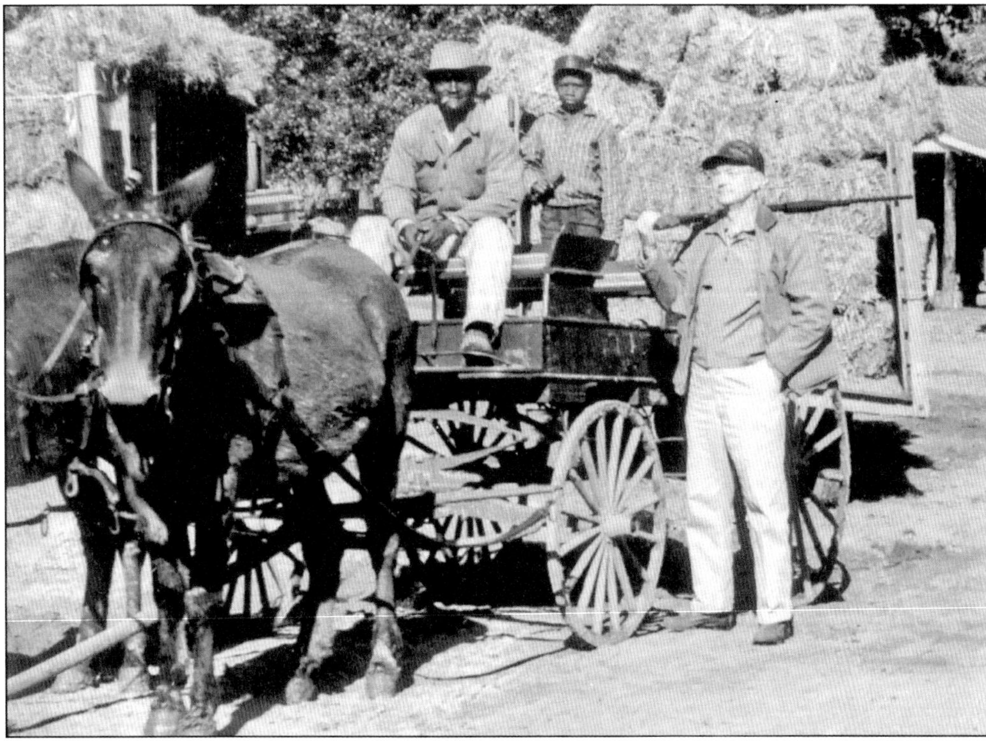

Dr. Ambrose Hertzog is seen here talking to John Vercher, who is seated on the hay wagon. Although stacking hay was a strenuous job for the men, it sometimes brought delights for the workers' children. As a young boy, Harry Jackson used to get haywire that was used for tying hay and make animal figurines like mules. Homemade toys were sometimes the only toys available. (Courtesy of Ambrose Hertzog Jr.)

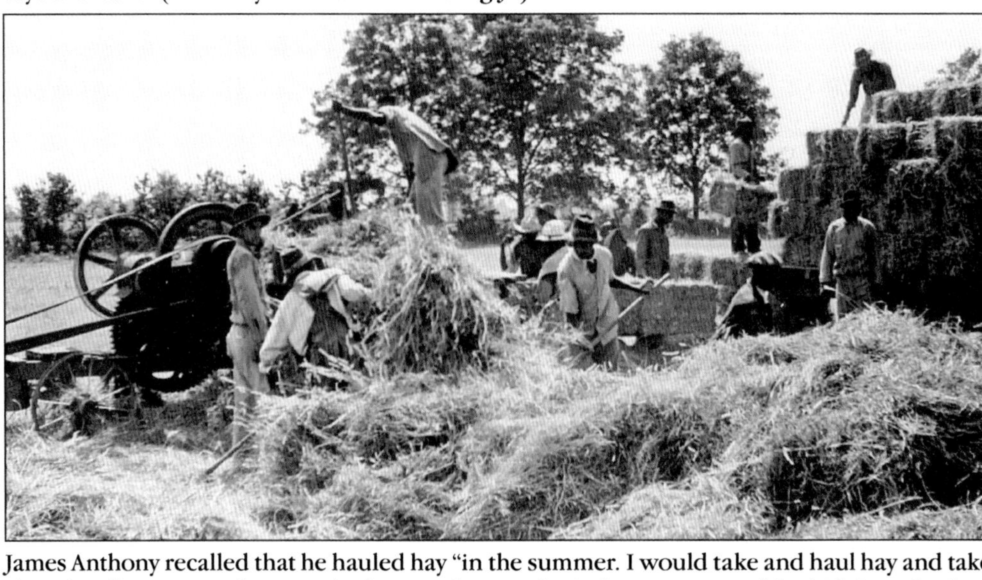

James Anthony recalled that he hauled hay "in the summer. I would take and haul hay and take the schoolboys. I put them on the hay truck. I say that's the way most of the kids bought their clothes and things that rode on my bus. The fact about it, that's where my daughter learned to drive in the hay field; she was seven years old." (Courtesy of Ambrose Hertzog Jr.)

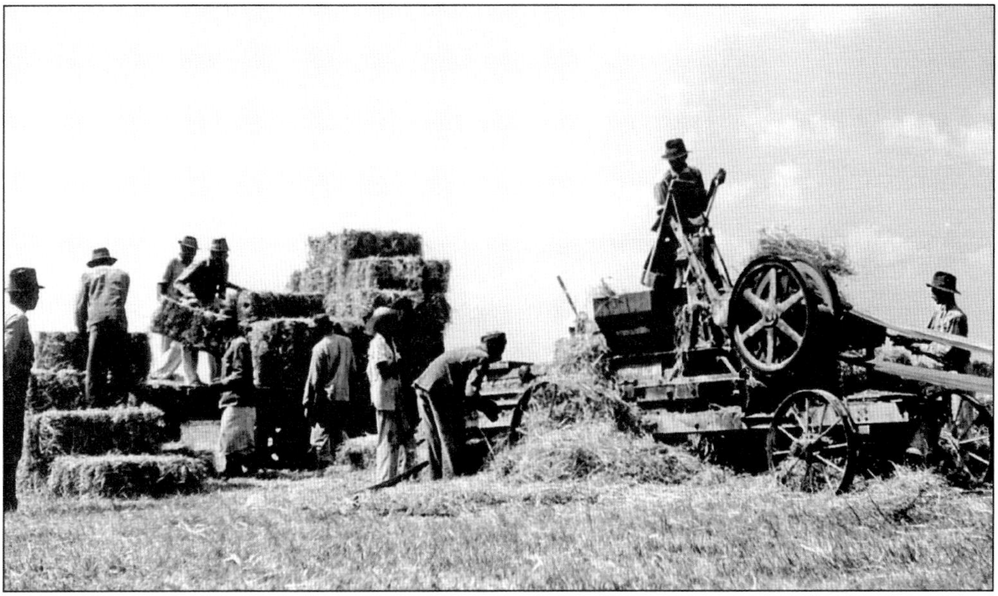

In 1865, only about 10 percent of African Americans left the plantations after emancipation. Most families stayed on or near the plantations that were most familiar to them. They continued to make a living off the land until the mechanization of cotton agriculture, at which time many farmers left to seek work in larger cities. (Courtesy of Ambrose Hertzog Jr.)

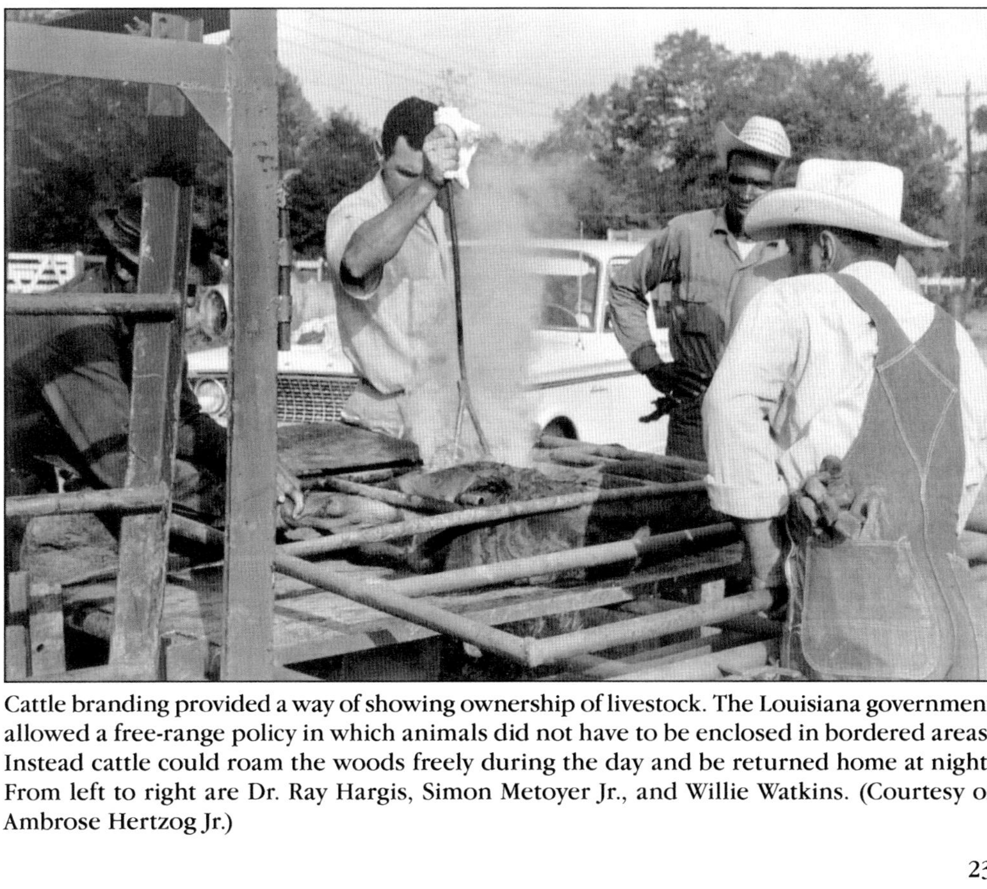

Cattle branding provided a way of showing ownership of livestock. The Louisiana government allowed a free-range policy in which animals did not have to be enclosed in bordered areas. Instead cattle could roam the woods freely during the day and be returned home at night. From left to right are Dr. Ray Hargis, Simon Metoyer Jr., and Willie Watkins. (Courtesy of Ambrose Hertzog Jr.)

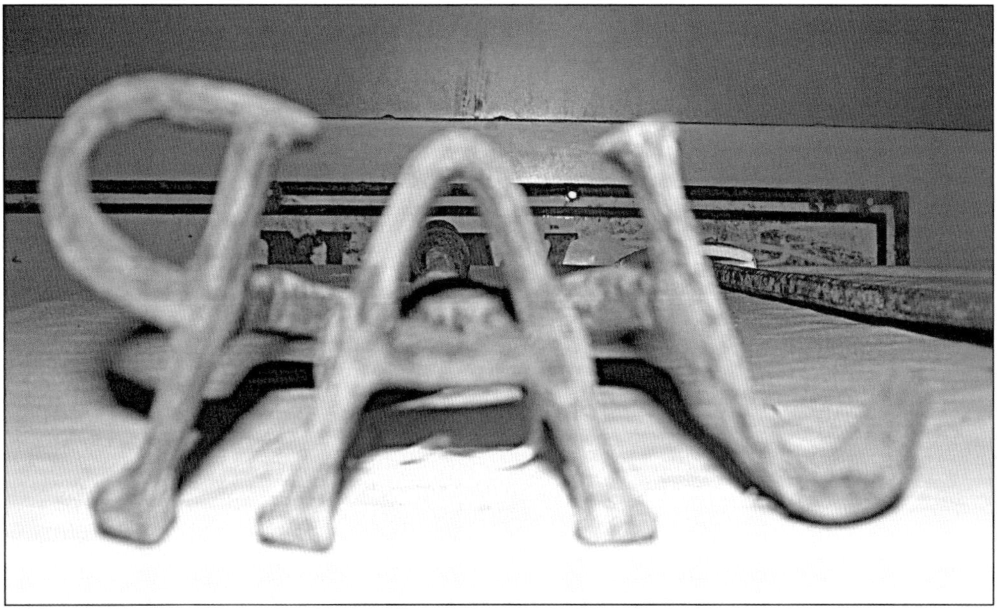

The branding iron above belonged to Jacques Alphonse Prud'homme (1838–1919), descendants of Oakland Plantation. In addition to marking cattle, landowners often marked their cotton sacks with a stencil to show ownership. The stencil below was designed to label the cotton sacks for the children of Narcisse Prud'homme (1788–1844). (Courtesy of Cane River Creole National Historical Park, photographer Rolonda Teal.)

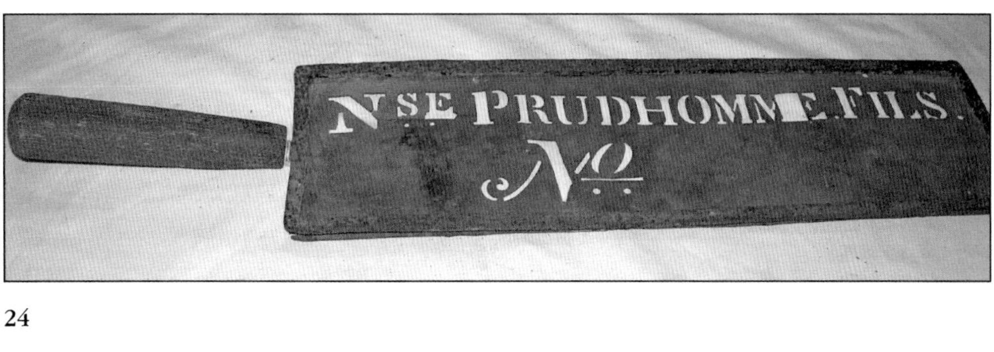

An elderly man picks cotton while wearing a hat, which provides protection against the harshness of the sun. His white cotton clothing helps his body to stay cool. Attached to him is a typical white cotton sack that drags the ground. (Courtesy of Cammie Henry Research Center, Northwestern State University.)

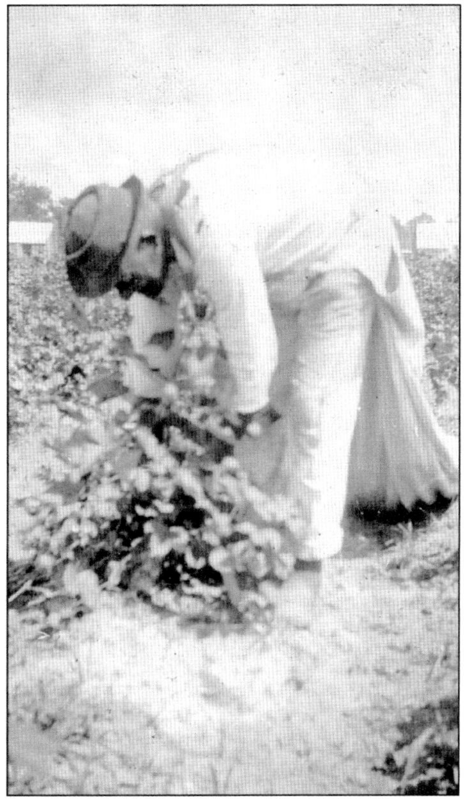

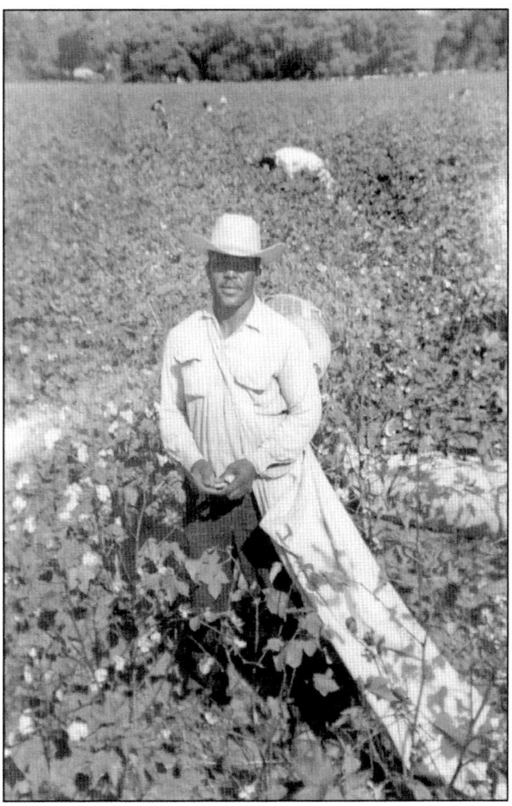

A man like Atrice Anthony, pictured here, would have been considered a prime worker. As an adult, he could be expected to pick, on average, 200 pounds of cotton per day. (Courtesy of Ambrose Hertzog Jr.)

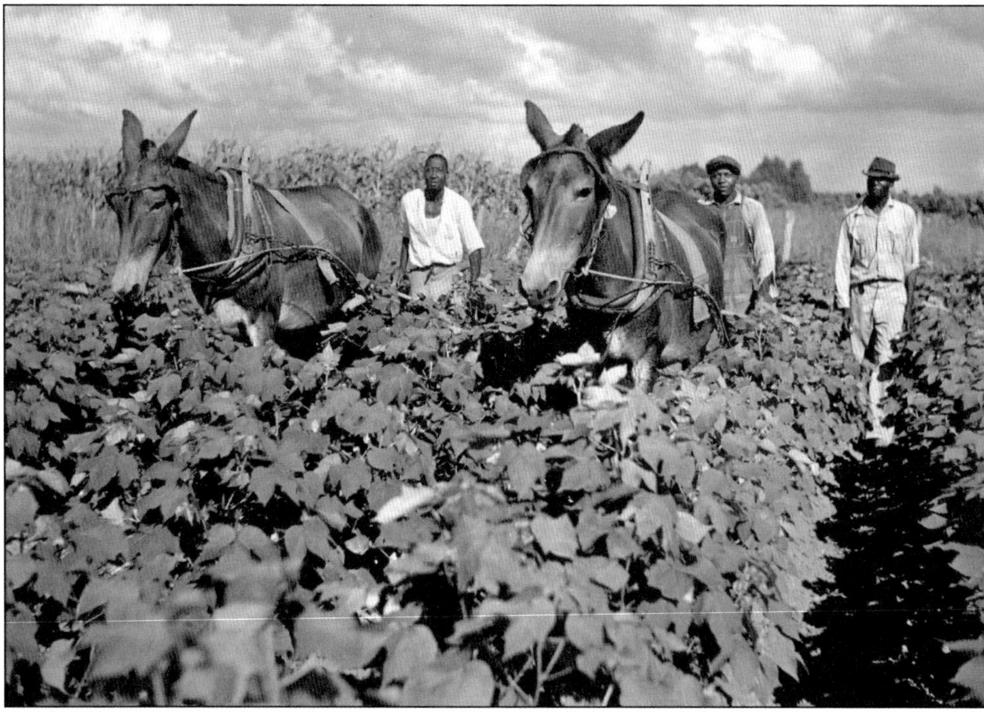

These men are caring for cotton crops in the middle of a field. The man without a mule is likely the overseer. This position had traditionally been reserved for whites and Creoles; however, by the early part of the 20th century, African Americans were employed as overseers. (Courtesy of the Library of Congress.)

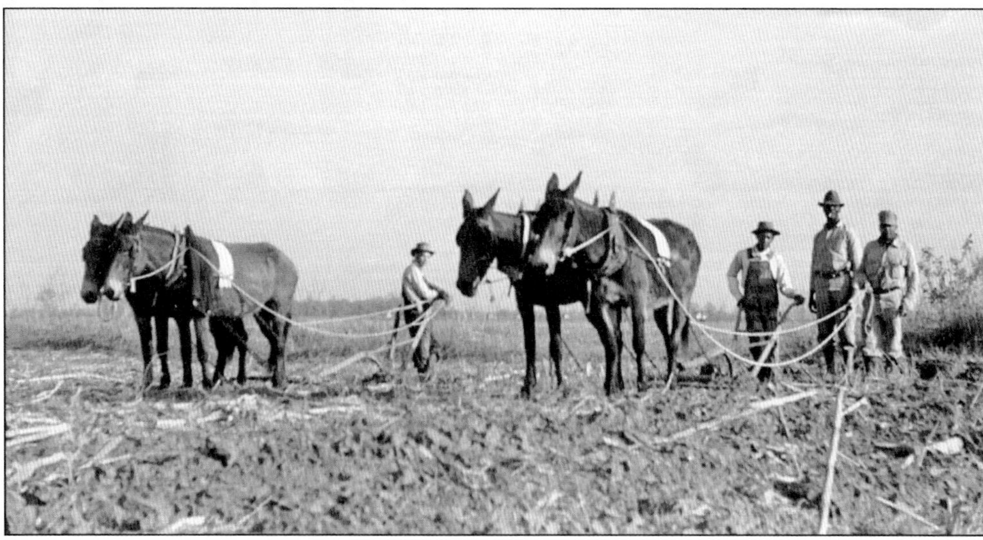

Four men stand in a harvested field, marking the end of the planting season. Mules were a significant part of farm labor before mechanization of farming practices. Wesley Johnson recalled that mules were often used on "moonshine nights." On those nights, the moon was full, providing enough light to work the fields. They would use one set of mules that night, go back to the barn the next morning, and then return to the fields with a new set of mules. (Courtesy of Ambrose Hertzog Jr.)

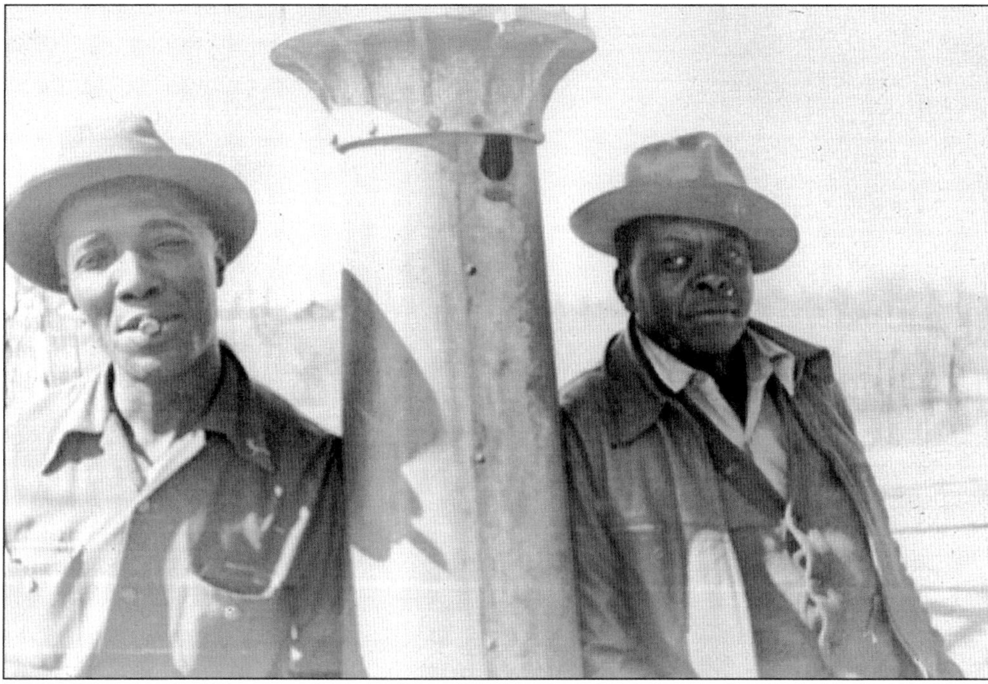

Matthew Johnson (left) and Walter Blackmon, the foreman at Magnolia Plantation, lean against a post. Blackmon worked for the Hertzogs during the 1950s. (Courtesy of Ambrose Hertzog Jr.)

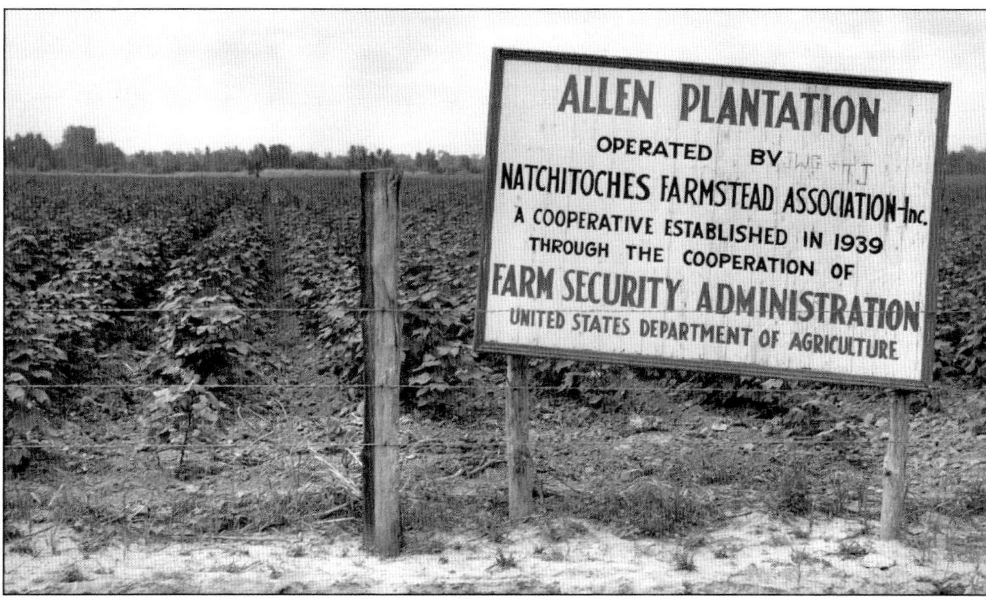

Allen Plantation Cooperative formed from a branch of the Farm Security Administration (FSA) in 1937. The FSA sought to bring struggling farmers together to work on large government-owned farms. Participants in the program could not own their own farms and were required to use modern techniques and equipment. Although FSA assistance was available to any poor farmer in the South, about a third of FSA clients were African Americans. (Courtesy of the Library of Congress.)

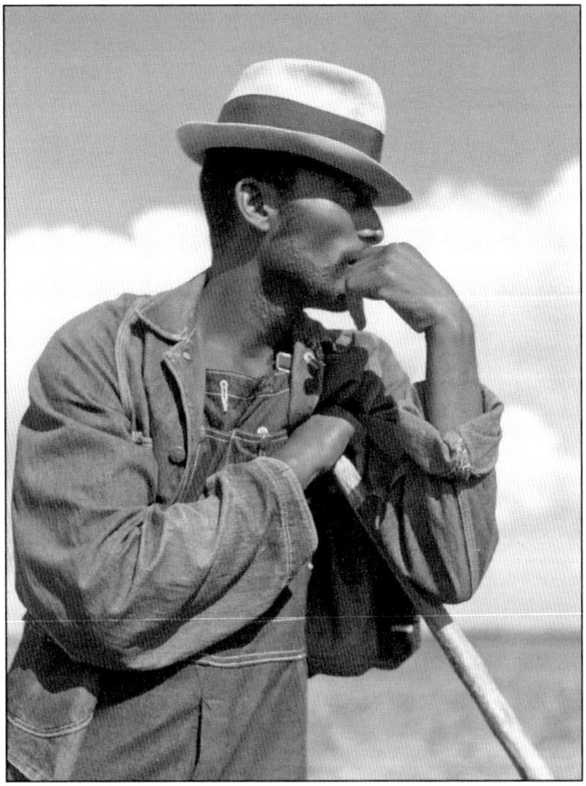

In addition to farm cooperatives, the FSA loaned money to tenant farmers at low interest rates. The loan program became the agency's focus so that thousands of tenant farmers could stay on the land they once worked. Through loan programs, many borrowers were able to earn enough to buy their own farms. (Courtesy of the Library of Congress.)

The FSA bought out small farms that were not economically viable and set up 34 subsistence homestead communities in which groups of farmers lived together under the guidance of government experts. This Allen Plantation Cooperative homestead depended on labor from several families. Lining the shelves of the store are pickled eggs, stewed tomatoes, and peas for sale. (Courtesy of the Library of Congress.)

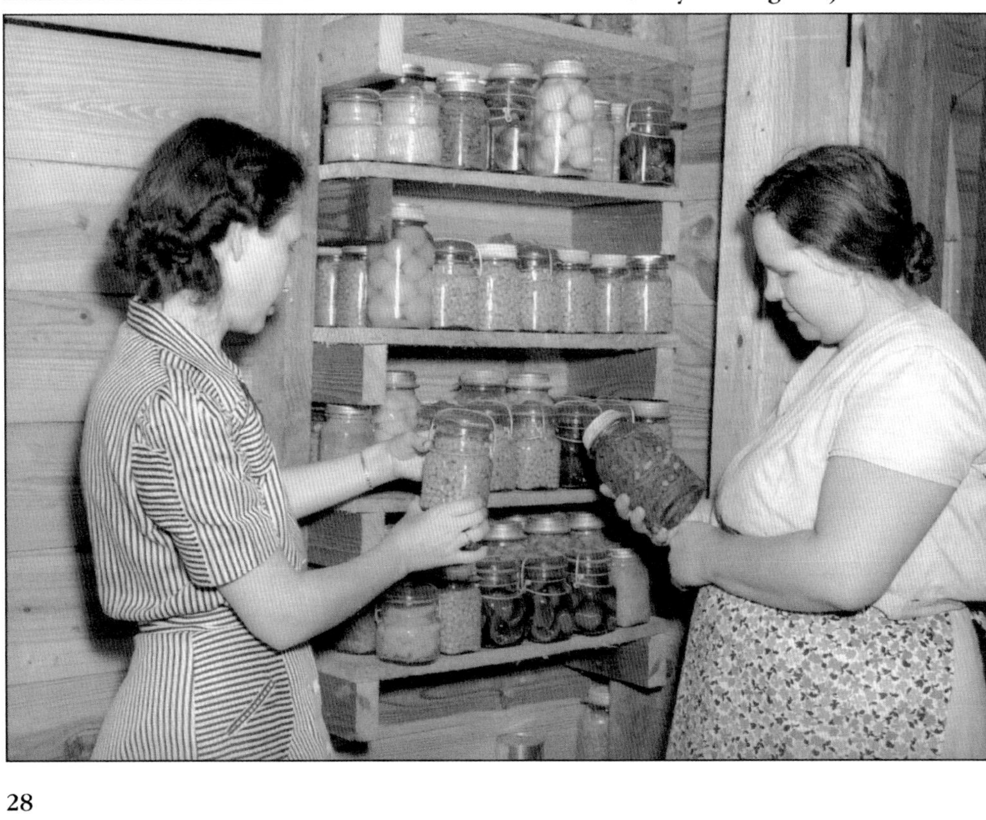

The FSA gave educational aid to 455,000 farm families from 1936 to 1943. In June 1936, Pres. Franklin Roosevelt noticed that educating farmers for self-sufficiency was proving successful. Farms that were once in disrepair had risen to a level of prosperity. This change in economic standing no doubt made it better for the farmers' children. (Courtesy of the Library of Congress.)

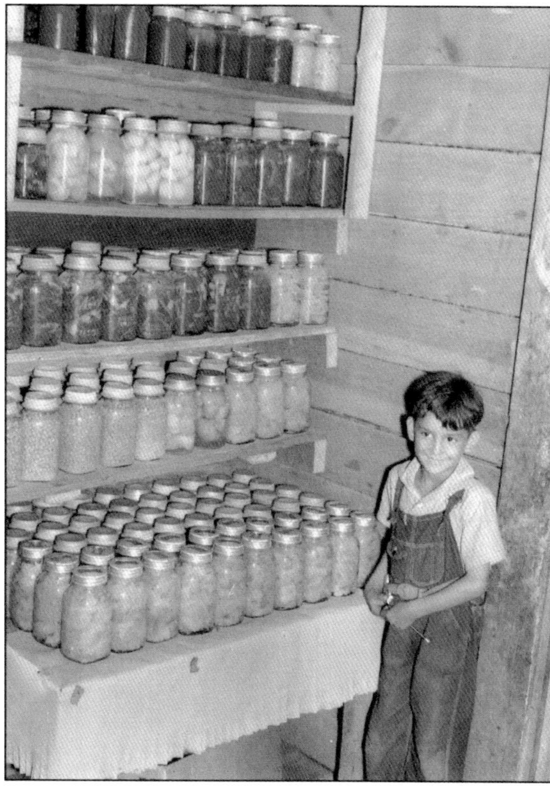

Julia Jones Lilly grew up in "a little shotgun house that had three rooms and a kitchen. It had no electricity, and we didn't have running water." The windows and front and back doors on this house, likely similar to Lilly's, were left open to allow a breeze to circulate through the home. (Courtesy of the Library of Congress.)

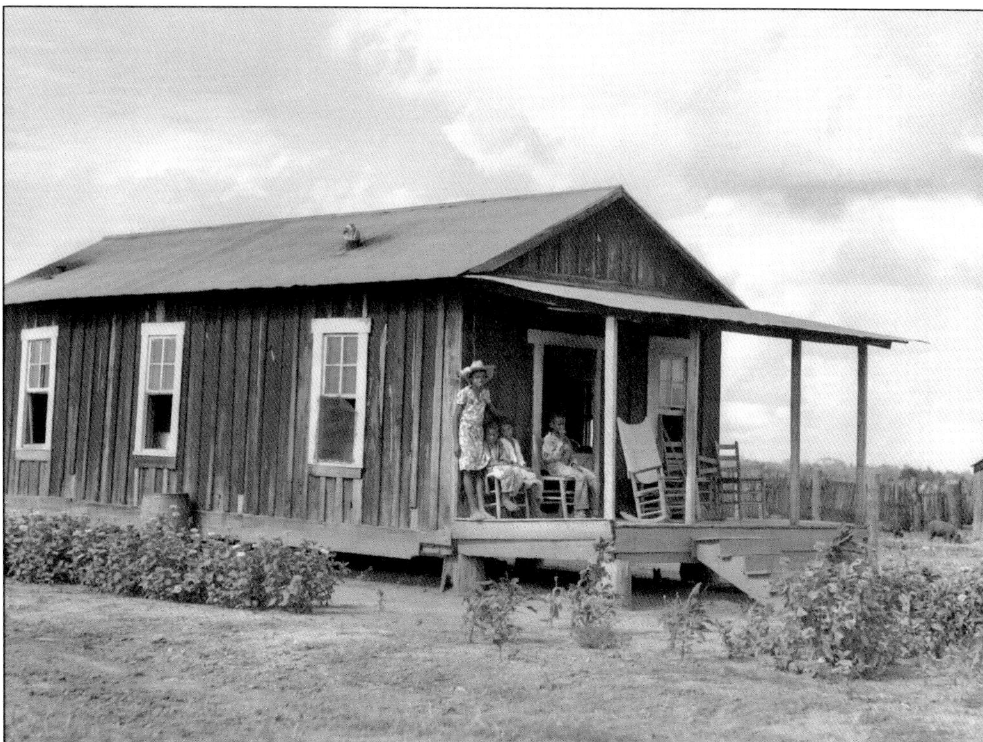

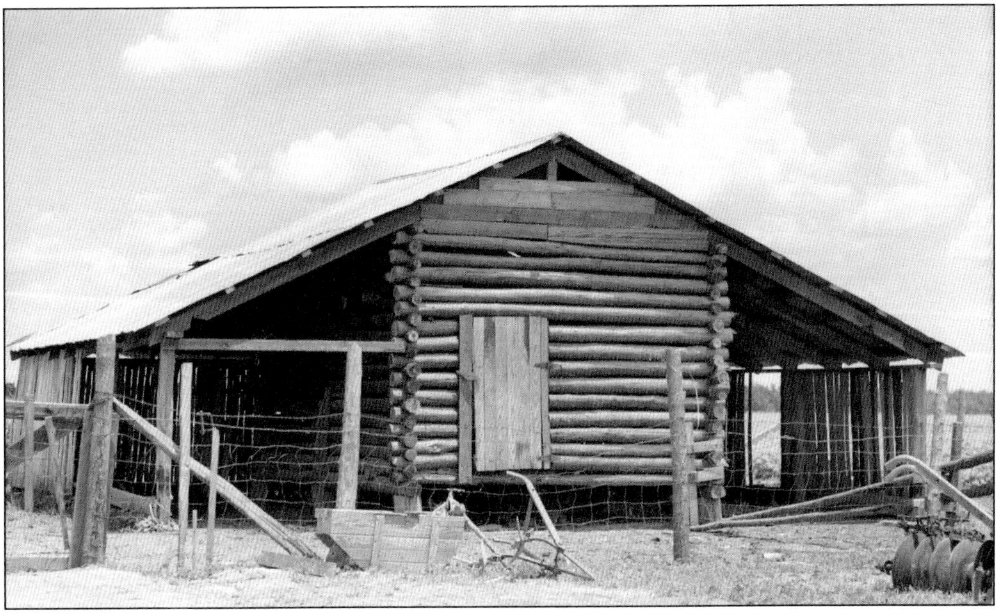

This old barn on Allen Plantation is a typical log crib structure. This type of construction provided a low-cost way to build since its intended use was limited to livestock, supplies, and food storage. This building was likely used to store hay. (Courtesy of the Library of Congress.)

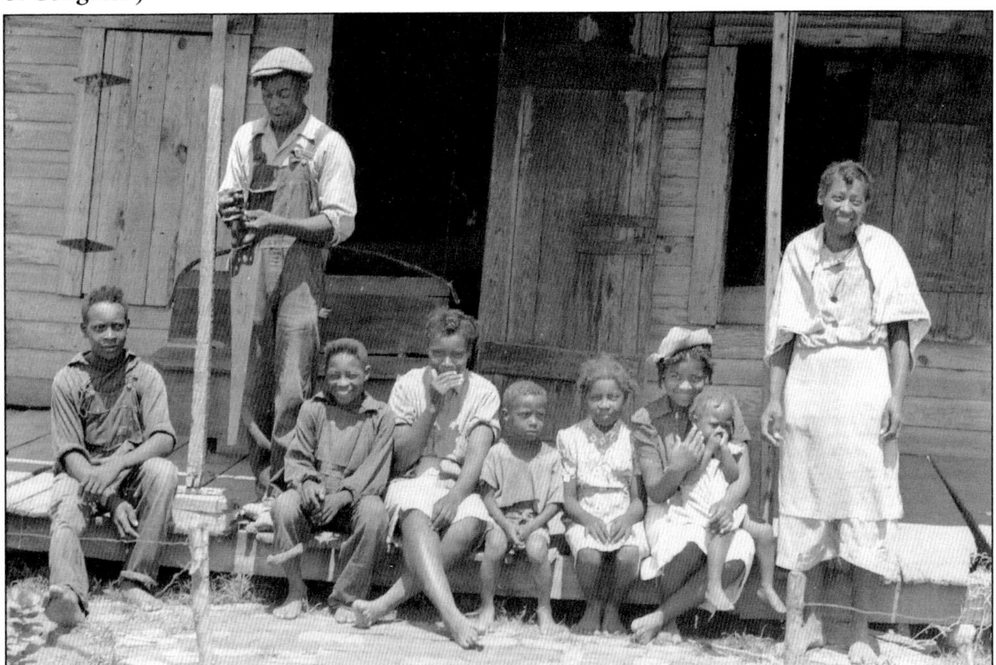

A family of nine sits outside their home at Bayou Bourbeaux Plantation. Families of this size were common and essential for rural living. Young children could assist in chores like feeding chickens and gathering firewood, while their older siblings helped with the planting and harvesting of crops. (Courtesy of the Library of Congress.)

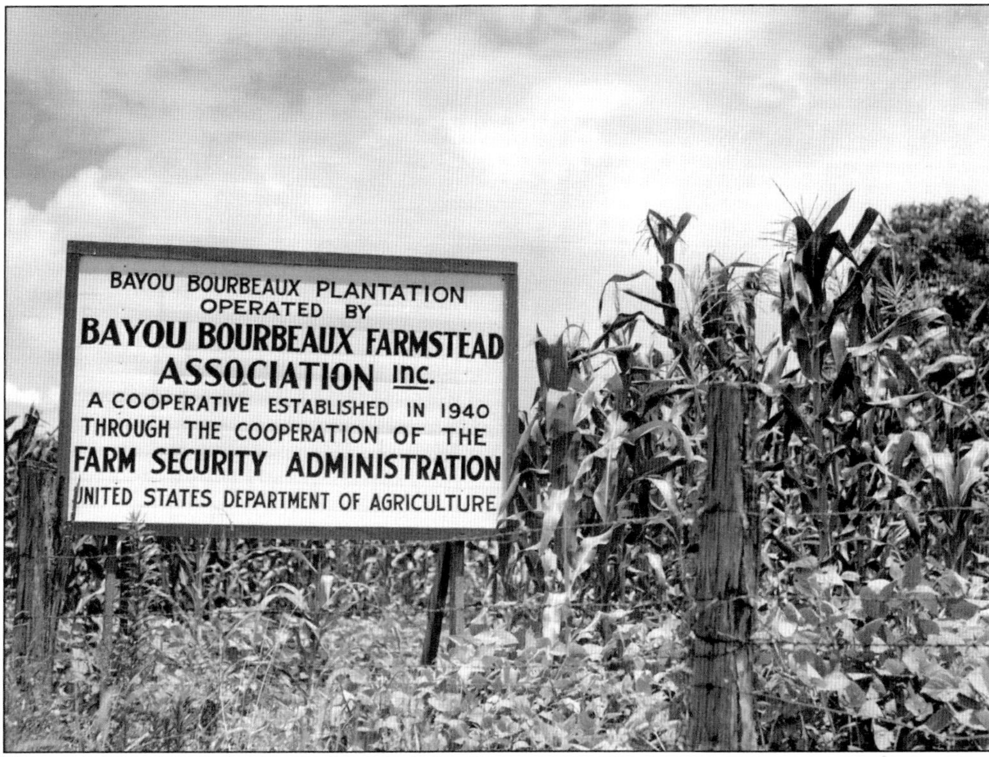

Bayou Bourbeaux Plantation, located in Clarence, Louisiana, about 15 miles northeast of Natchitoches, also participated in a FSA program. Although successful for a while, most cooperatives and associations were discontinued by the mid-1940s. (Courtesy of the Library of Congress.)

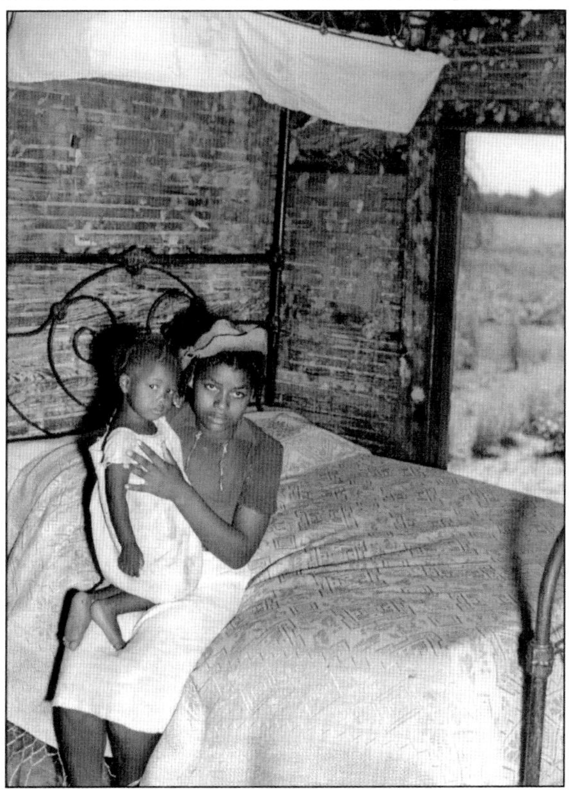

The benefit of belonging to a FSA cooperative is visible inside this family's home. A wrought-iron bed frame is decorated with store-bought covers. The canopy on top, while decorative, likely provided a space to hang mosquito netting. (Courtesy of the Library of Congress.)

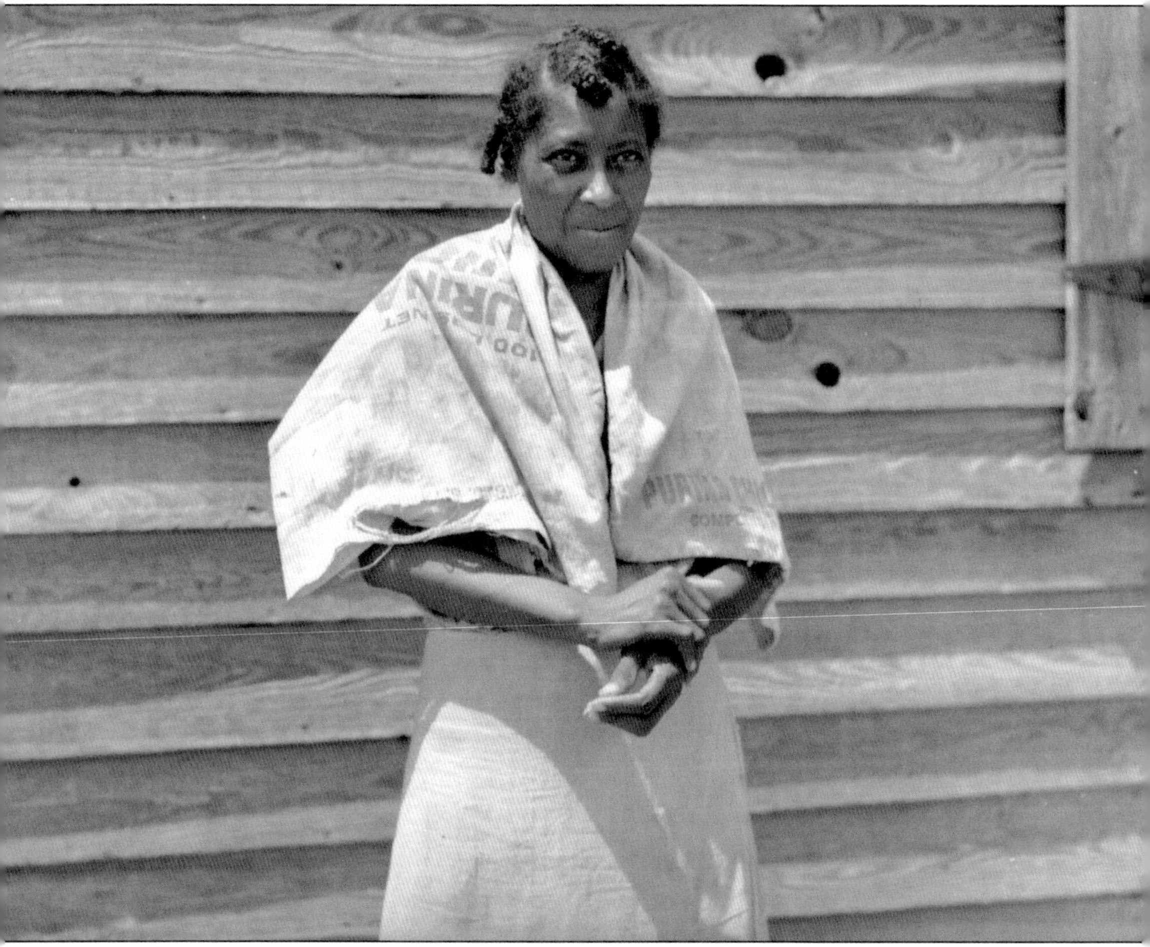

This woman wears a feed sack as a shawl. Draped over her shoulders, it provides a cover for her bare arms and offers protection from the sun. Feed sacks, when decorated in flowered or striped patterns, were also used to make dresses and blouses. (Courtesy of the Library of Congress.)

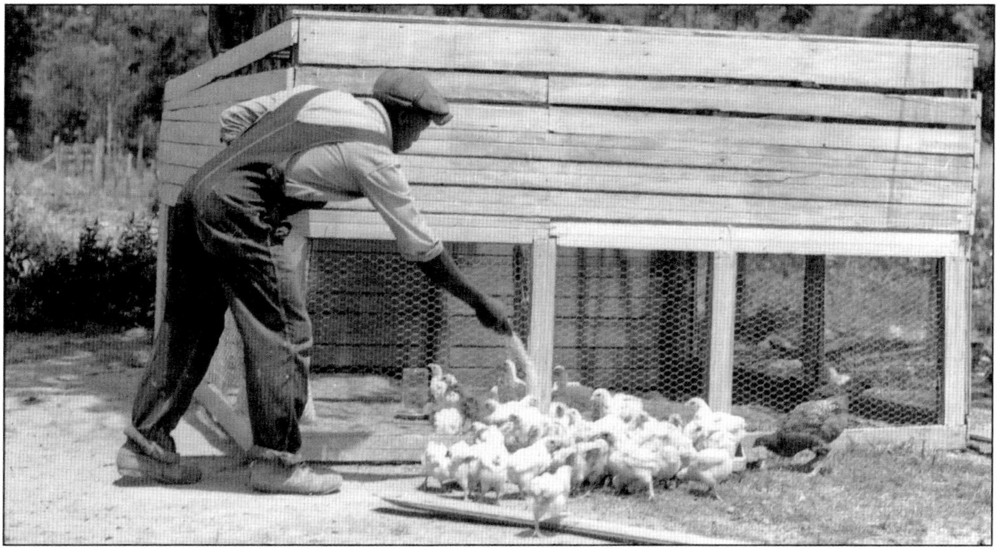

This man feeds chickens that belong to his family. Chickens were part of many tenant farmer diets because they provided meat and eggs, which also could be sold for a profit. Isaac Brosette remembers that, as a child, he had a big backyard with many chickens. Those chickens, according to Brosette, were helpful in keeping the yard clean since they ate insects and debris. (Courtesy of the Library of Congress.)

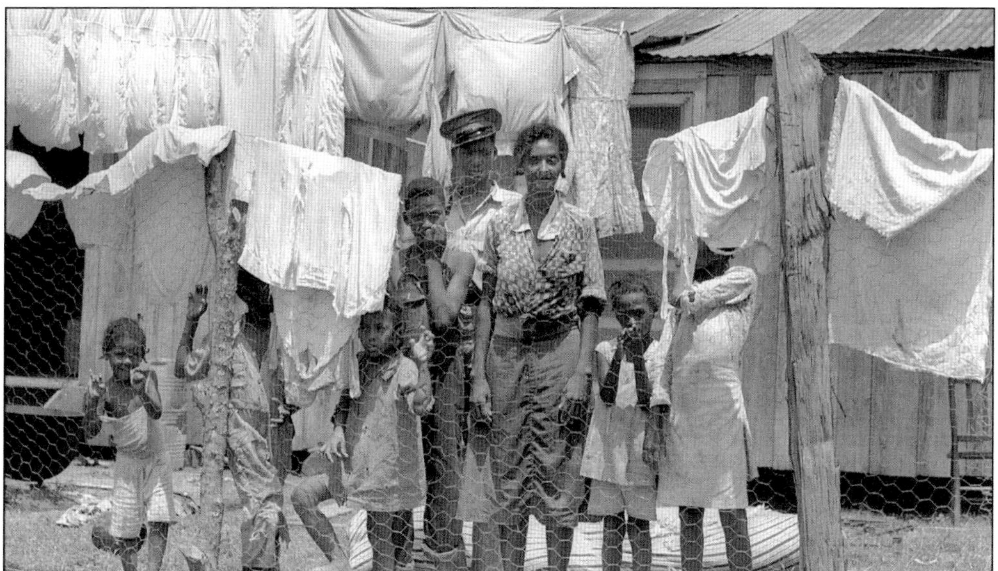

The black kettle in the yard and numerous white undergarments on the clothesline suggest this family provided a laundry service to bring in additional income. One important component in washing clothes was the use of lye soap. Although not shown in this image, Lucindy Helaire recalled how her grandmother and mother made lye soap. According to Helaire, they used old fat grease that was mixed with lye and water. The mixture cooked in a big pot that they continuously stirred until everything was ready. After being poured into tubs, the soap sat on a back porch to cool. Once hard, it was ready to be cut into blocks. (Courtesy of the Library of Congress.)

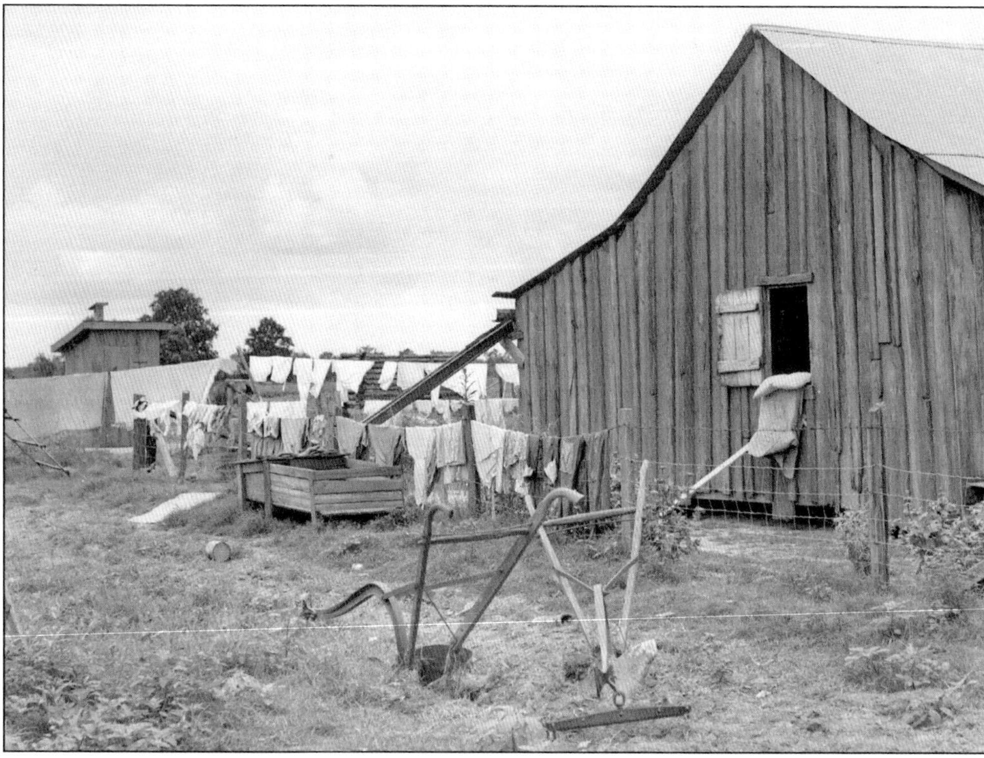

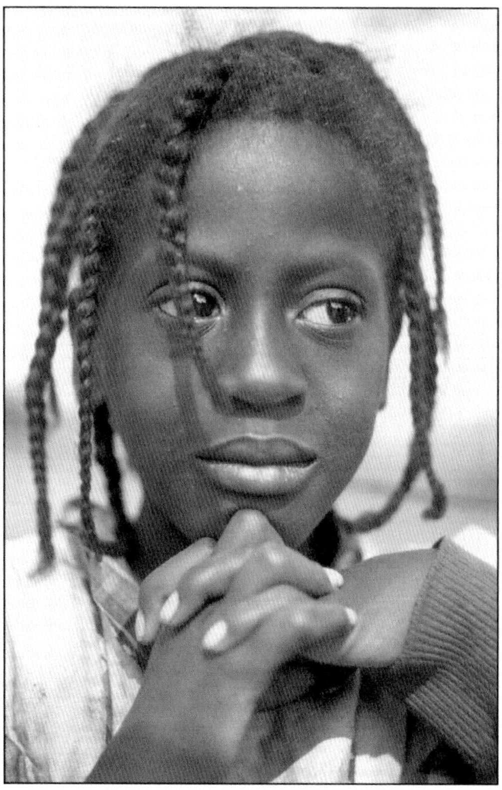

One goal of FSA cooperatives was to take families who once received assistance (now called welfare) and make them economically self-sufficient. This panoramic view of a farmstead shows the workings of a complete laundry facility. Water for washing is collected in gutters attached to the roof, while house windows allow the airing out of bed linens. (Courtesy of the Library of Congress.)

Minnie Randolph, shown here, from Magnolia Plantation represents many young people who were absent from school in order to help with family responsibilities. Another local resident, Earnest Charles, remembers that he, like many other children in the rural South, "had to miss school to gather the crops . . . and many times we had to miss school to haul wood, pull the corn, shell corn, and take [it] to the mill to grind. Sometimes we had to miss school on Friday so that we could take the [crops to the] mill on Saturday because the mill was only open on Saturday mornings." (Courtesy of John Thomas Guillet.)

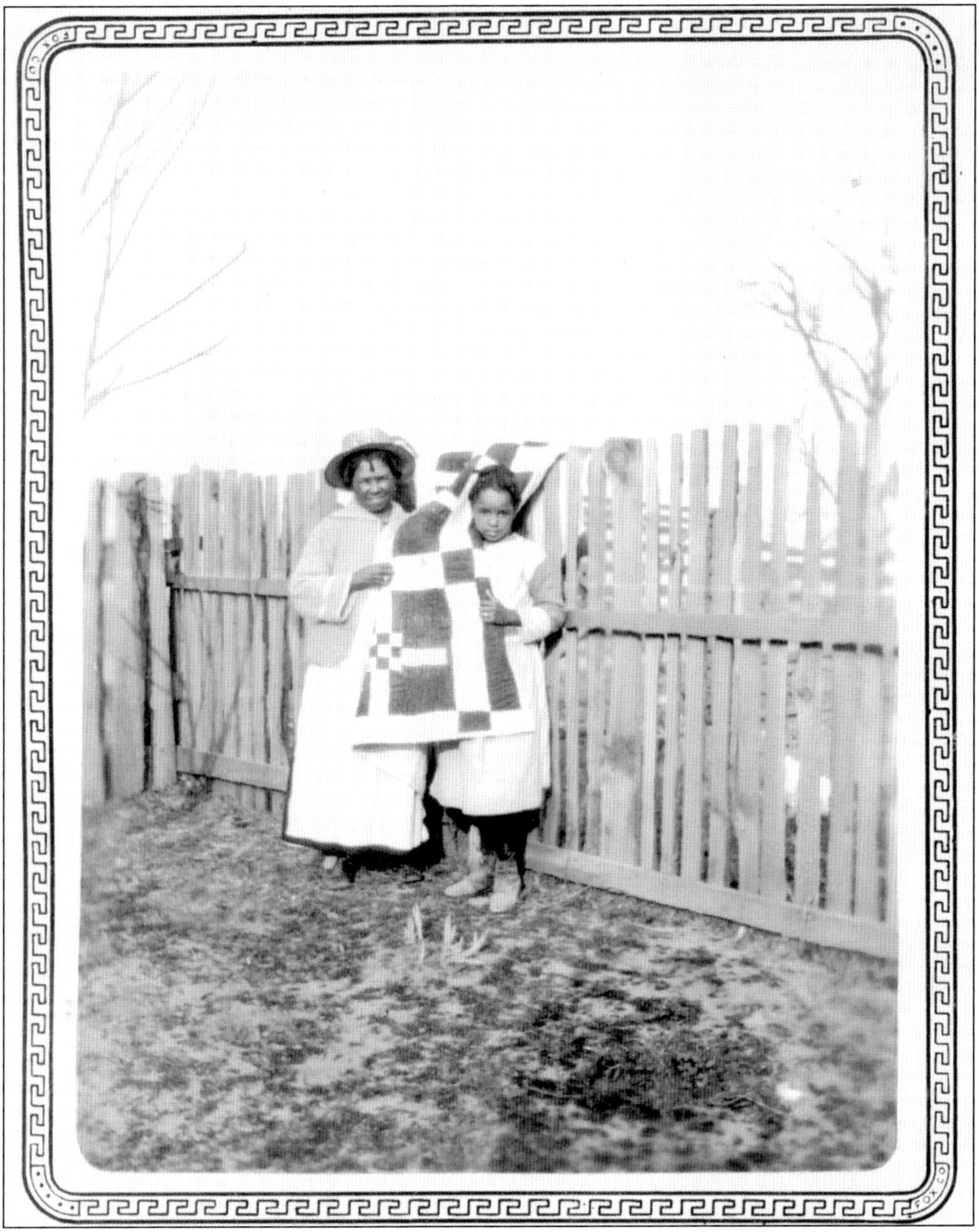

Cotton was a way of life on the plantation and was commonly used in the production of quilts. During winter months, every bed had one or more quilts. Bennie Allen recalls how his mother prepared for quilt making: "She had four poles, and she would put them together on the floor first, the bottom of the quilt on the floor. Then she would get the cotton and put the cotton all through it. Then she would put the top [part of the quilt] down on [the cotton]. She would pin it and take it and put it in the frame. It was ready to quilt then." (Courtesy of Cammie Henry Research Center, Northwestern State University.)

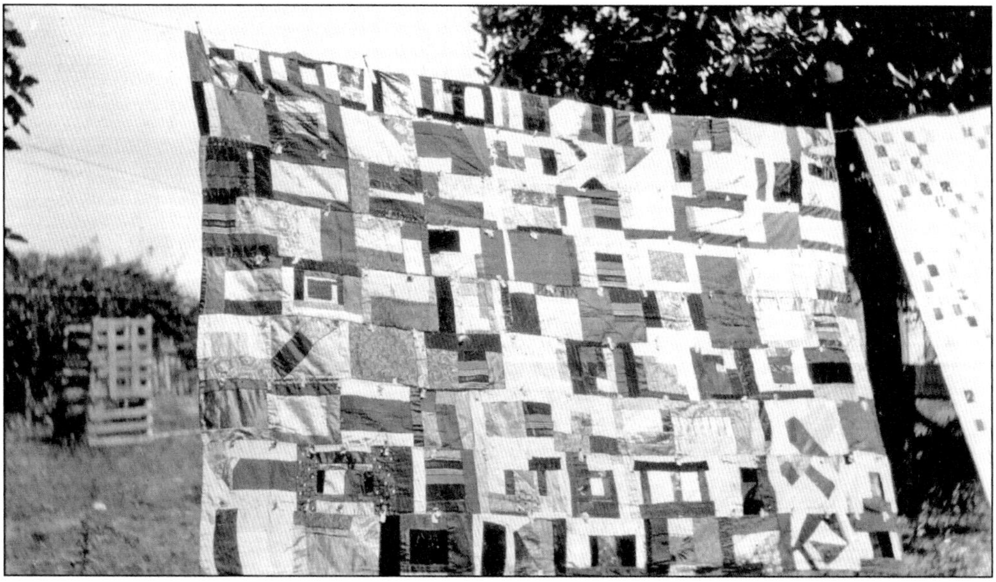

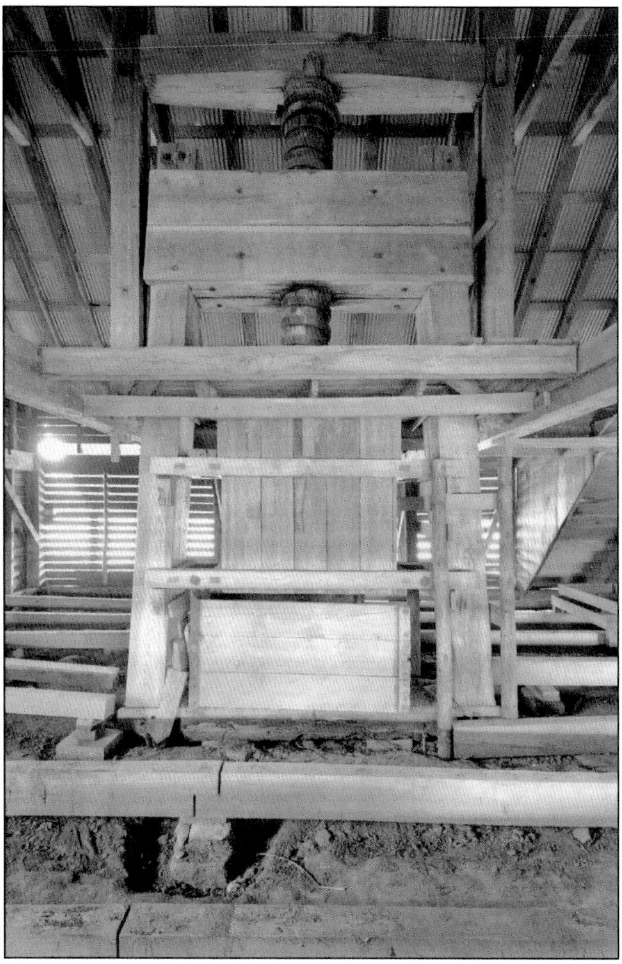

Women quilted with two basic design types: appliqué and patchwork. Aesthetically, African American quilts are thought to hold some common elements that are not visible in other quilts. Those commonalities are the use of vertical stripe organization, bold color, large design elements, asymmetry, and multiple patterning. A small group of skilled quilters could complete a quilt in one night. (Courtesy of Cammie Henry Research Center, Northwestern State University.)

By 1850, most plantations had switched to steam-powered cotton presses, unlike the manual one featured here at Magnolia Plantation. After a tornado destroyed the original mule-driven press, this press was built sometime between 1890 and 1900. Today it holds the distinction of being one of half a dozen similar presses in the United States and the only press in its original location. (Courtesy of the Library of Congress.)

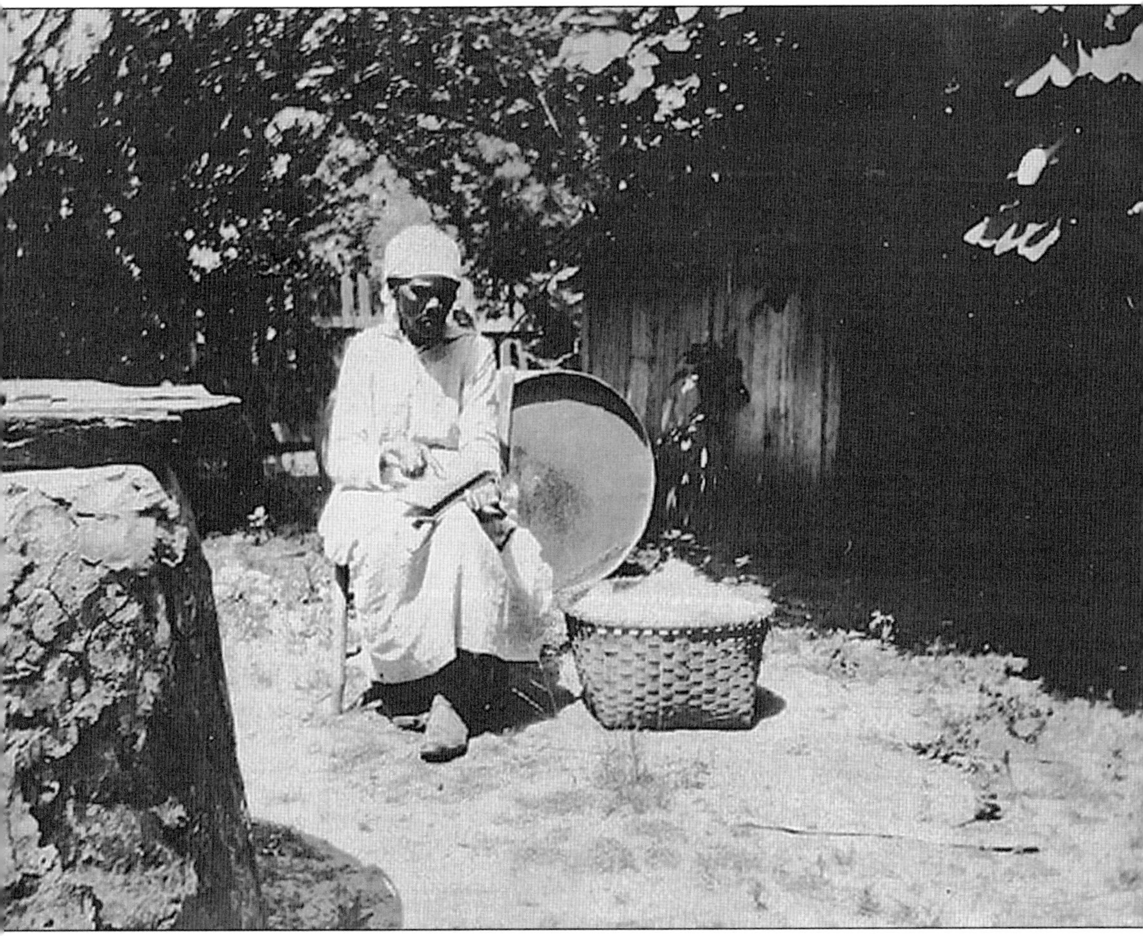

Too old to work at some of the more strenuous jobs, this woman is combing cotton to pick out the seeds in preparation for weaving. Plantation life required many job specializations. Spinning and weaving were occupations in which both men and women worked. (Courtesy of Cammie Henry Research Center, Northwestern State University.)

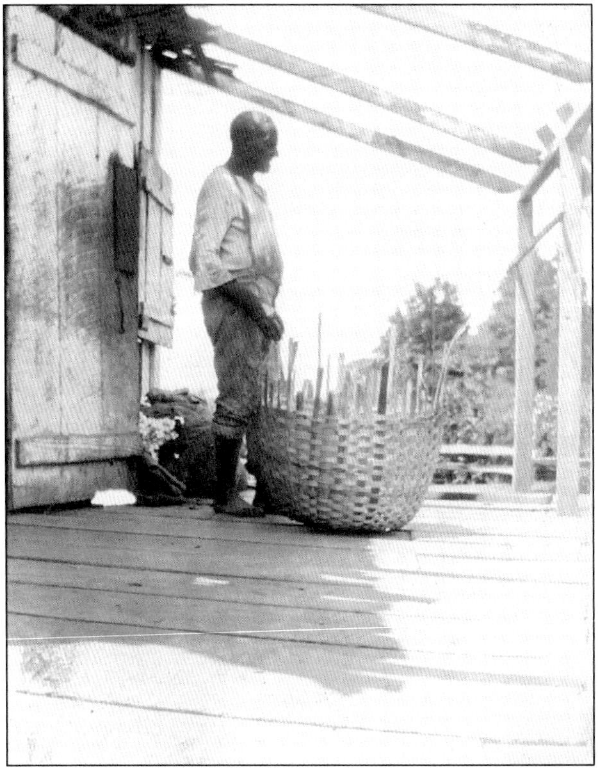

Basket maker Clement Claiborne, a former slave at Oakland Plantation, settled at Melrose Plantation in his later years. Claiborne was known throughout the region for the beautiful, handcrafted white-oak baskets he made. (Courtesy of Cammie Henry Research Center, Northwestern State University.)

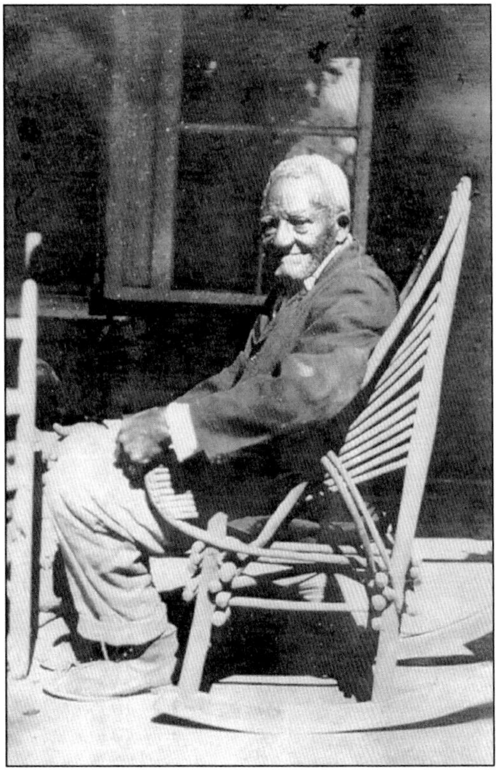

Clement Claiborne poses in a handcrafted rocking chair. Many items were made on the plantation, including furniture, baskets, and cloth. Several of Claiborne's descendants currently live in Natchitoches Parish. (Courtesy of Cammie Henry Research Center, Northwestern State University.)

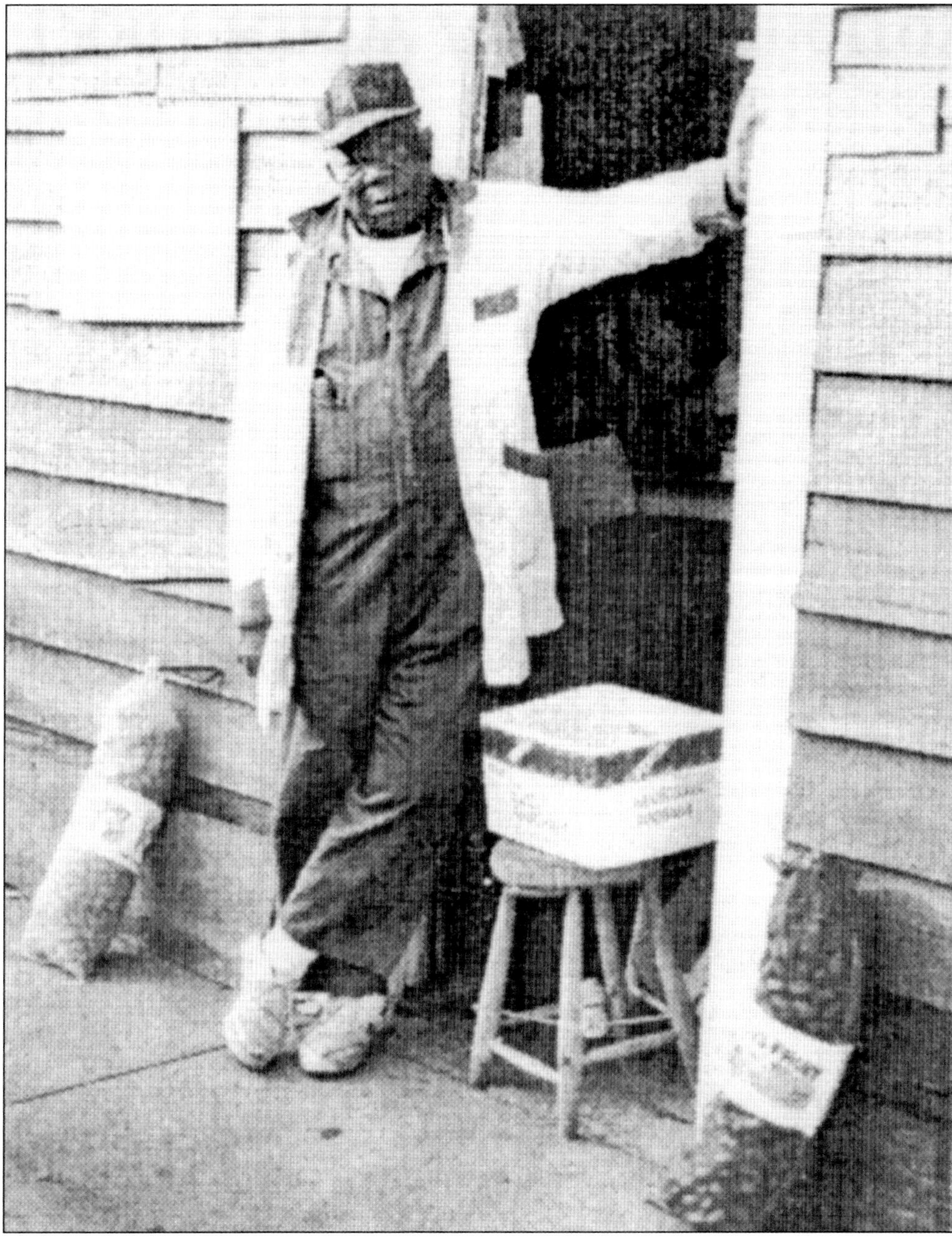

In the early 20th century, Jim Crow segregation laws restricted the ability of African Americans to conduct business in the city. Consequently, African Americans gathered behind the Ford automobile dealership located on the corner of Lafayette and Front Streets. This area became affectionately known as the "Ape Yard" and was equivalent to a black business district. Less than a full block in size, this area was bounded by Horne and Lafayette Streets to the south and north and by an unnamed lane to the west. Inside the "Ape Yard" was a barbershop, blacksmith shop, shoeshine stand, and several small marketplaces. In this image is Sam Cole, who operated the shoeshine stand and sold vegetables for several years before working for Sears, Roebuck, and Company. (Courtesy of the Cole family.)

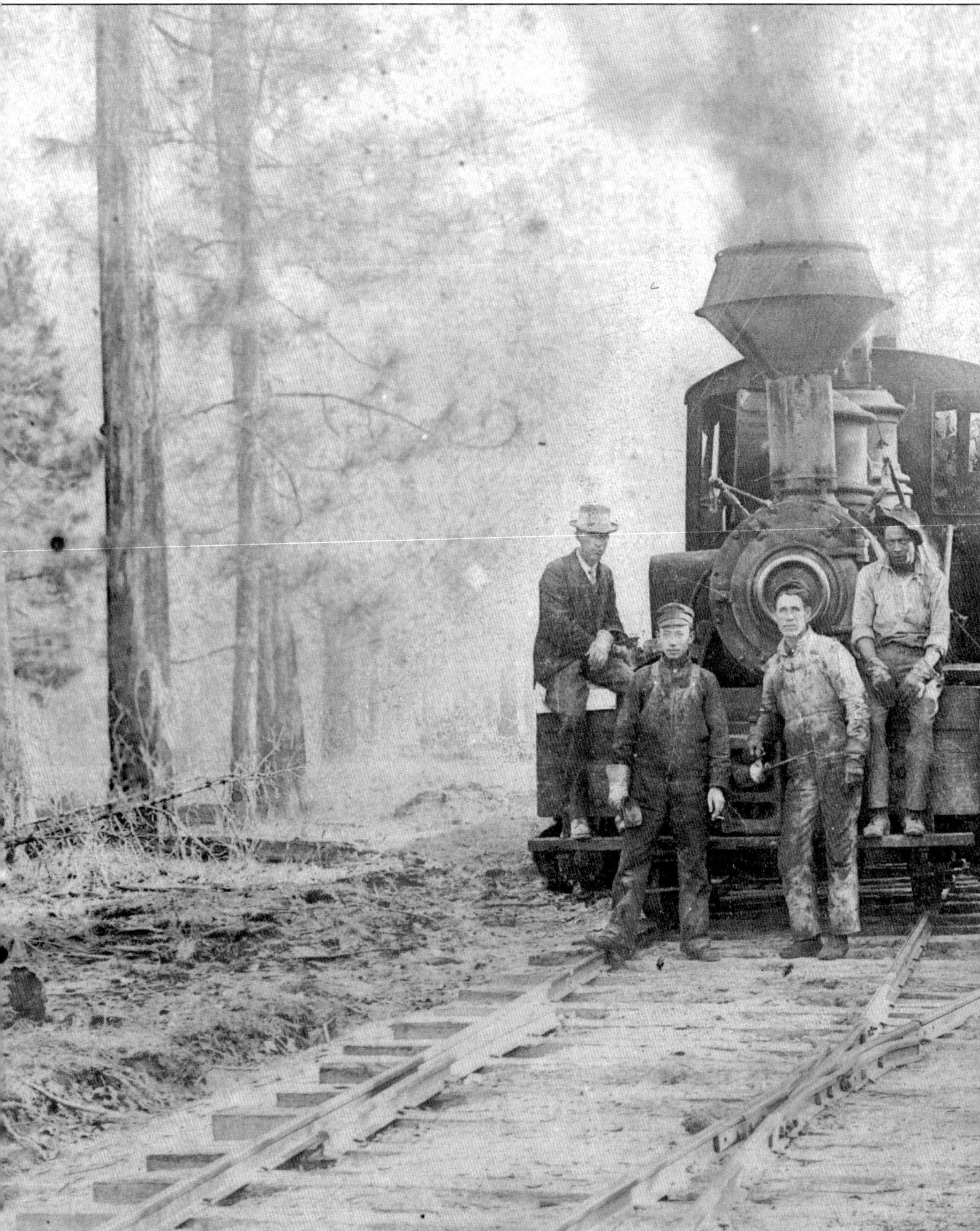

Albert Morris, who worked in railroad construction, describes the strenuous conditions of this work: "We had to tote them old long rails on your shoulders. It ain't no tale about working on a railroad. That's the hottest day looks like it ever was. We used to call [the rails] 'them

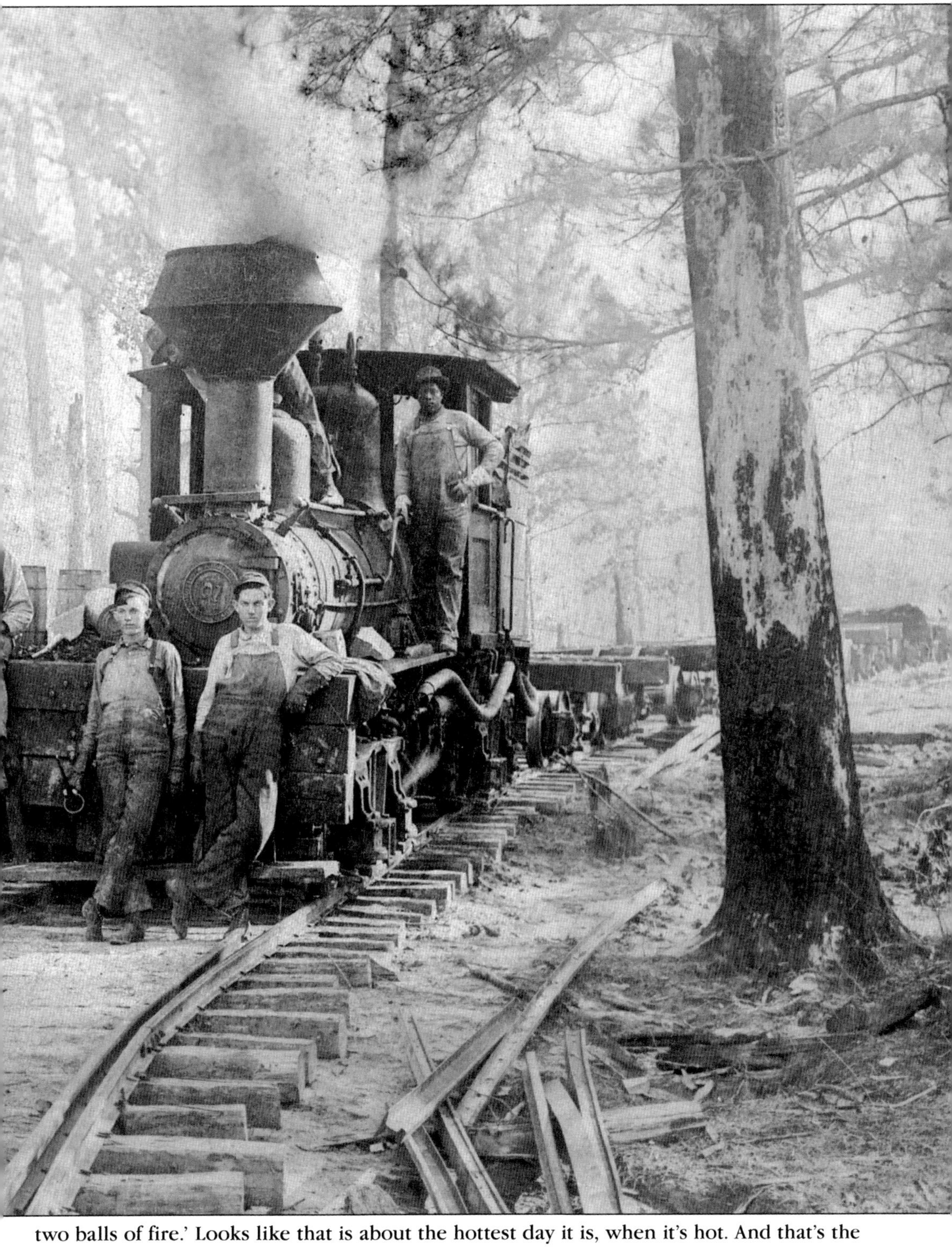

two balls of fire.' Looks like that is about the hottest day it is, when it's hot. And that's the coldest place when it's cold. It feels like you don't have no hands or feet they be so cold." (Courtesy of Cammie Henry Research Center, Northwestern State University.)

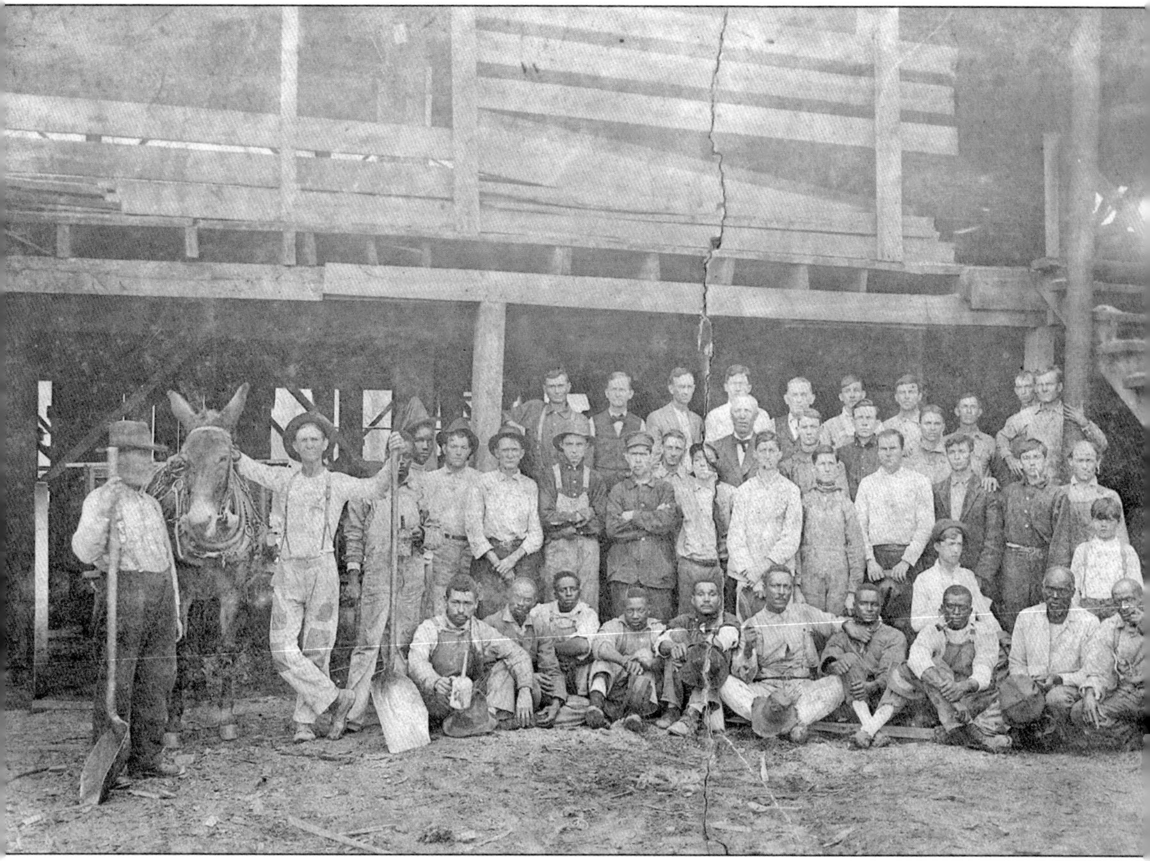

The Weaver Brothers' Sawmill crew takes time from their workday to pose for this photograph taken in 1915. Burton D. Weaver Sr. opened the mill, located in Flora, Louisiana, in the southwestern portion of the parish, after migrating to the state from Georgia. The mill closed during World War II and sent most of its scrap metal and building materials to the war effort. The sawmill industry was perhaps the only profession that defied Jim Crow policies and paid equal wages for work. (Courtesy of the Weaver family.)

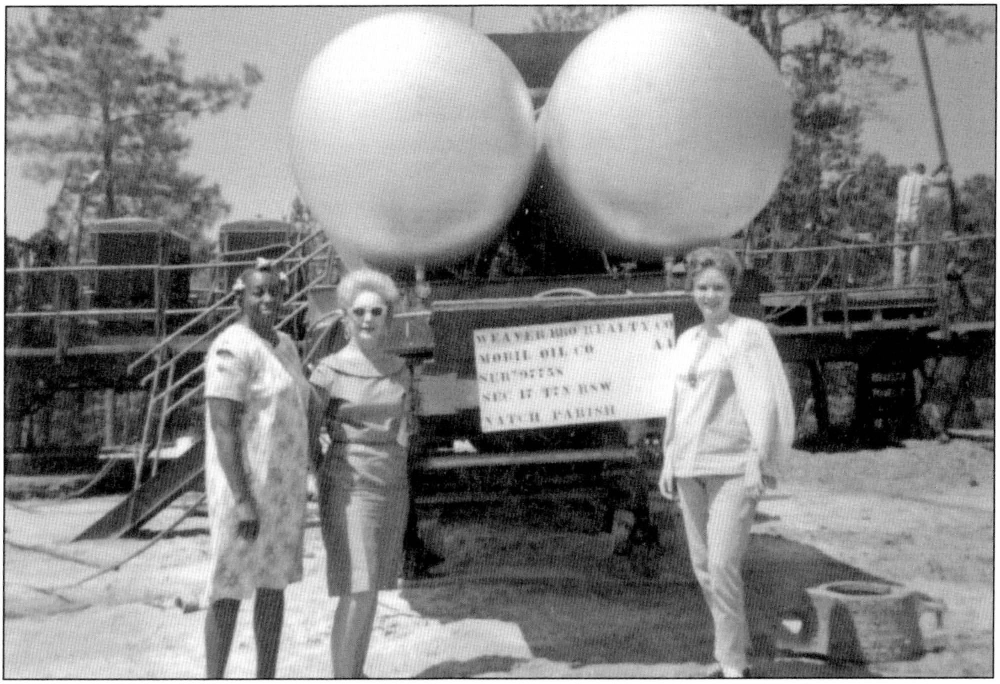

Next the family opened the Weaver Brothers Realty Company. They have also operated several companies under the name Weaver Brothers, including the current business, Weaver Brothers Land and Timber Company. Standing from left to right are Emma Lee Page Manning, who raised two generations of Weavers; Lois Boone Weaver, a schoolteacher; and her daughter-in-law, Jerri Roberts Weaver. (Courtesy of the Weaver family.)

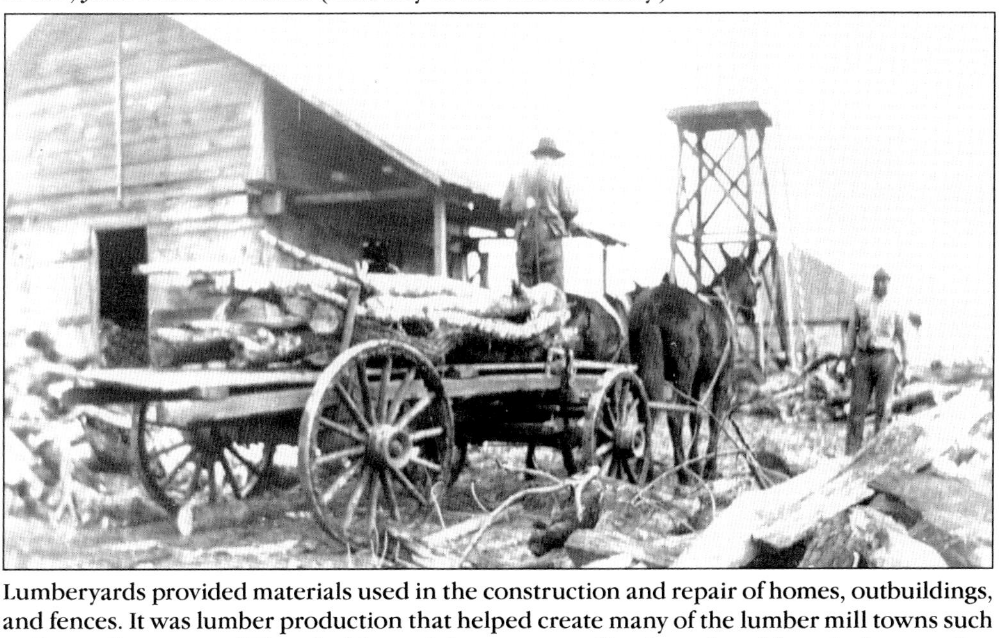

Lumberyards provided materials used in the construction and repair of homes, outbuildings, and fences. It was lumber production that helped create many of the lumber mill towns such as Derry, Cypress, and Victoria. Many of those towns still exist today, although there are few remnants of the prosperity that once existed there. (Courtesy of Cammie Henry Research Center, Northwestern State University.)

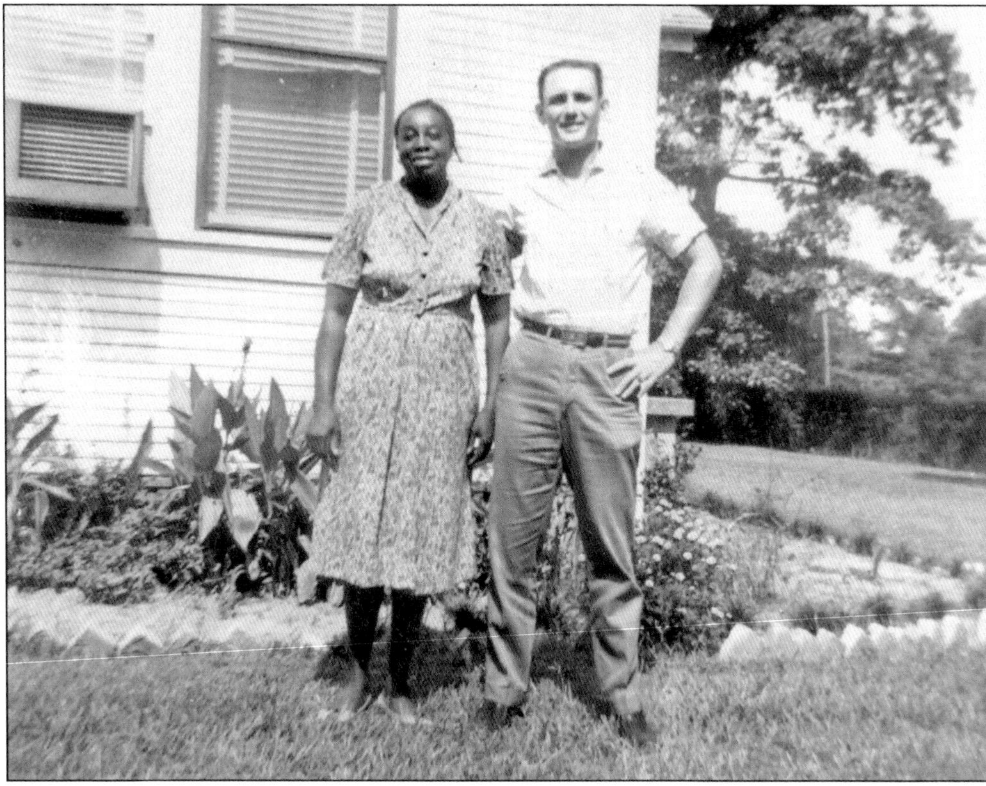

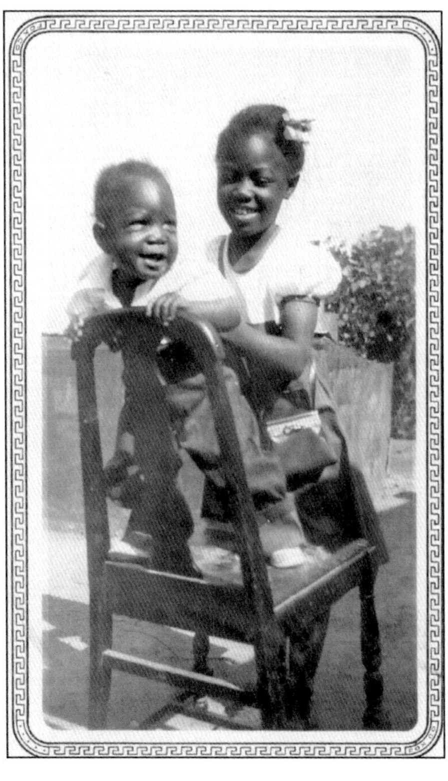

This 1955 image of Emma Lee Page Manning and Burton Weaver Jr. attests to the longevity of her employment with the Weaver family. Manning went to work for the family when Weaver was a baby. Here he stands as a business administration student at Northwestern State University. (Courtesy of the Weaver family.)

Johnnie Mae and Frank Manning, both children of Emma Lee Page Manning, are dressed for a special occasion. Johnnie Mae currently resides in Los Angeles, California, where she practices law. Her brother Frank lives in St. Louis, Missouri, and owns several nursing homes. (Courtesy of the Weaver family.)

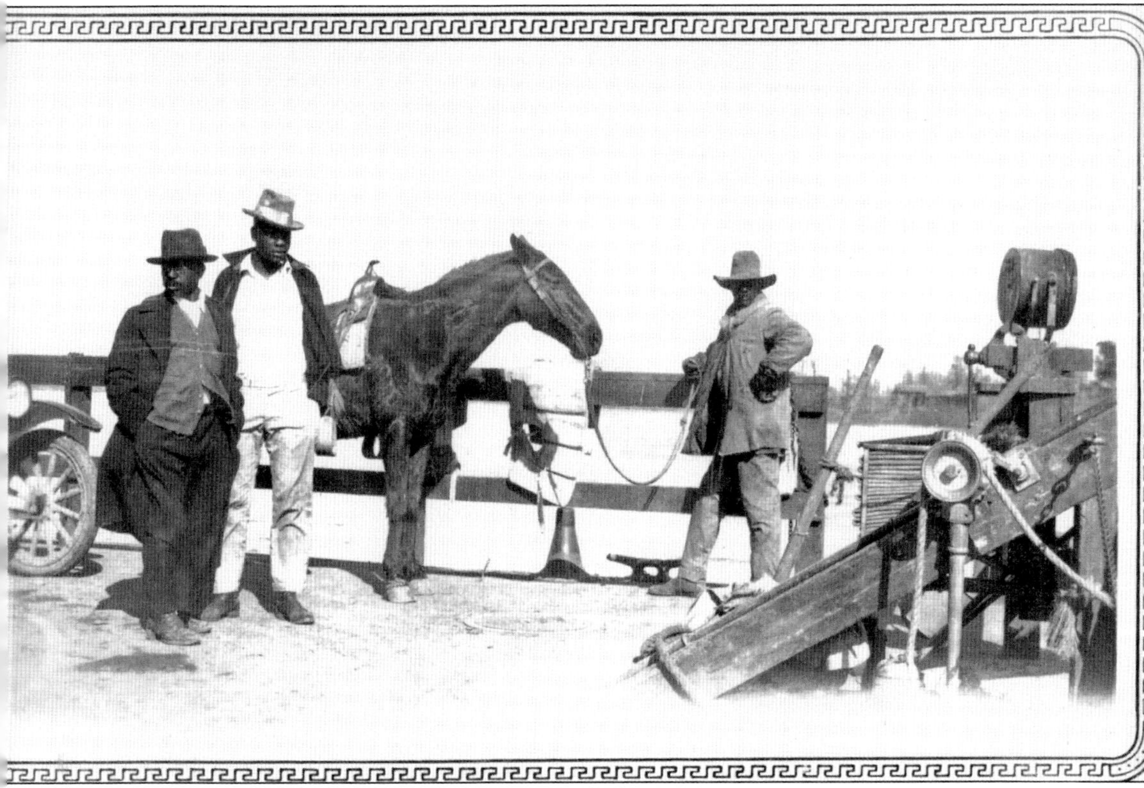

Alfra Wade (not pictured here) tells of one ferry service that was available when he was a young man: "You probably heard of Monnett Ferry. Well that's where we was to go across to [the towns of] Montgomery and Colfax. We would cross Red River at Montgomery on a ferry that would take people on the east side to the west side." These men are waiting for a ferry to travel across the river. (Courtesy of Cammie Henry Research Center, Northwestern State University.)

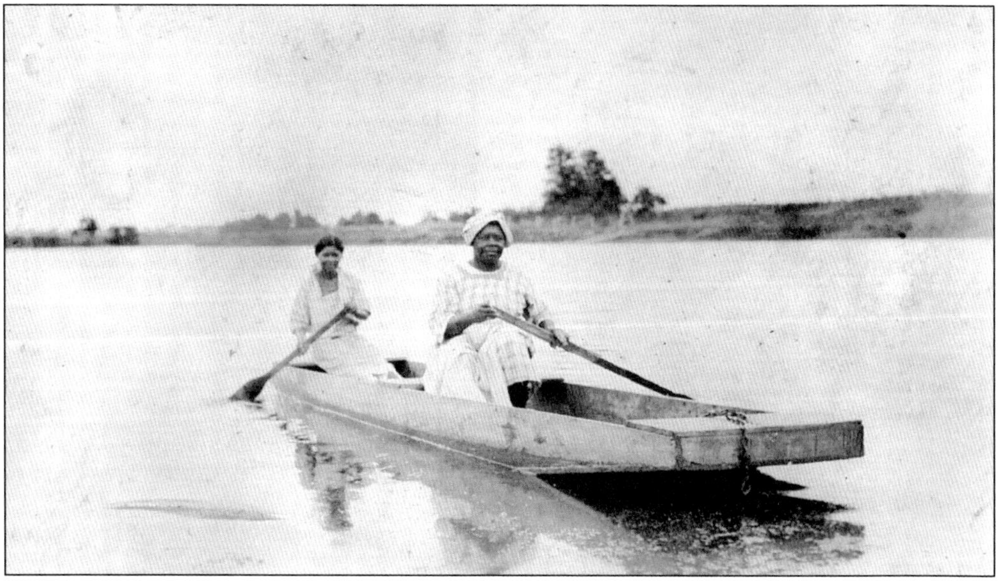

Water transportation was almost as important as land transportation. People in Natchitoches used waterways to go to work, school, and church. Several African American churches were physically moved from one location to another by boat. (Courtesy of Cammie Henry Research Center.)

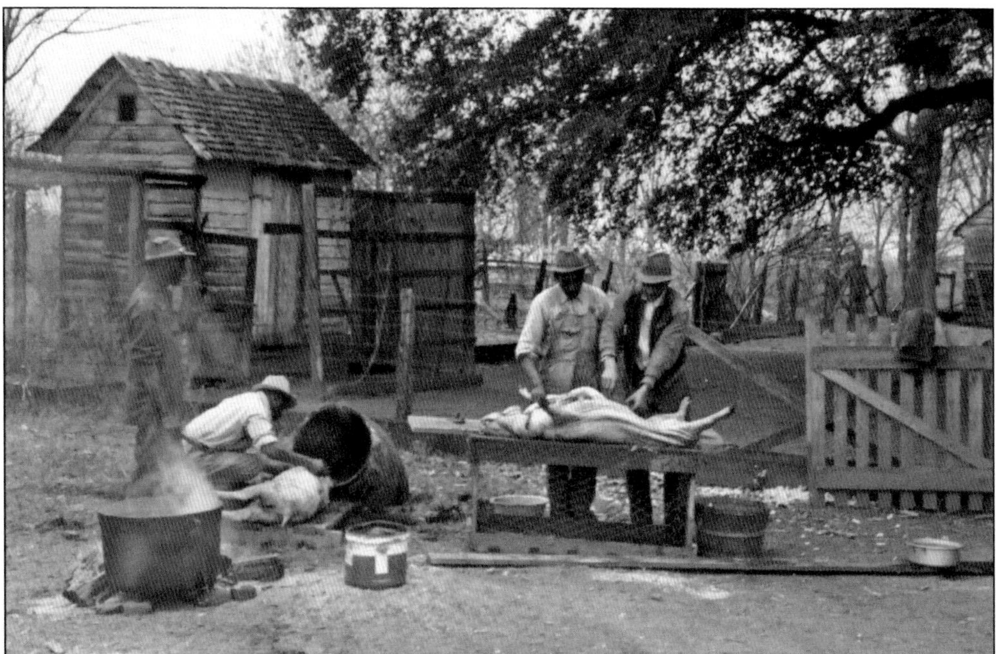

Hog-killing time generally occurred twice a year—once in the spring and once in the winter. Rev. Moses Rawland recalls hog-slaughtering time: "It was set apart, that day. Everybody would come at a designated spot, a designated house. They would come, and it was considered a festive time." Cliff Lemell, second from right, used to preach for the Magnolia Plantation residents. Also seen are John Vercher (kneeling) and Brindie Gallien (far right). (Courtesy of Ambrose Hertzog Jr.)

Rev. Moses Rawland describes the process of preparing a hog after slaughter: "They would get the old black pot and get the water hot. Then pour that hot water on it [the hog]. Then they would scrape him. They would hang him and gut him. My mother and them would be cleaning chitlins, and my daddy would be dressing the hog out. They would take the chitlins and they would cut it and wash it." (Courtesy of Ambrose Hertzog Jr.)

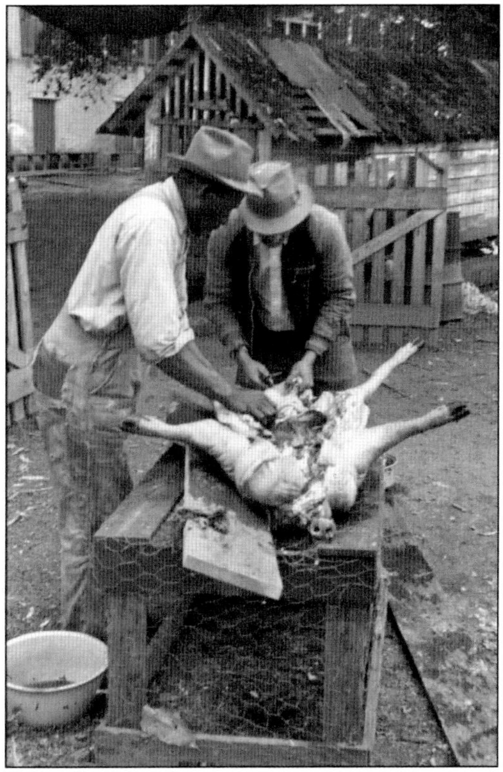

John Vercher trained horses for the Hertzog family at Magnolia Plantation. During the 1940s, the Hertzogs sponsored and participated in several horse races. Alphonse Metoyer told of races in which people came from Alexandria, Shreveport, and parts of Oklahoma. Many of the horse owners had substantial landholdings, worked in the oil field business, or were car dealers. At a well-attended race, a horse owner could make $26,000. (Courtesy of Ambrose Hertzog Jr.)

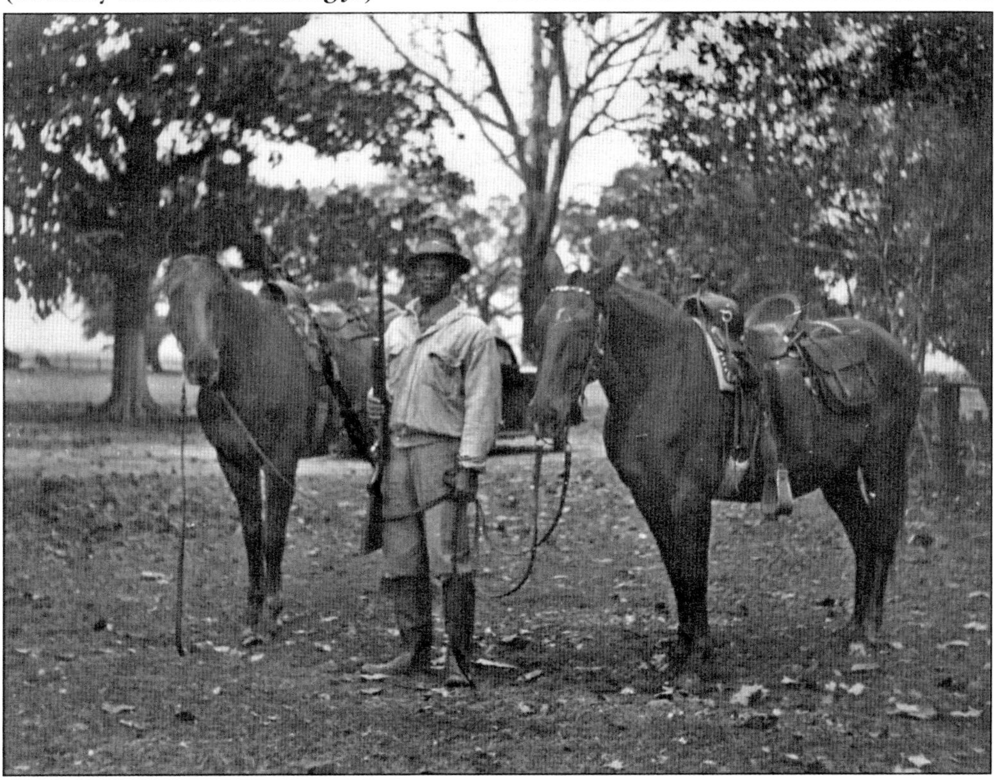

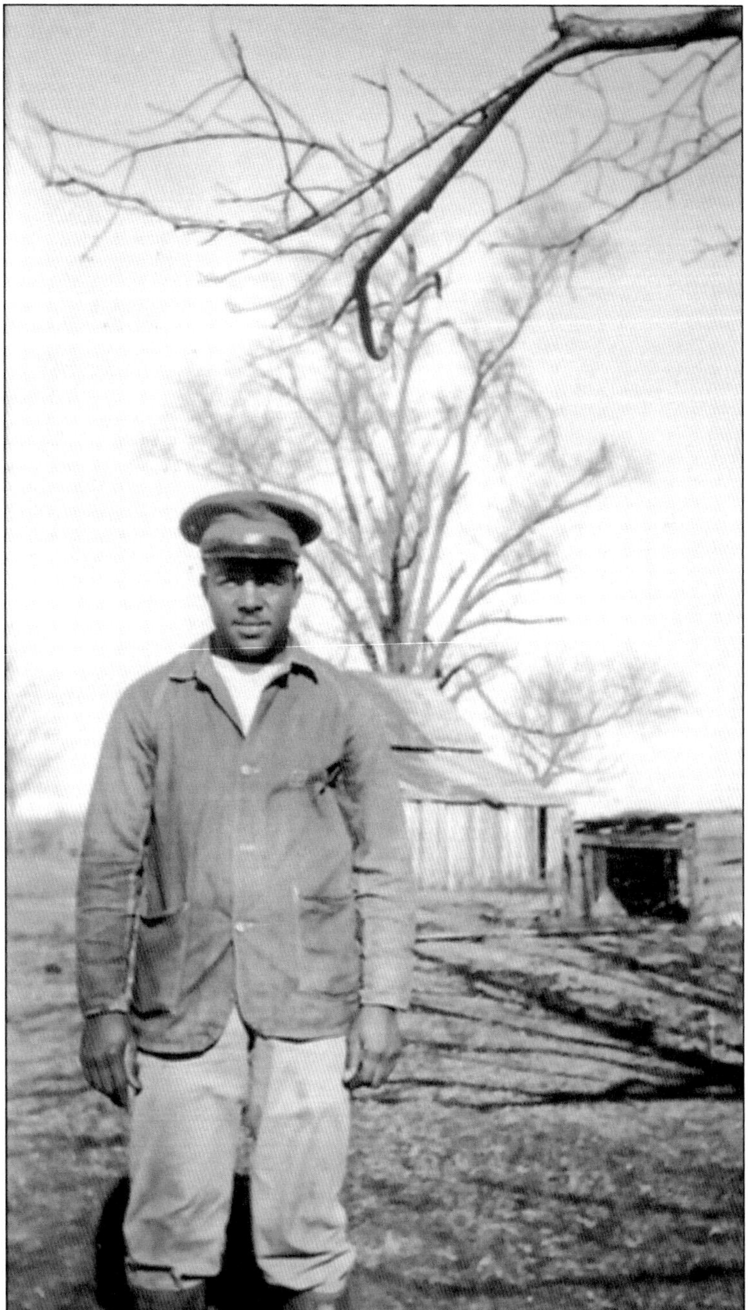

Many African American men from Natchitoches Parish spent time in a branch of the armed forces, like this unidentified man. Another local resident, Wesley Johnson, remembers being discharged from the army in 1945. He attended Grambling State University for six months before being called back to Fort Bragg in North Carolina. From Fort Bragg, Johnson traveled to Washington, D.C., and from Washington, D.C., back overseas. He received his final discharge papers in 1950. (Courtesy of Cammie Henry Research Center, Northwestern State University.)

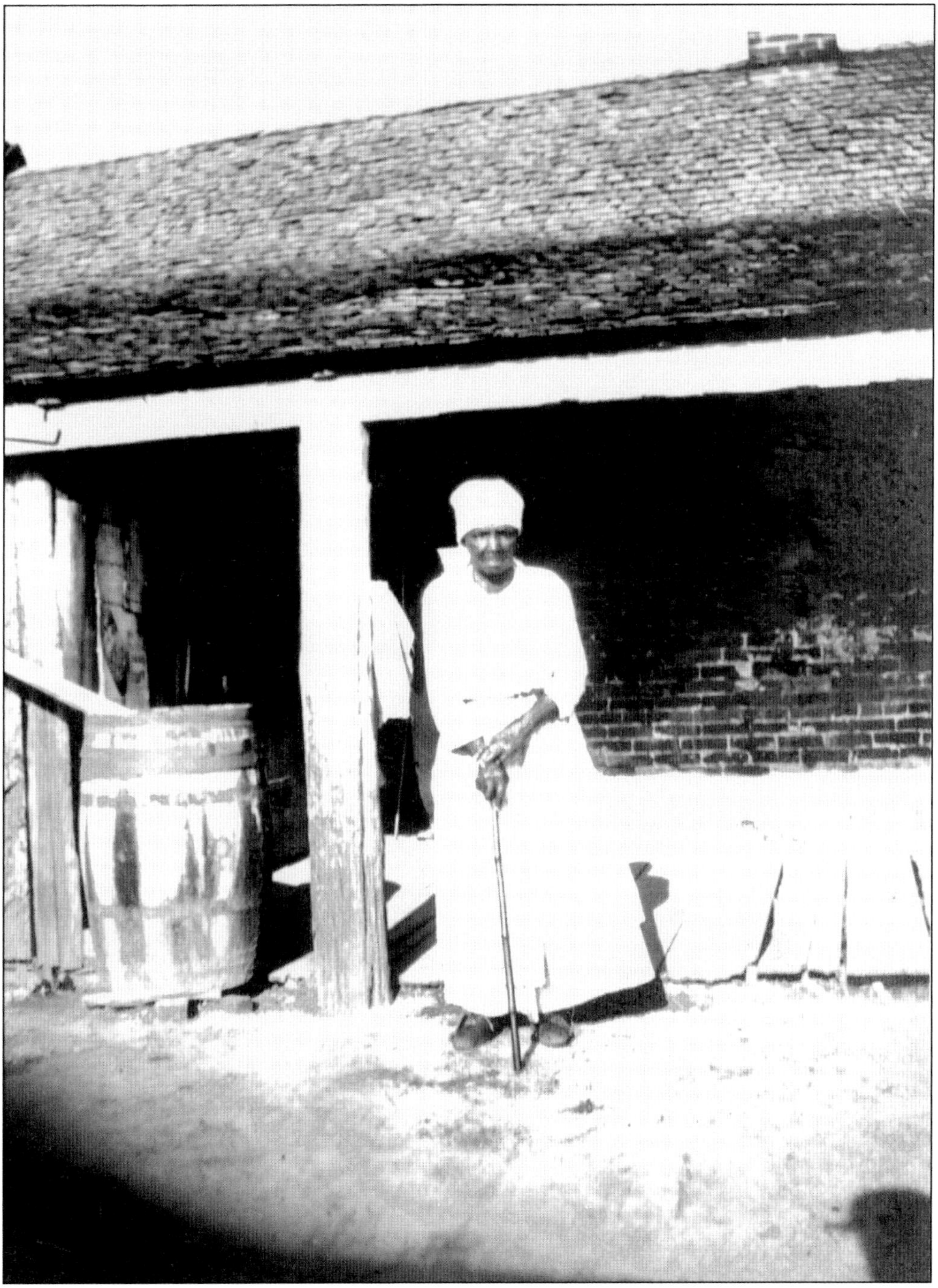

Aunt Agnes, an old midwife, was thought to be 119 years old when she died. Midwives delivered most of the babies in rural Natchitoches. In the 1950s, women were given the option of going to Confederate Memorial Hospital, now a part of Louisiana State University in Shreveport, or having a midwife deliver the baby at home. (Courtesy of Cammie Henry Research Center, Northwestern State University.)

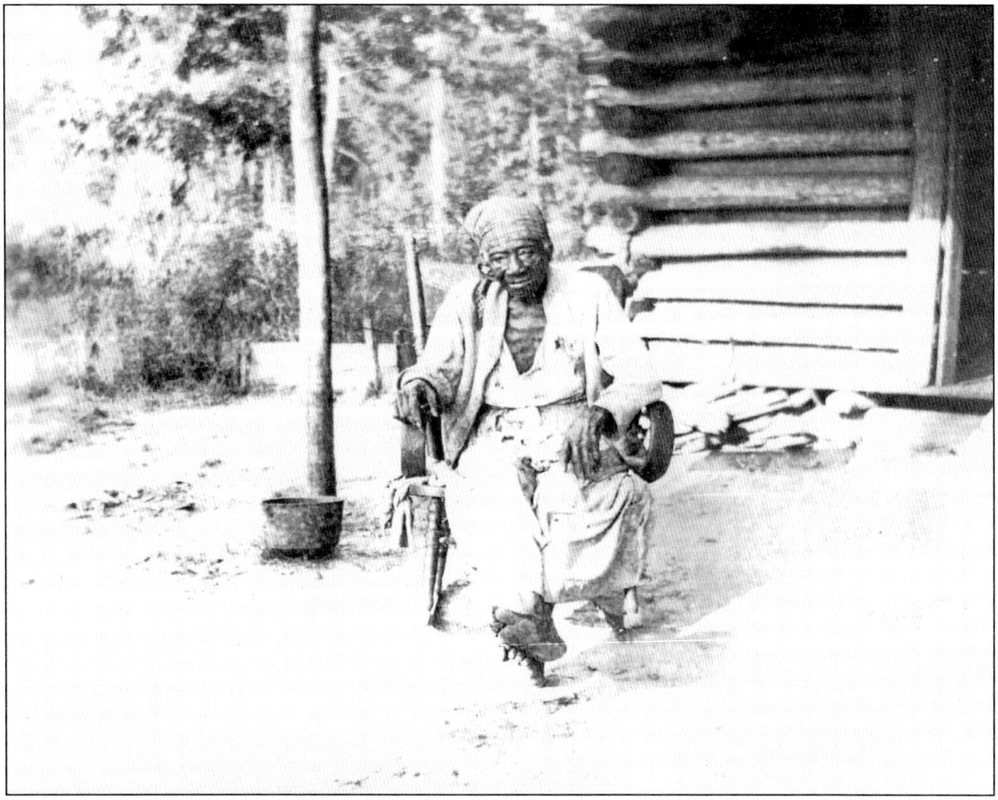

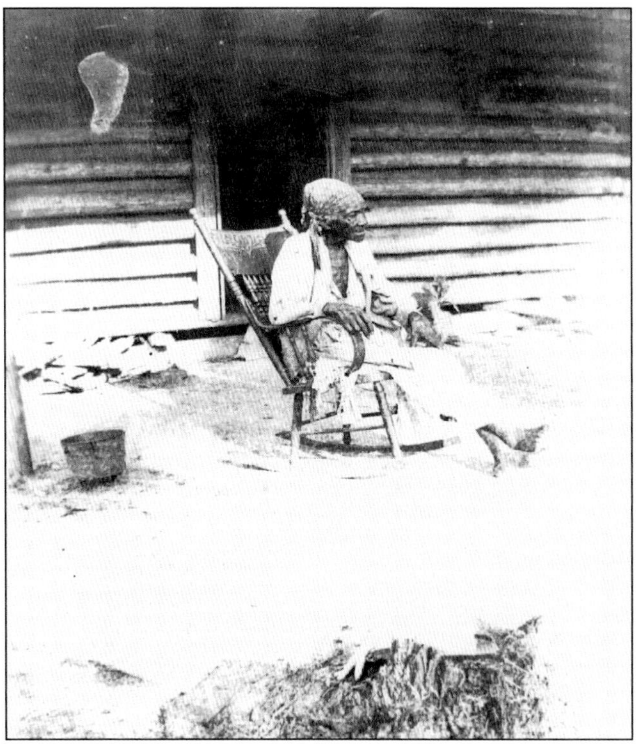

Aunt Winnie was at least 100 years old when these photographs were taken in the 1940s. She sits in the yard, perhaps resting after performing some minimal chore. Too old to care for herself, she may have lived with a child or relative. As was customary in Aunt Winnie's day, in the absence of family, community elders were generally cared for by community members. (Courtesy of Cammie Henry Research Center, Northwestern State University.)

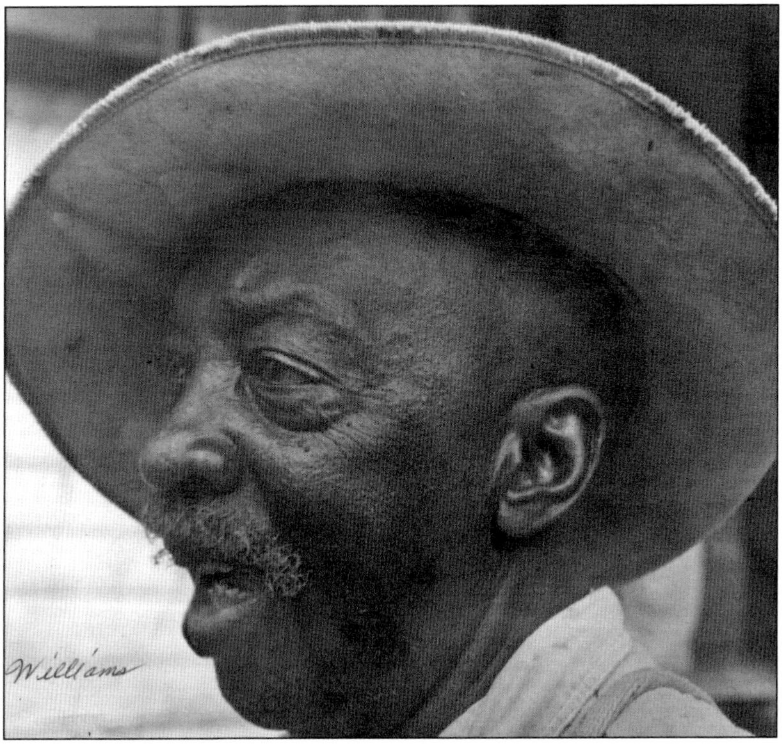

Cotton Williams, pictured here, had a son named Jack. Folks living at the Hertzog place nicknamed him "Jack of Cot" in reference to his status as Cotton's son. Jack of Cot became a cowboy as an adult. (Courtesy of Ambrose Hertzog Jr.)

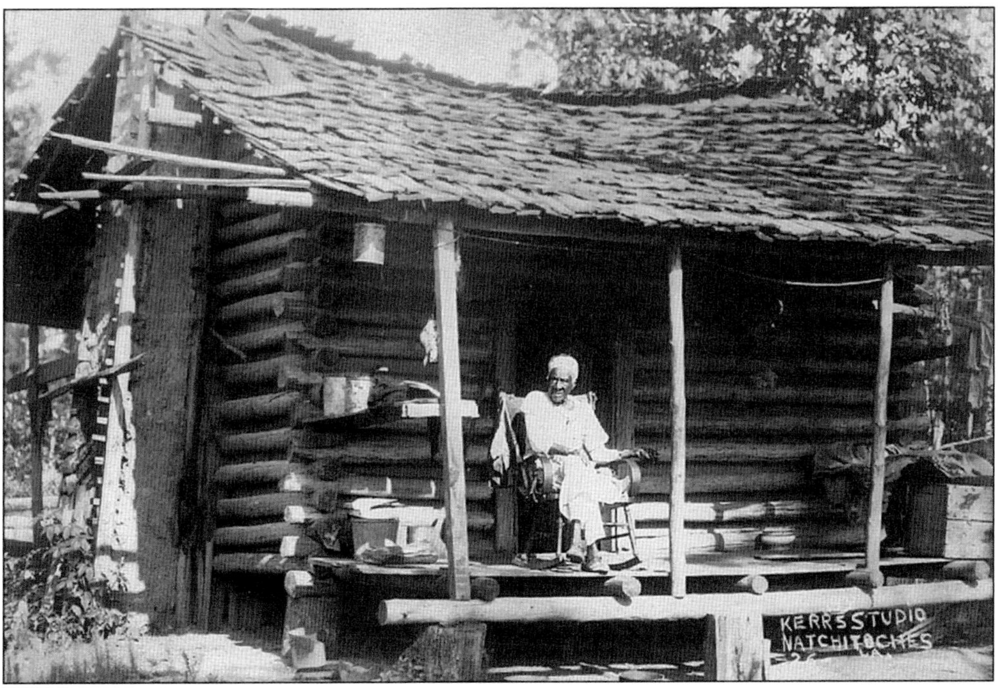

Black Lake, located approximately 15 miles northeast of Natchitoches, is home to many species of birds, fish, and turtles. This unidentified woman lived near the lake when Arthur Babb, a civil engineer for Texas and Pacific Railway, captured this image in the 1940s. (Courtesy of Cammie Henry Research Center, Northwestern State University.)

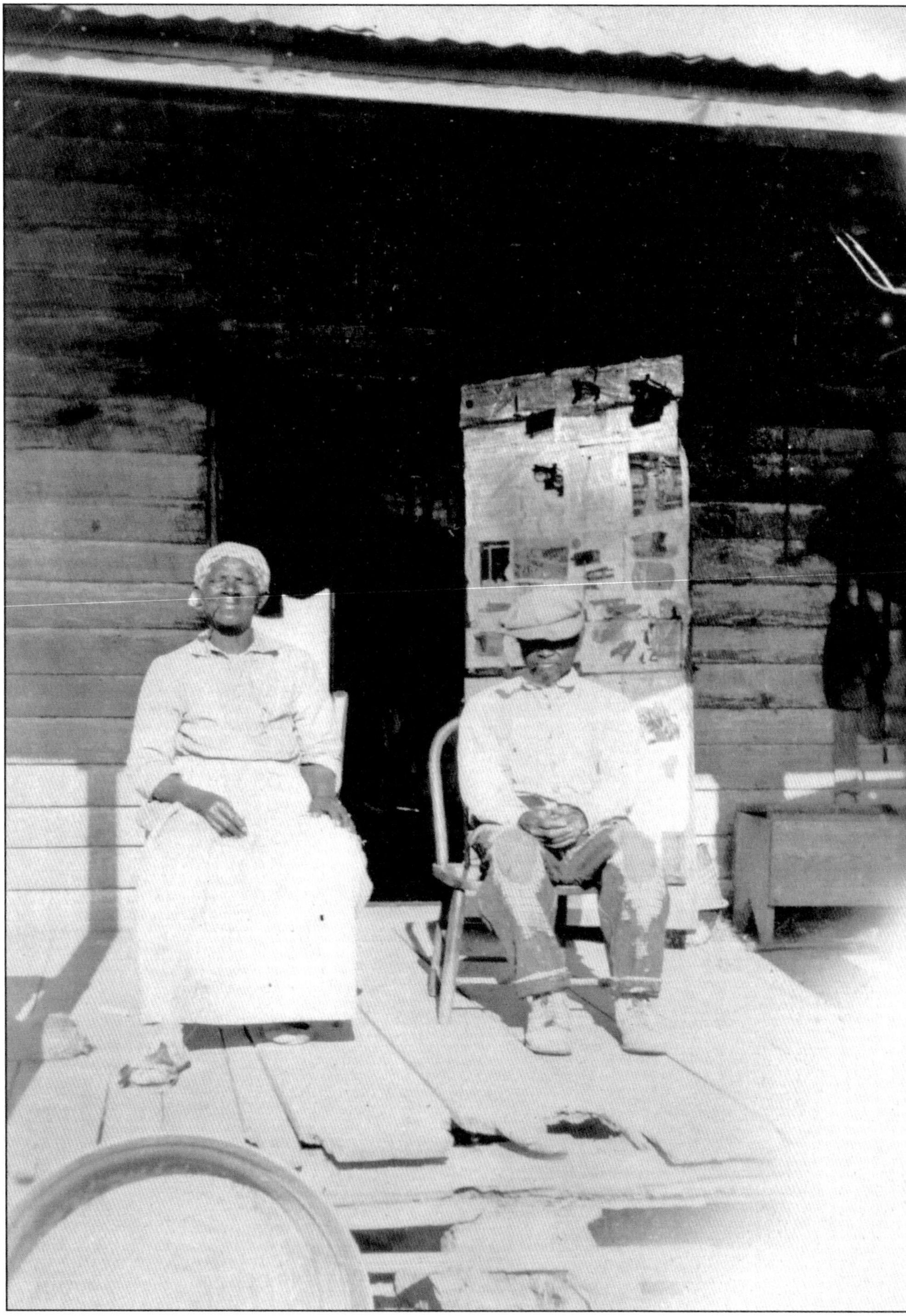

Rural farmers from the 1940s to the 1960s used newspaper advertisements and magazine pages as wallpaper. The most popular decorations were fashion and religious images. Interestingly, this couple has chosen to enhance their home with pages of farming equipment and other machinery. (Courtesy of Cammie Henry Research Center, Northwestern State University.)

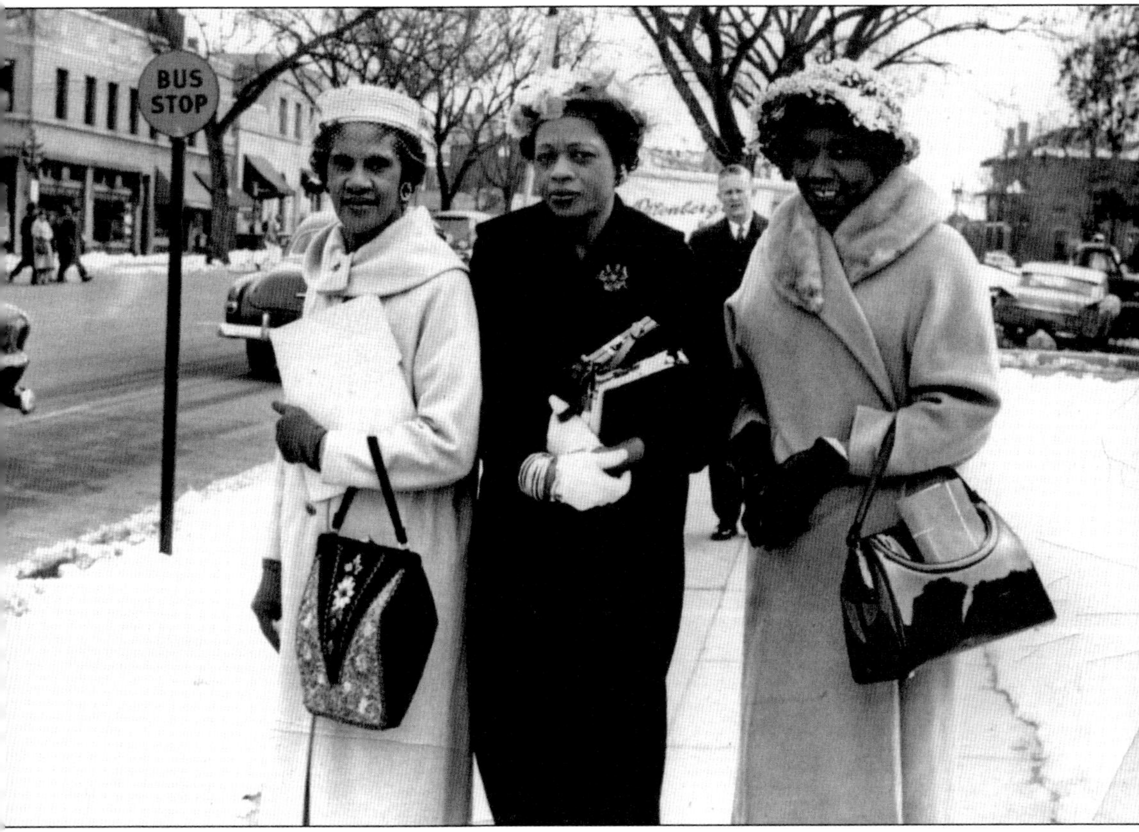

The Jeanes Foundation, created by Anna T. Jeanes of Philadelphia, donated $1 million in 1907 for the purpose of helping Southern states educate African Americans. The foundation focused mostly on rural schools. Seen here are several Jeanes supervisors from Natchitoches while on a trip to Washington, D.C. (Courtesy of Edward Ward Jr.)

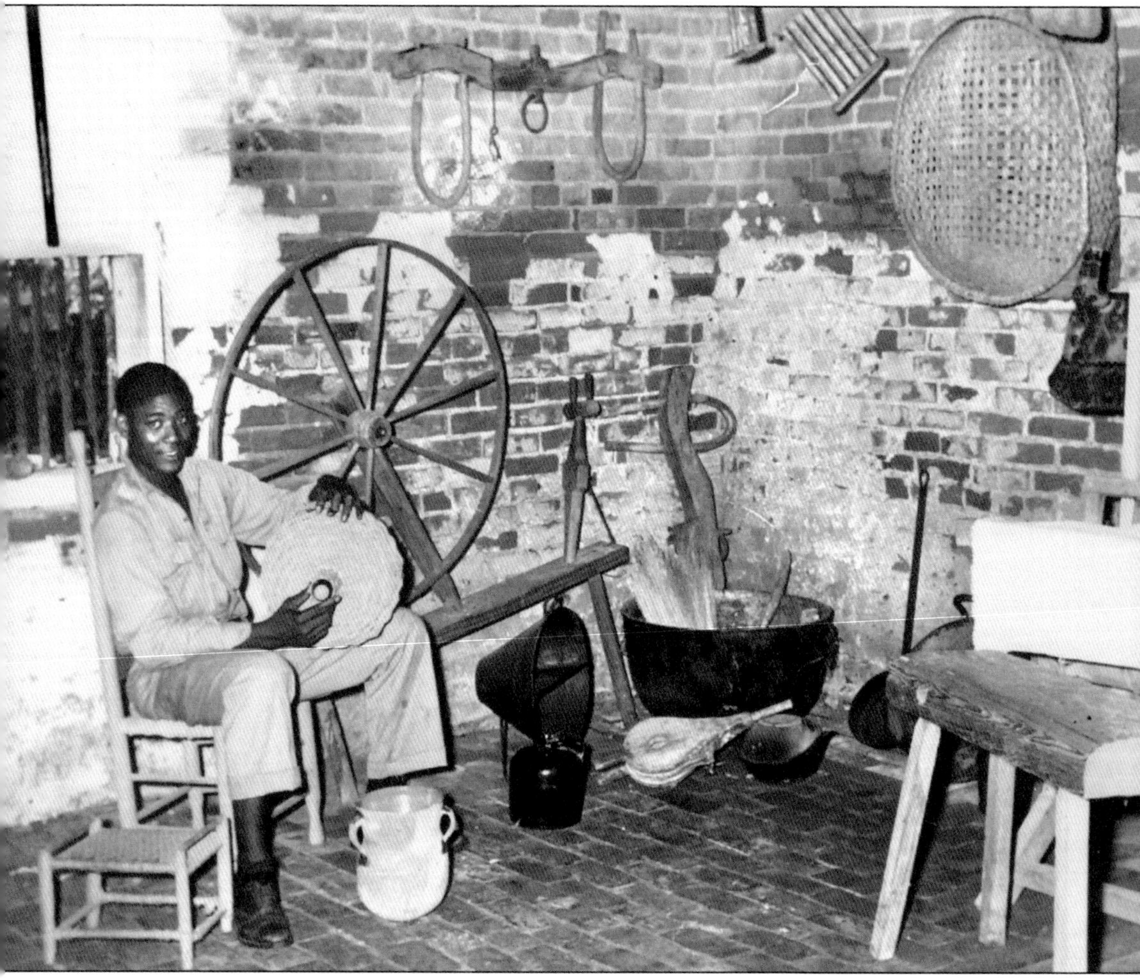

This gentleman sits inside a building on Melrose Plantation. This area contains old equipment used during or shortly after slavery. Cammie Henry, the plantation mistress during the early 20th century, at one time used the facility as a museum. (Courtesy of Cammie Henry Research Center, Northwestern State University.)

Two

The Power of the Good Book

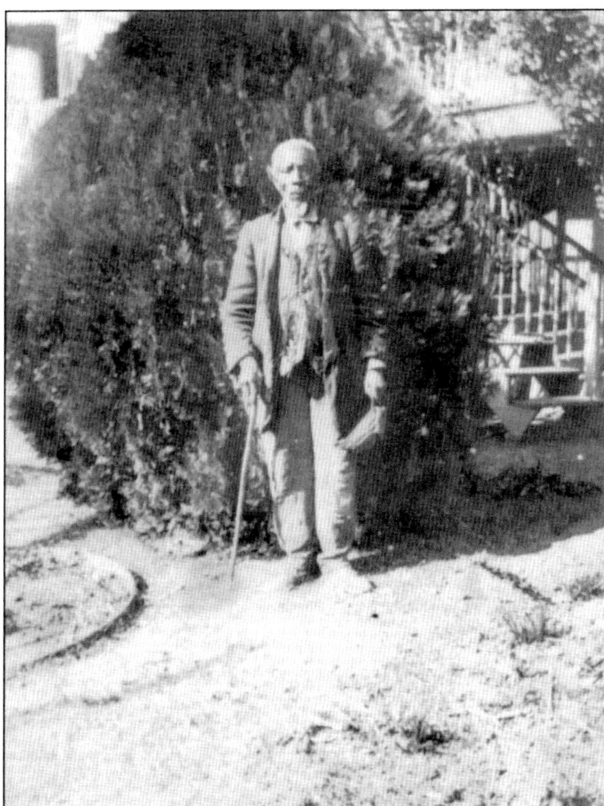

Israel Suddeth, a former slave at Melrose Plantation, remained on the plantation after emancipation. As plantation minister, he was responsible for baptizing converts and regulating religious behavior. The Primitive Rock Church located across the river from the plantation is where Reverend Suddeth conducted services. (Courtesy of Cammie Henry Research Center, Northwestern State University.)

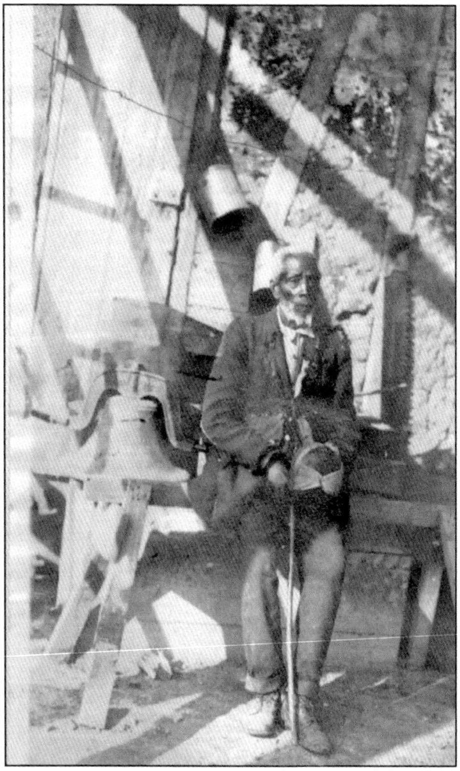

Until the mid-19th century, African American religious leaders were forbidden by law to preach in Louisiana. However, the popularity of Protestantism and the unwillingness of plantation owners to have strangers preach to their slaves led to the "plantation minister." (Courtesy of Cammie Henry Research Center, Northwestern State University.)

Israel Suddeth's wife, Jane, is shown here holding mail near Melrose Plantation's African House. Ministers' wives were also important figures in the community. (Courtesy of Cammie Henry Research Center, Northwestern State University.)

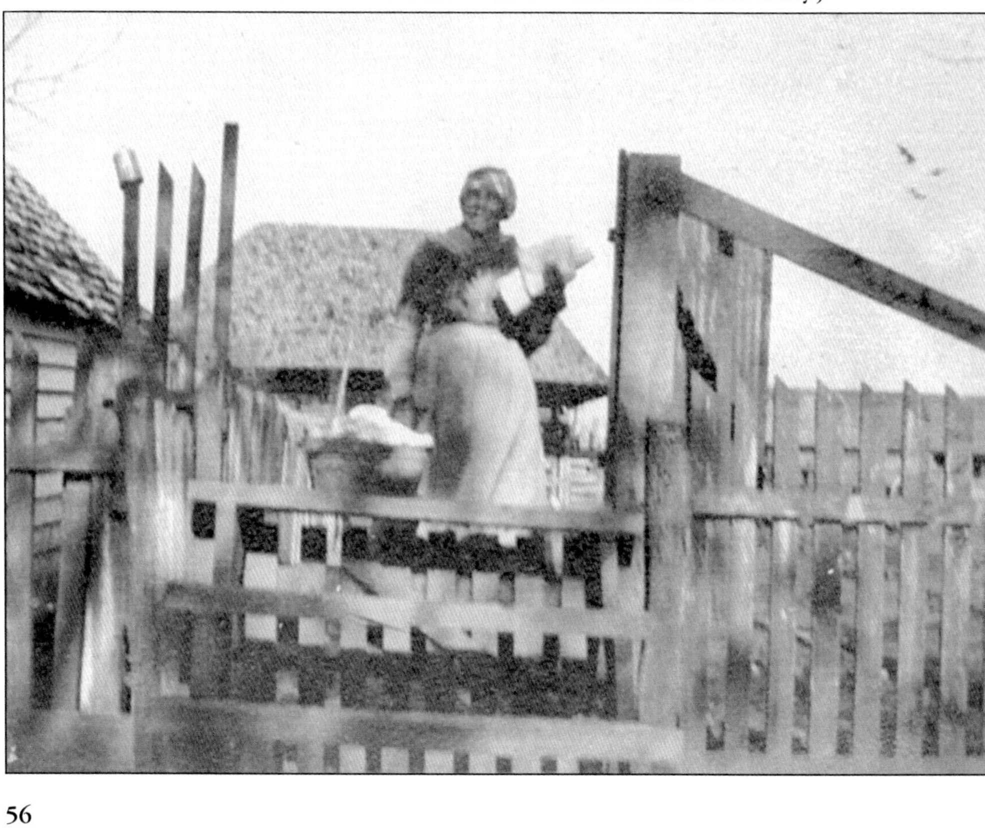

This pastor and his wife stand in front of the bell tower at church. Bells were used as a form of communication to announce special occasions such as a baptism, an emergency, or a death. (Courtesy of Cammie Henry Research Center, Northwestern State University.)

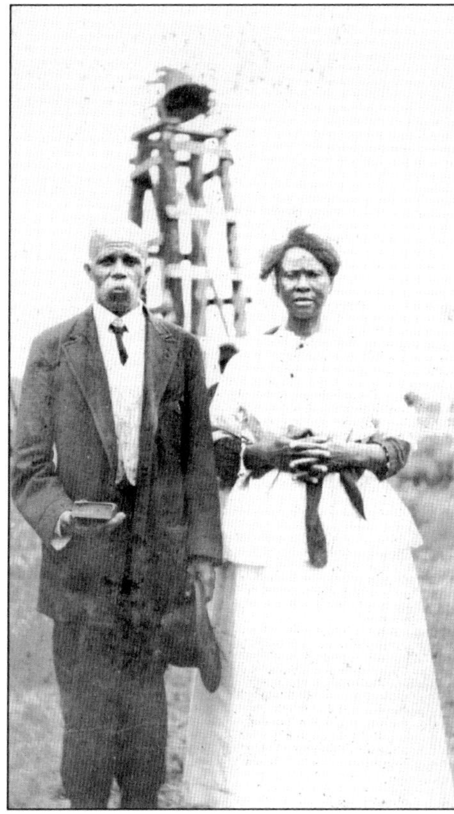

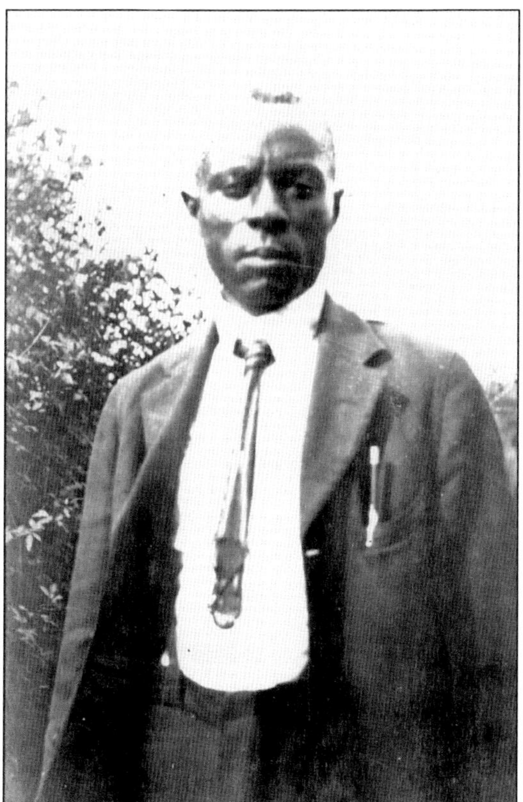

Rev. Jessie Davis was a preacher listed on the 1930 census as neighboring the Hertzog family of Magnolia Plantation. Reverend Davis and his wife, Victoria, had seven children whom they raised in the tradition of farming. Two of the eldest children received some college training. (Courtesy of Cammie Henry Research Center, Northwestern State University.)

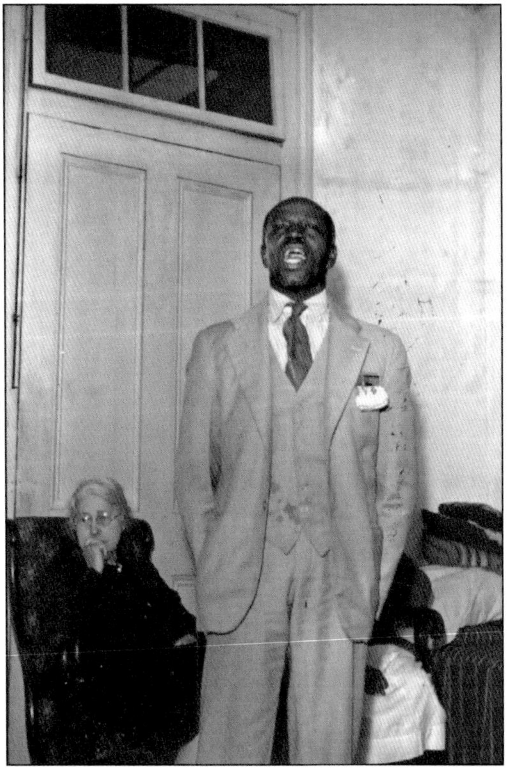

As a minister in the African American community, Reverend Cheatam held multiple roles as a leader, politician, and orator. On this Christmas Day, Reverend Cheatam, from the African Methodist Episcopal Church, stopped in to visit with the Hertzog family at Magnolia Plantation. (Courtesy of Ambrose Hertzog Jr.)

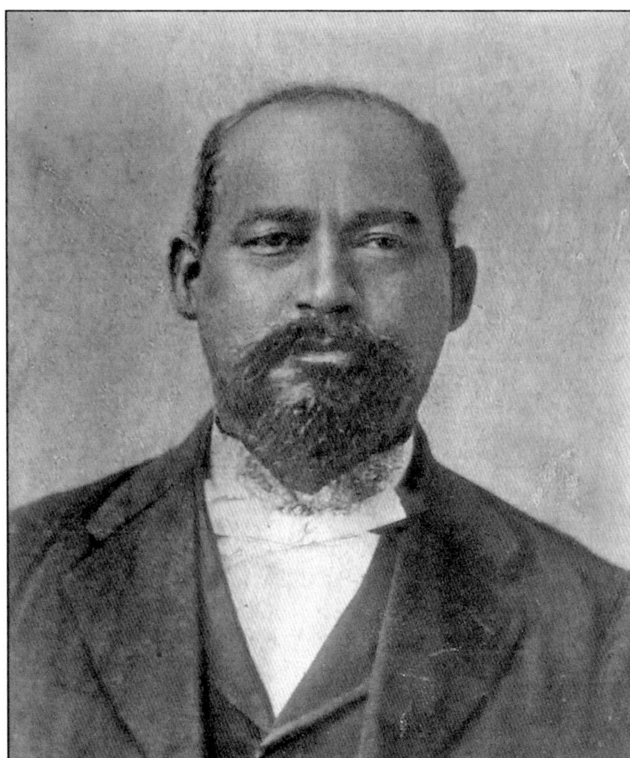

In 1866, Rev. Rayford Blount helped establish the First Baptist Church, located on Second Street in Natchitoches. This church provided classes for African American students in town. Blount is also credited with developing several other churches within the parish. He later became a state legislator and used his position to advocate for human rights. The First Baptist congregation split into two churches after the Second Street church burned. Today one is located on North Street and one is located on Amulet Street. (Courtesy of First Baptist Church, North Street.)

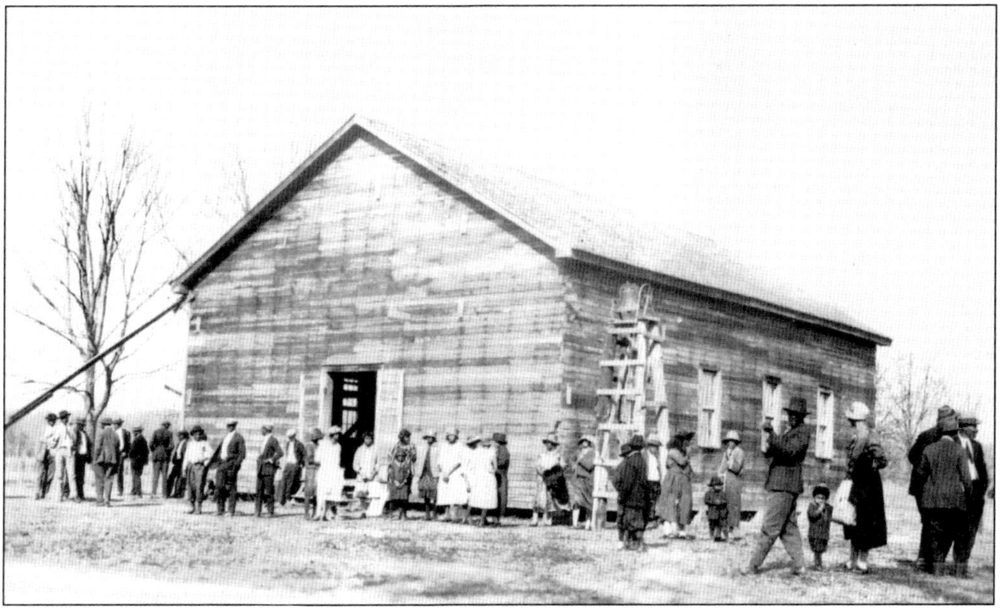

A congregation gathers outside the church on a cool day. After a service, it was common for people to socialize. Many church congregants were related, so gathering at the church afforded time to catch up on family chitchat. (Courtesy of Cammie Henry Research Center, Northwestern State University.)

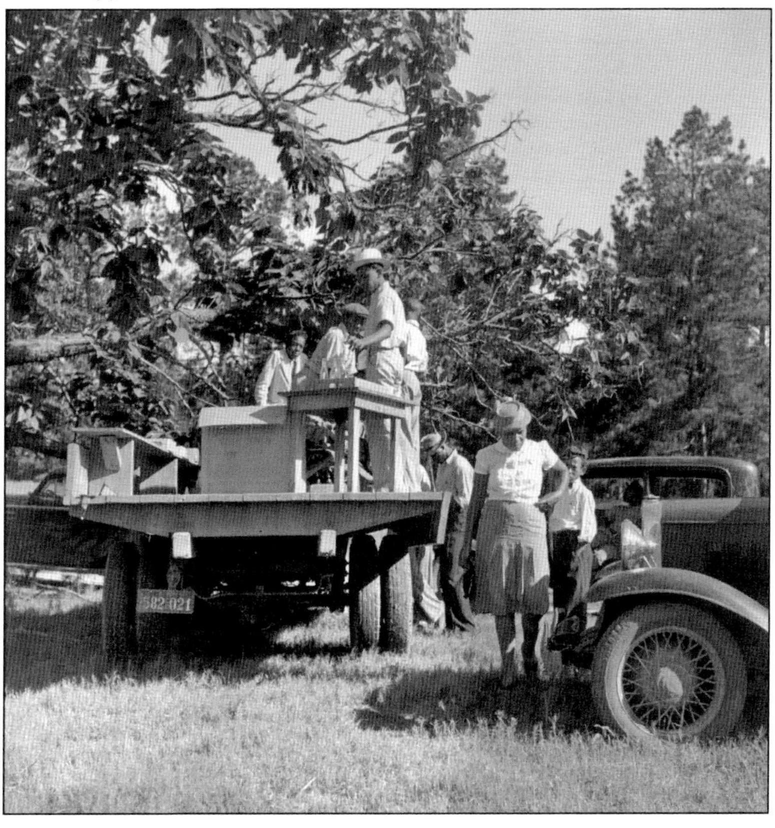

Black churches were largely responsible for generating their own funds. This church decided to sell ice cream and cool drinks as part of the church fund-raiser. Izola Bryant recalled that her church sometimes sold cakes and pies or had a gumbo supper. (Courtesy of the Library of Congress.)

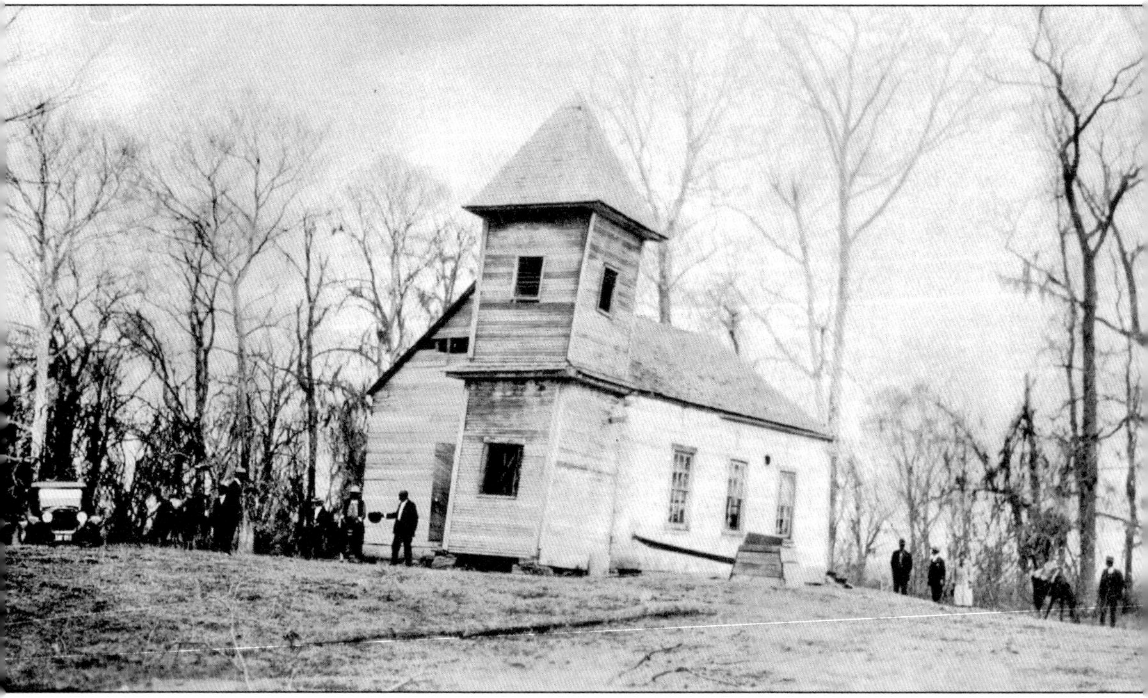

This African Methodist Episcopal Church is believed to have been the only one of its kind in the parish. Located on the northern end of Melrose Plantation, it faced St. Andrew Baptist Church, which was accessible by way of a footbridge that crossed the Cane River. Members of the two churches were generally descendants of Melrose Plantation and sometimes held services together. (Courtesy of Cammie Henry Research Center, Northwestern State University.)

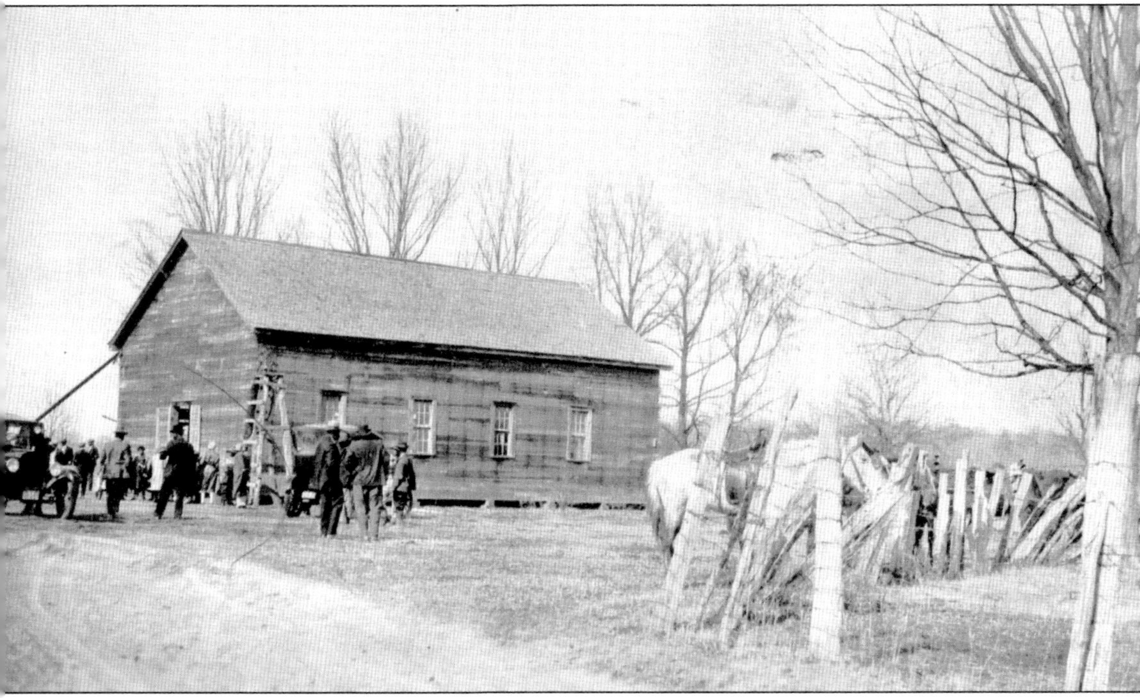

Most folks, according to Harry Jackson, would walk to church. People sometimes walked miles to get to church, and a lucky few had horses for transportation. The vehicle likely belonged to the minister. (Courtesy of Cammie Henry Research Center, Northwestern State University.)

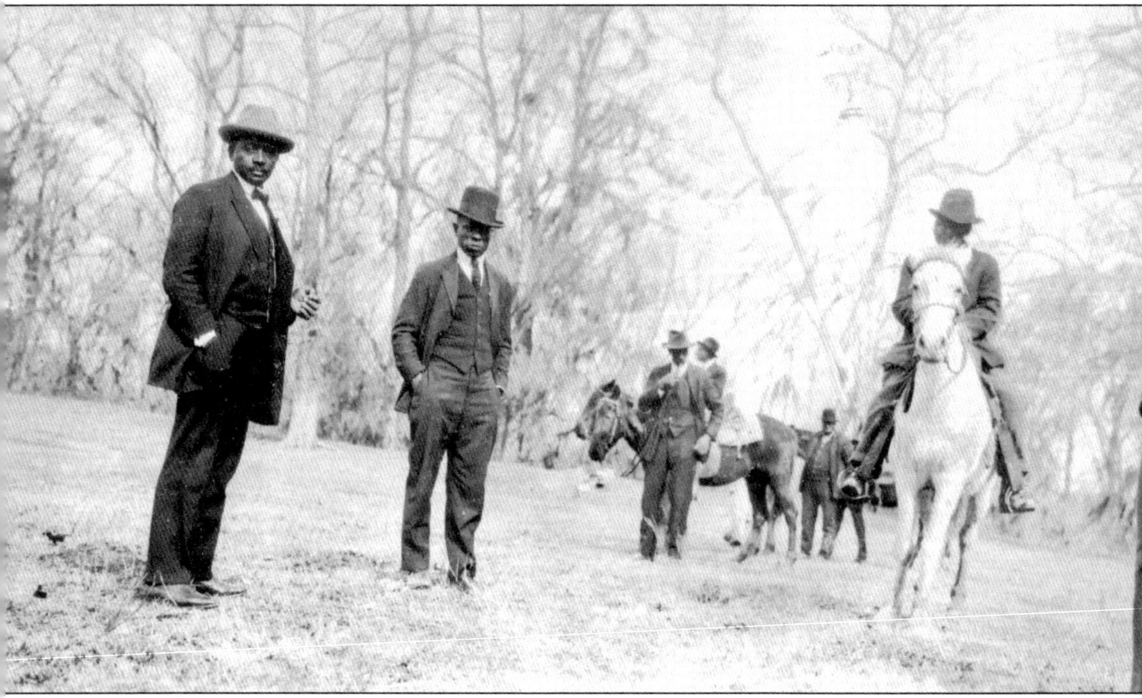

Some of these gentlemen were probably deacons of a church. Deacons were often instrumental in providing the backbone for social change in the black community. Ben Johnson recalled that deacons from various churches helped form the Winnfield Colored Burial Association, which provided burial assistance to poor people. (Courtesy of Cammie Henry Research Center, Northwestern State University.)

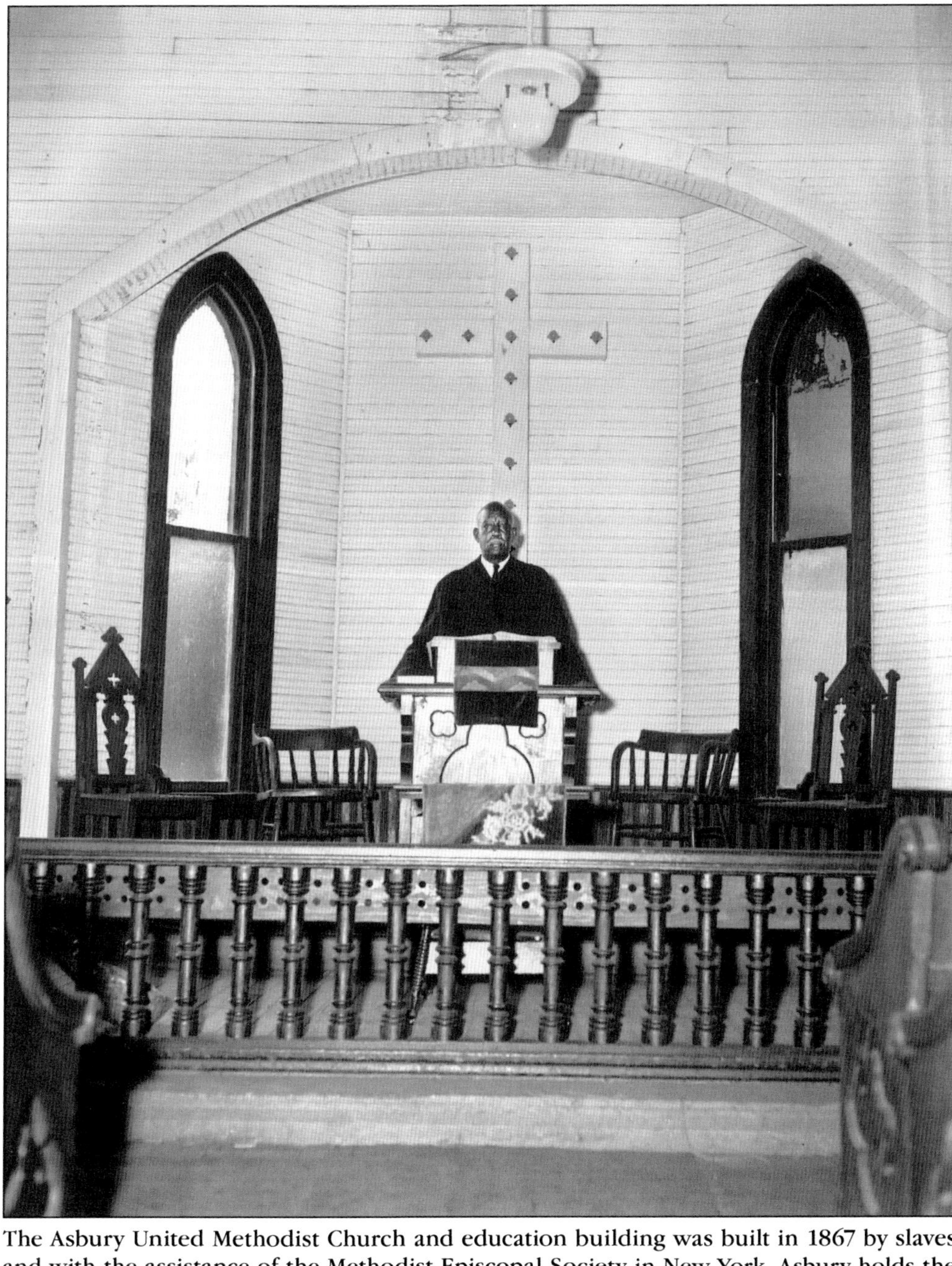

The Asbury United Methodist Church and education building was built in 1867 by slaves and with the assistance of the Methodist Episcopal Society in New York. Asbury holds the distinction of being the first Methodist church built in Natchitoches. Shown here is Rev. J. S. Dickson, who led the first service in the new sanctuary on July 14, 1957. In 1998, the congregations of Williams Chapel and St. Mark joined with the congregation of Asbury. Services are still conducted at the church, which is located at 704 Fifth Street. (Courtesy of John Thomas Guillet.)

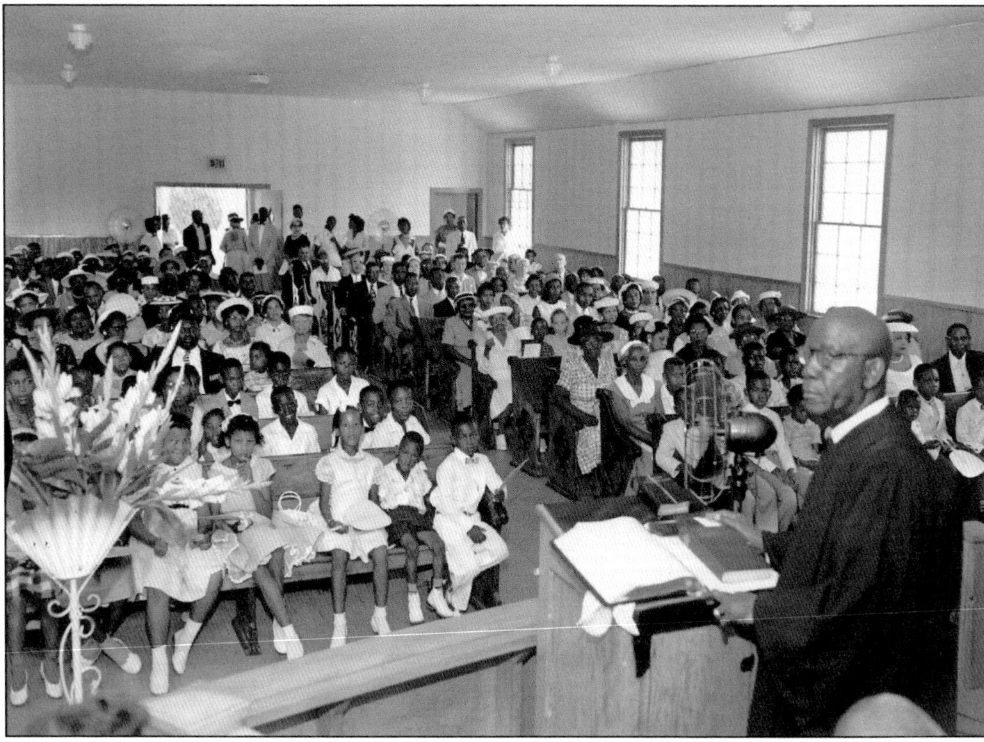

Easter Sunday morning at Asbury Church is marked by a full house, including standing room only. Easter, along with Christmas, was one of the most important holidays in African American communities. Notice the seating arrangement of children in the front, with the adults sitting behind them. (Courtesy of John Thomas Guillet.)

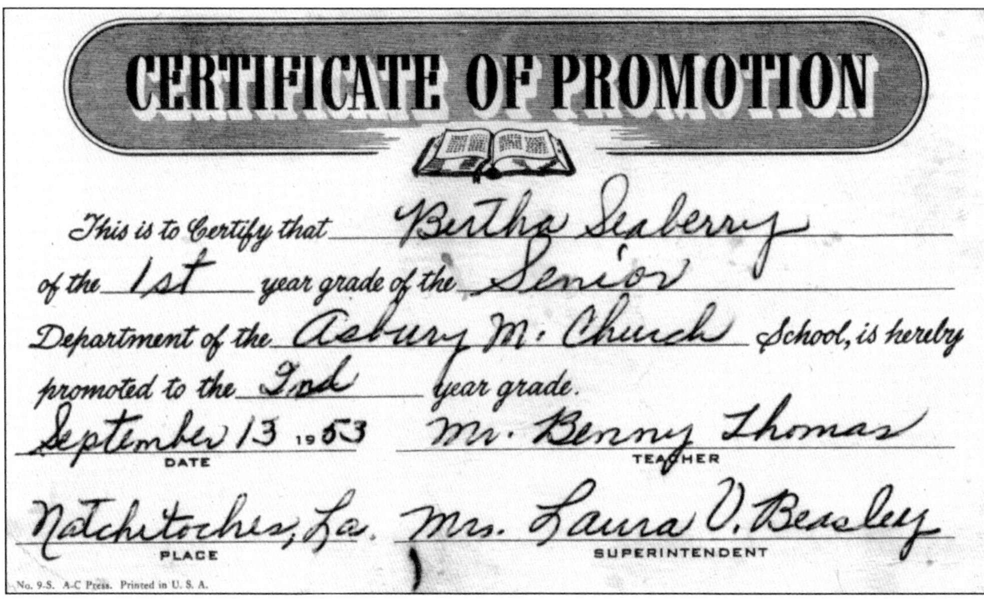

CERTIFICATE OF PROMOTION

This is to Certify that Bertha Seaberry
of the 1st year grade of the Senior
Department of the Asbury M. Church School, is hereby
promoted to the 2nd year grade.
September 13 1953 — DATE
Mr. Benny Thomas — TEACHER
Natchitoches, La. — PLACE
Mrs. Laura V. Beasley — SUPERINTENDENT

No. 9-S. A-C Press. Printed in U. S. A.

According to this certificate, Bertha Seaberry received a promotion from first to second year at the senior level of the church school. The church offered in-depth biblical instruction so that members could better understand the teachings of God. (Courtesy of Edward Ward Jr.)

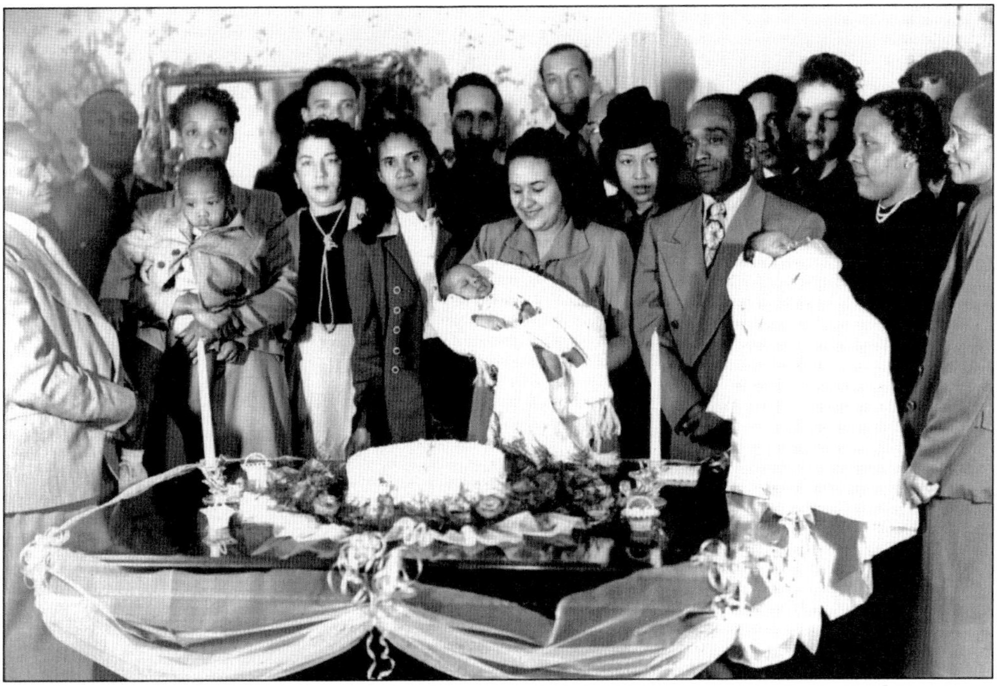

Family and friends of two infants gather for a double christening ceremony being held within Asbury United Methodist Church. Methodist teachings allowed for the religious conversion of babies, as opposed to the Baptist tradition of only converting youths and adults. (Courtesy of Edward Ward Jr.)

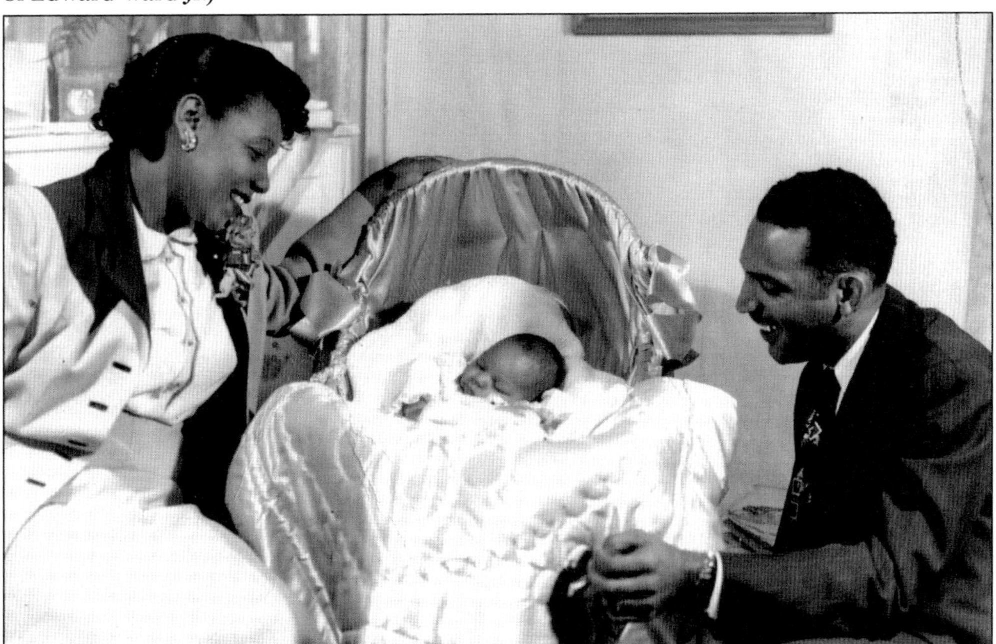

Edward Ward Sr. and his wife, Odile, sit next to their son, Edward Jr., who was just christened. The parent's clothing and decorated baby crib speak to the celebratory nature of the occasion. (Courtesy of Edward Ward Jr.)

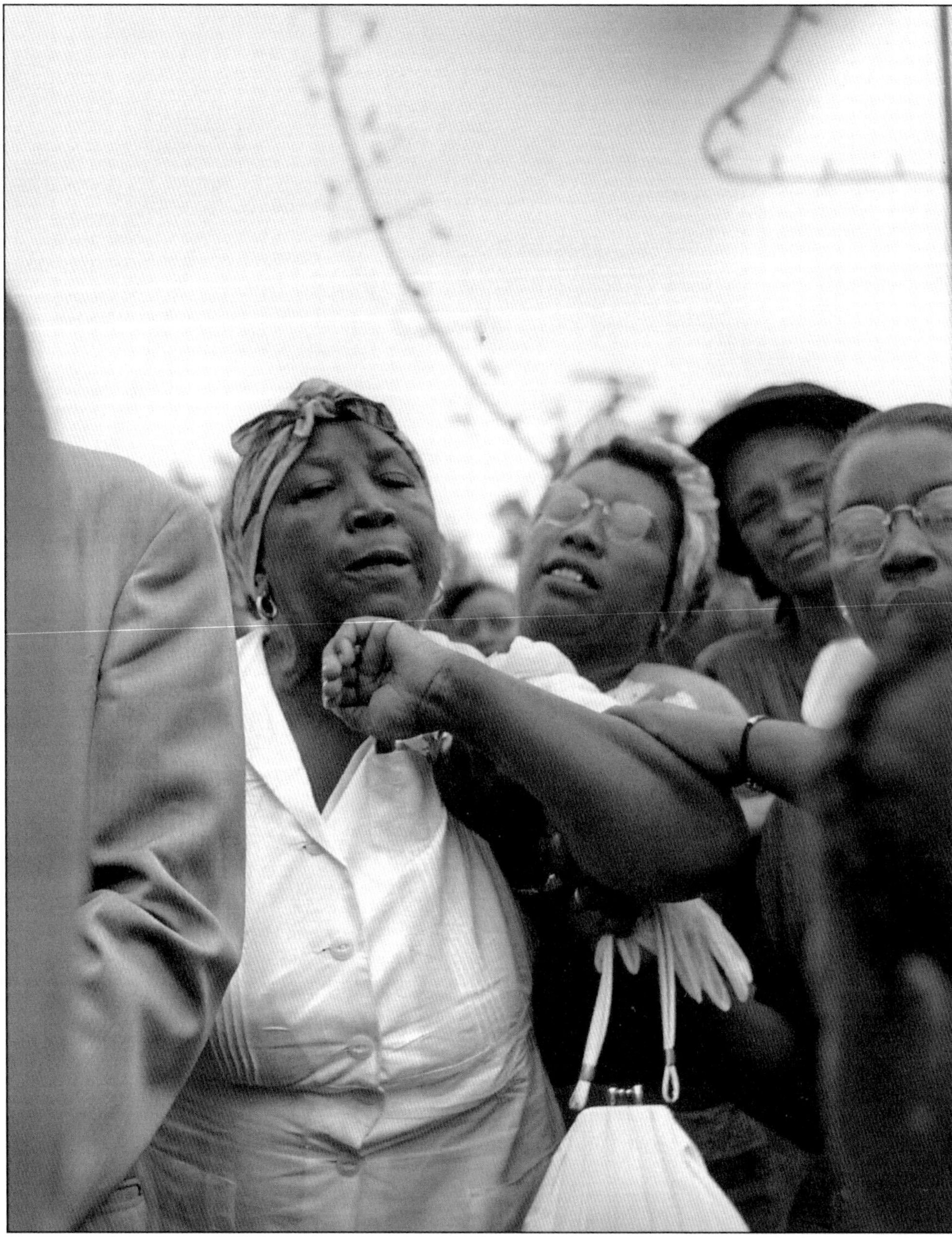

This crowd gathered for a baptism in the Cane River shows several women who are mentally preparing for the upcoming ritual. Baptisms were a community celebration, and sometimes there were hundreds of people gathered at this location along Front Street in Natchitoches. (Courtesy of John Thomas Guillet.)

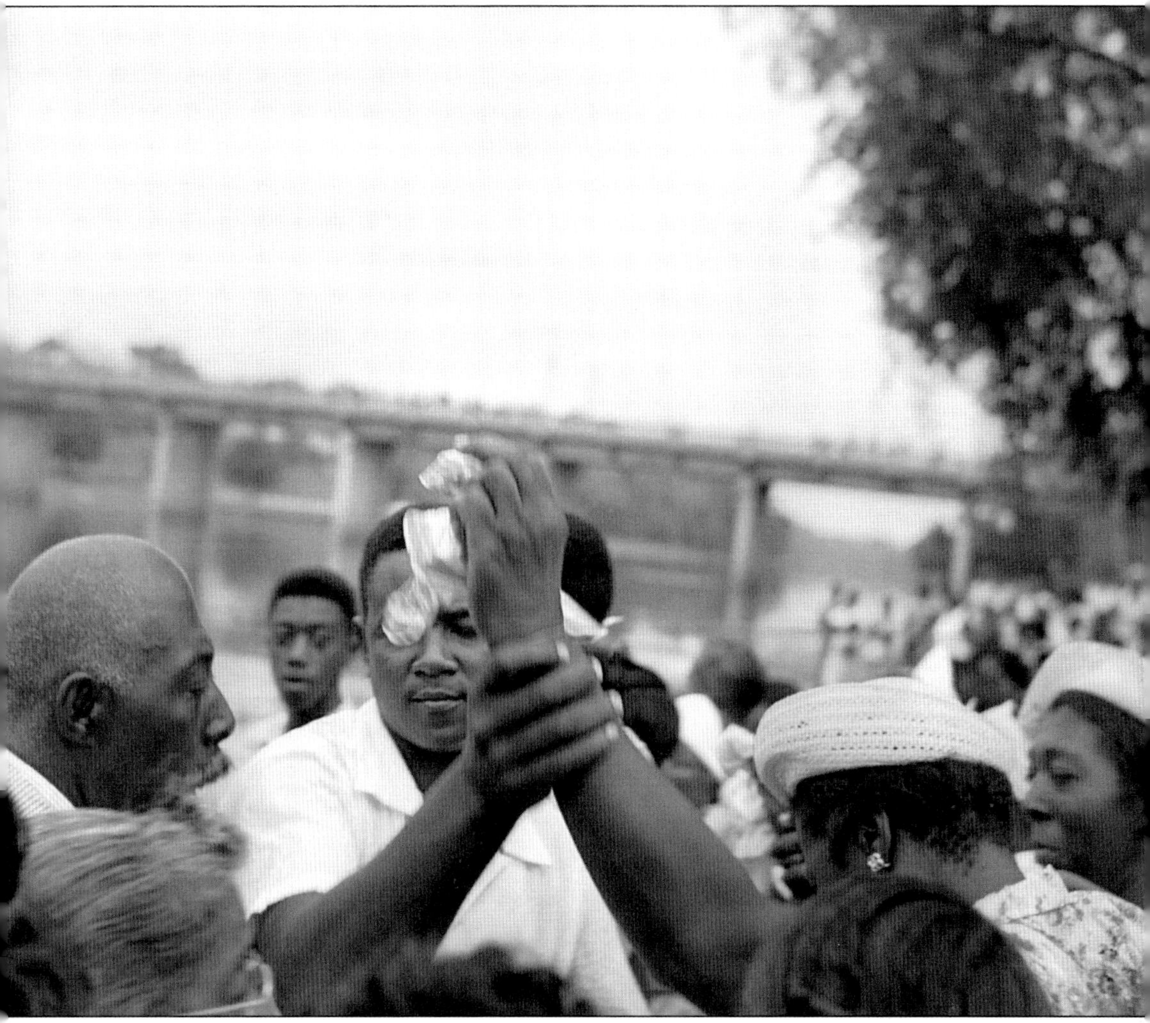

A woman receives individual prayers from one of the deacons participating in the ceremony. The Church Street Bridge, which connects east and west Natchitoches, is visible in the background. (Courtesy of John Thomas Guillet.)

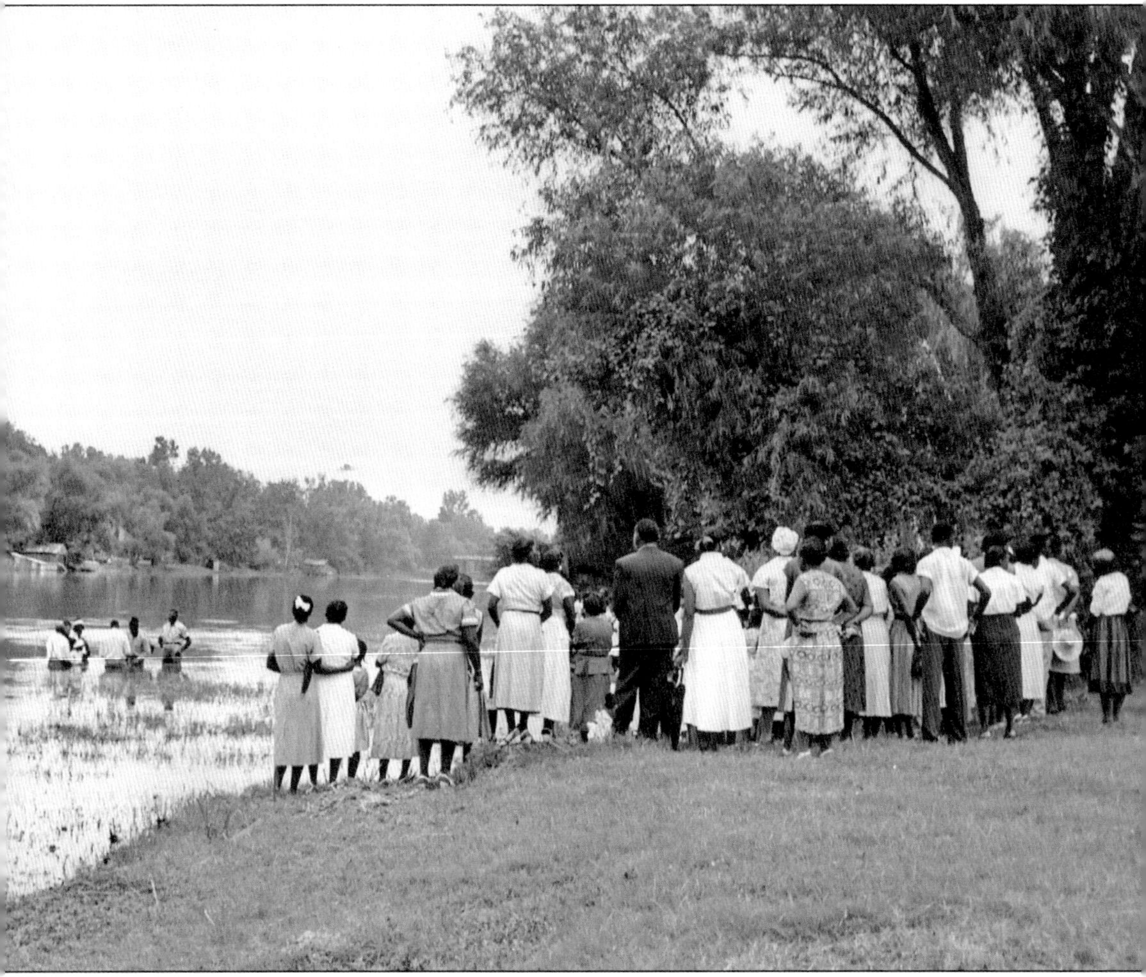

The baptism ceremony is also marked by the attendance of family and friends. A large crowd has gathered on the banks of the river to witness a baptism, which generally occurred in the month of August. (Courtesy of John Thomas Guillet.)

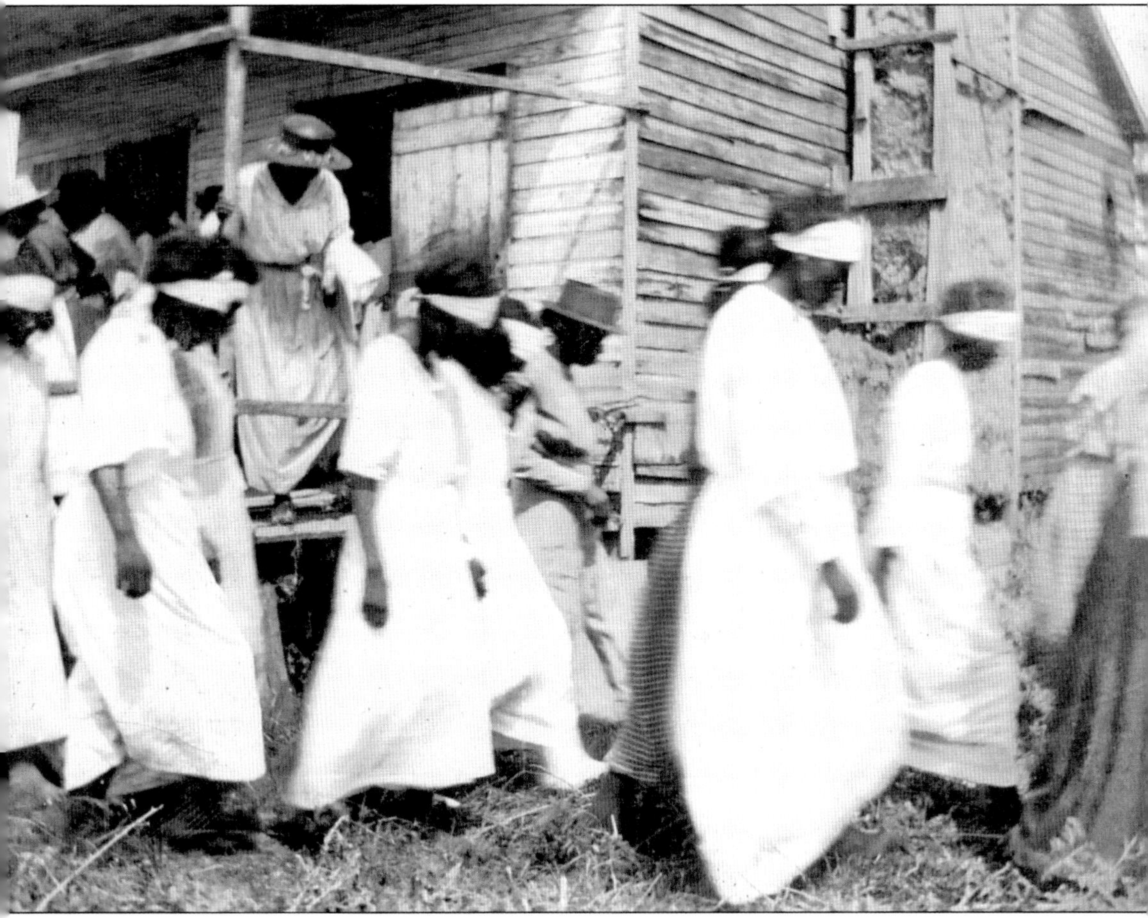

At this Baptist baptism ceremony, candidates are being led from the church to the water's edge. Each candidate wears white clothing and a matching head wrap to signify the death of the sinner and subsequent rebirth of the spiritual person. (Courtesy of Cammie Henry Research Center, Northwestern State University.)

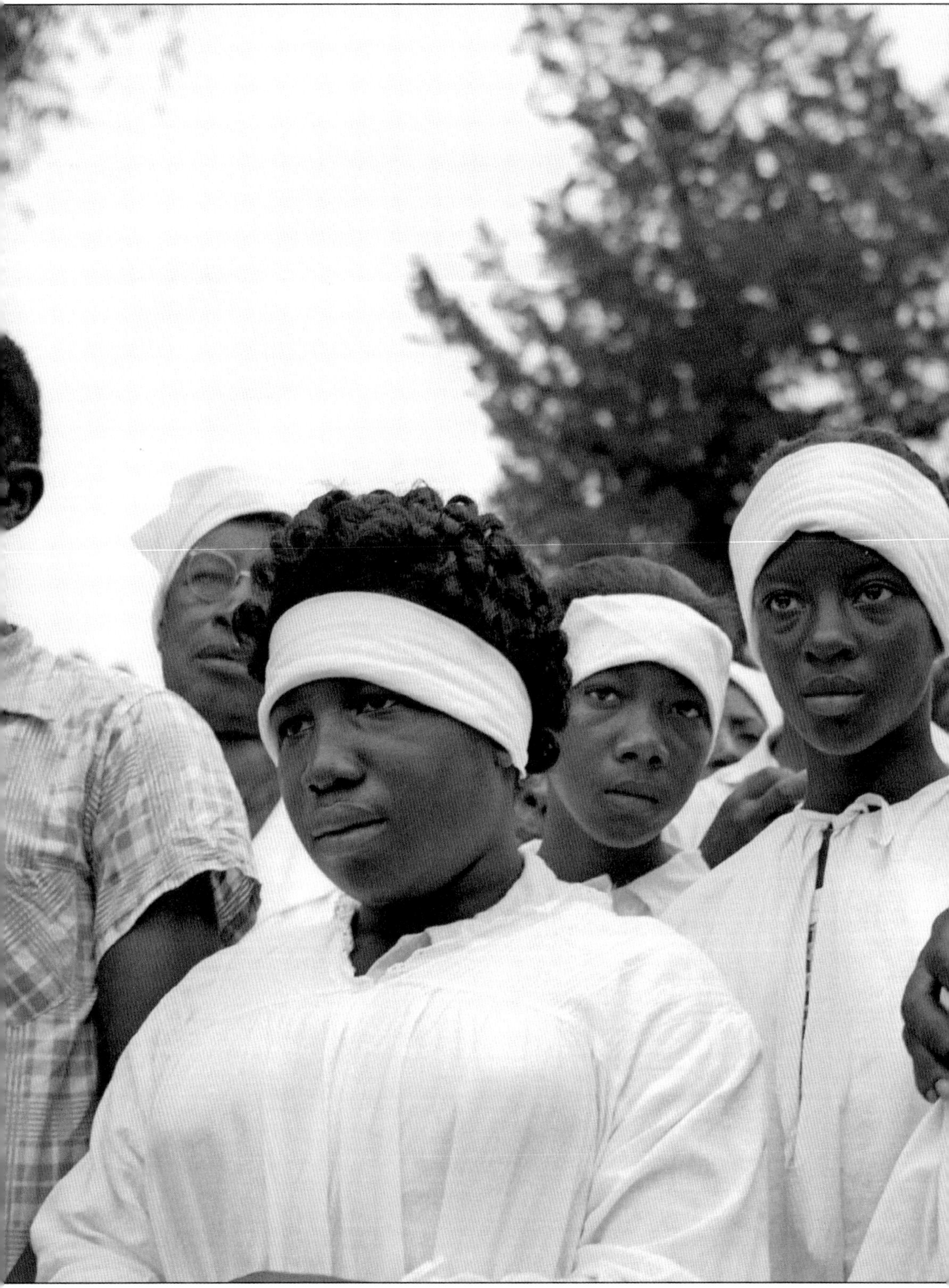

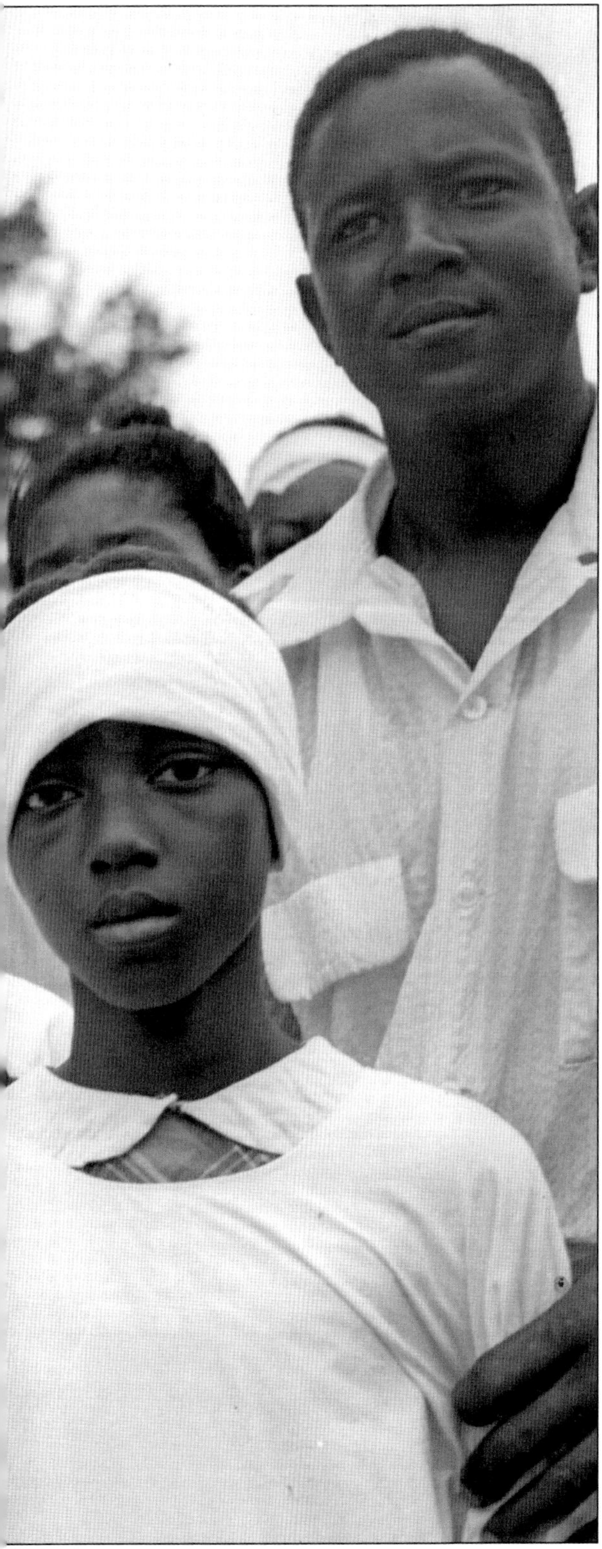

These young girls have not yet entered the water. They stand and wait their turn while family members and church deacons lend emotional support. (Courtesy of John Thomas Guillet.)

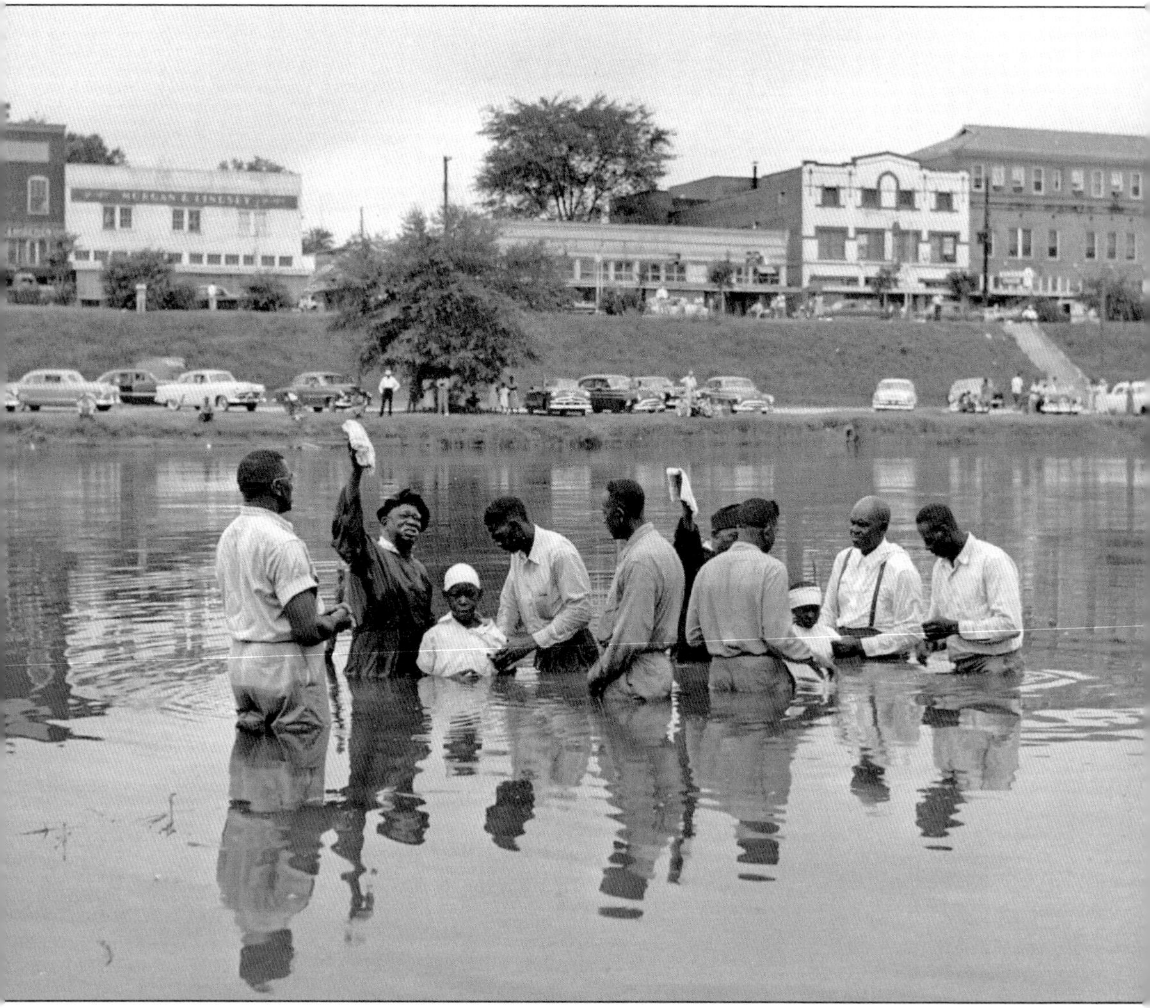

Along the river's banks stand onlookers who often gathered to watch and listen to the spirituals that the congregation sang. In the background are several buildings on Front Street in the city of Natchitoches. In the foreground are two ministers, six deacons, and two candidates. (Courtesy of John Thomas Guillet.)

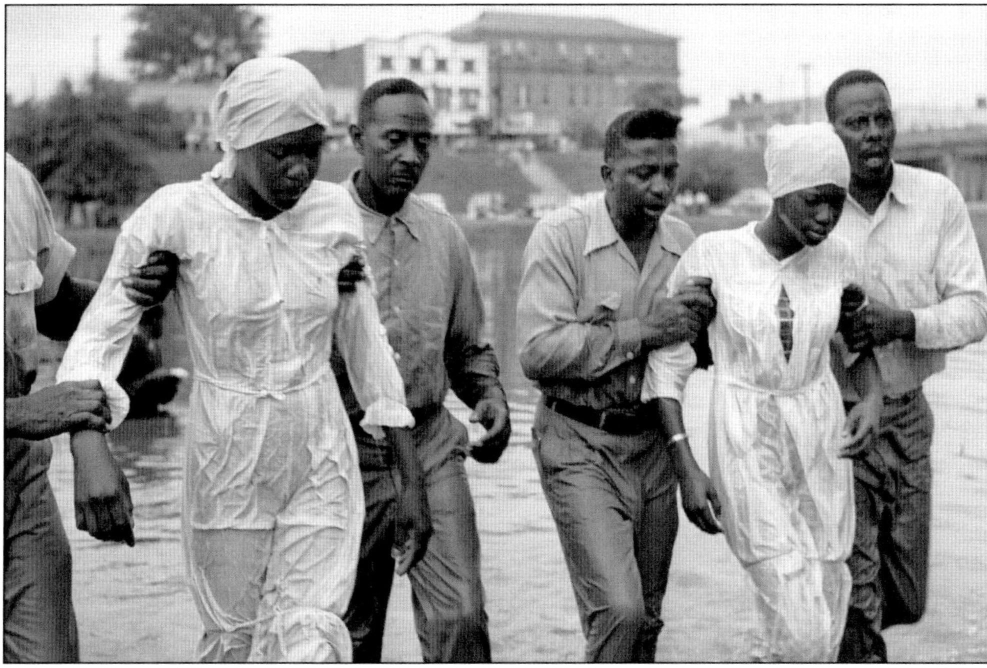

Deacons escort candidates from the water by holding each girl's arms. Sometimes after receiving a full submergence in water, candidates, according to Idell Snowden, "would come up shouting." The escorts ensured the safety of the candidate as they experienced a religious transformation. (Courtesy of John Thomas Guillet.)

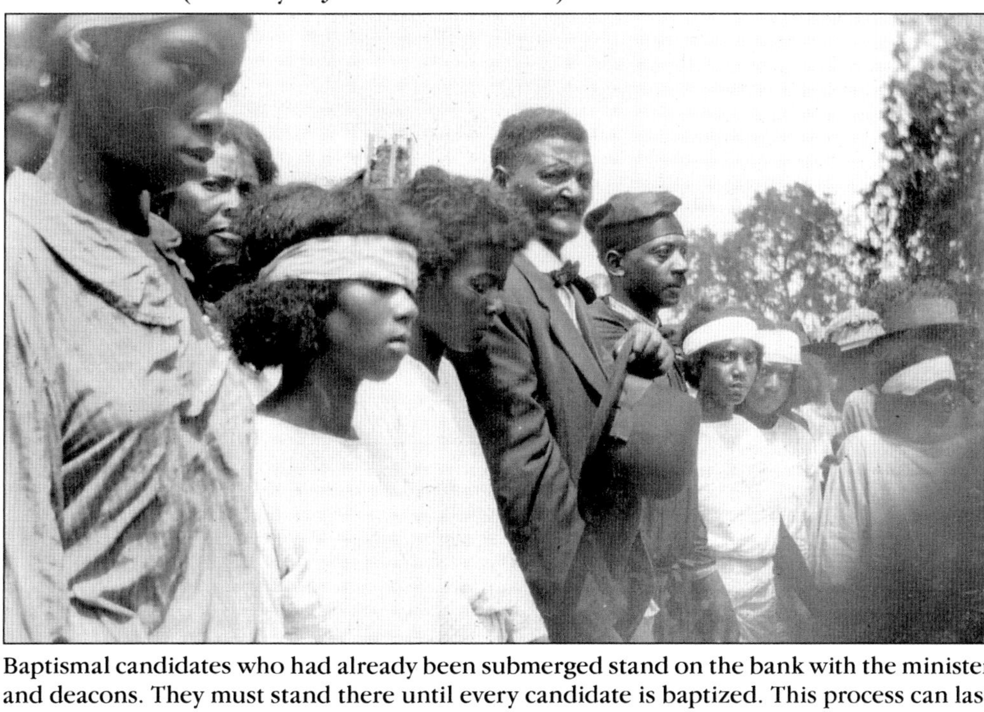

Baptismal candidates who had already been submerged stand on the bank with the minister and deacons. They must stand there until every candidate is baptized. This process can last from 30 minutes to several hours depending on the number of candidates. (Courtesy of John Thomas Guillet.)

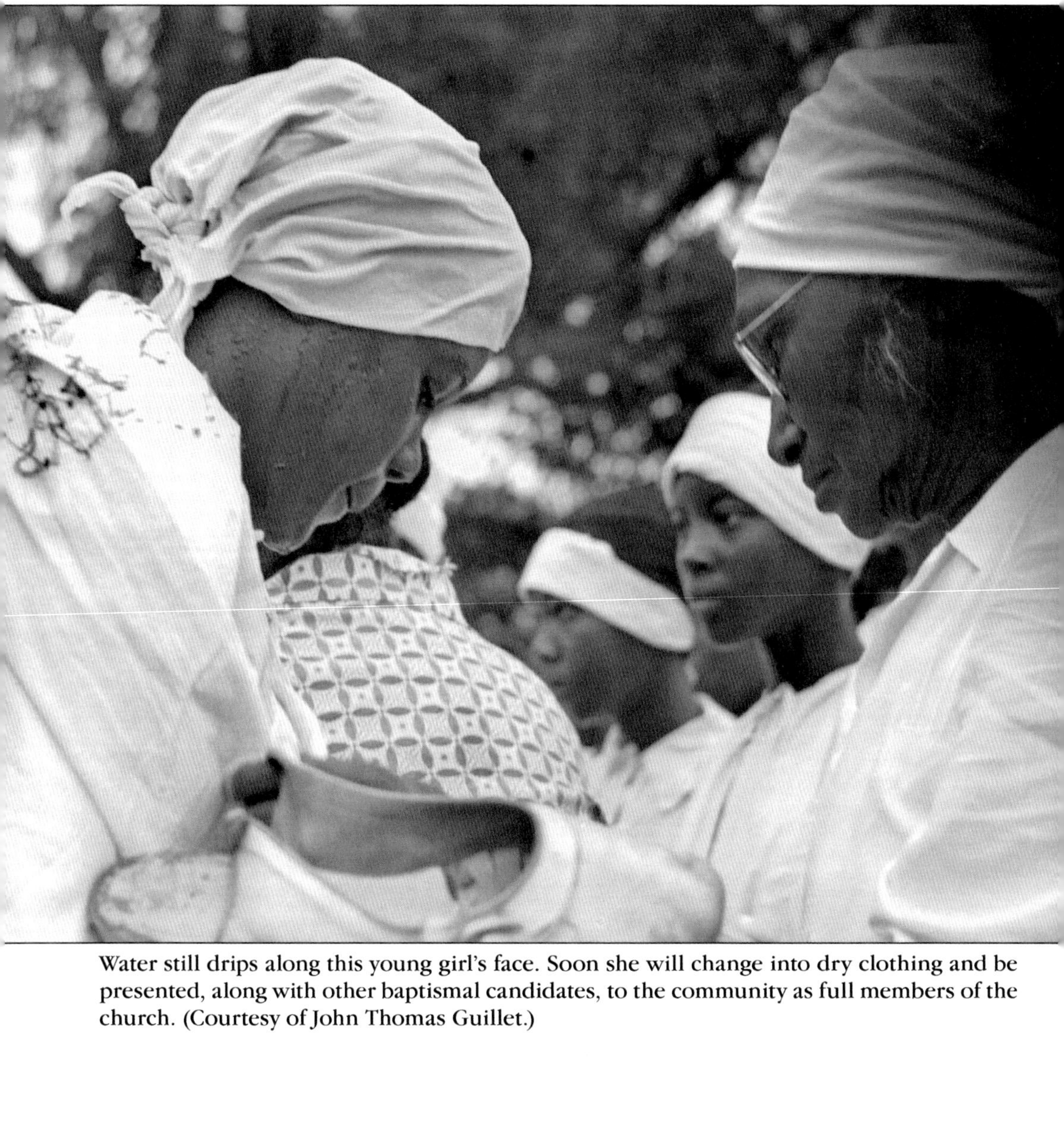

Water still drips along this young girl's face. Soon she will change into dry clothing and be presented, along with other baptismal candidates, to the community as full members of the church. (Courtesy of John Thomas Guillet.)

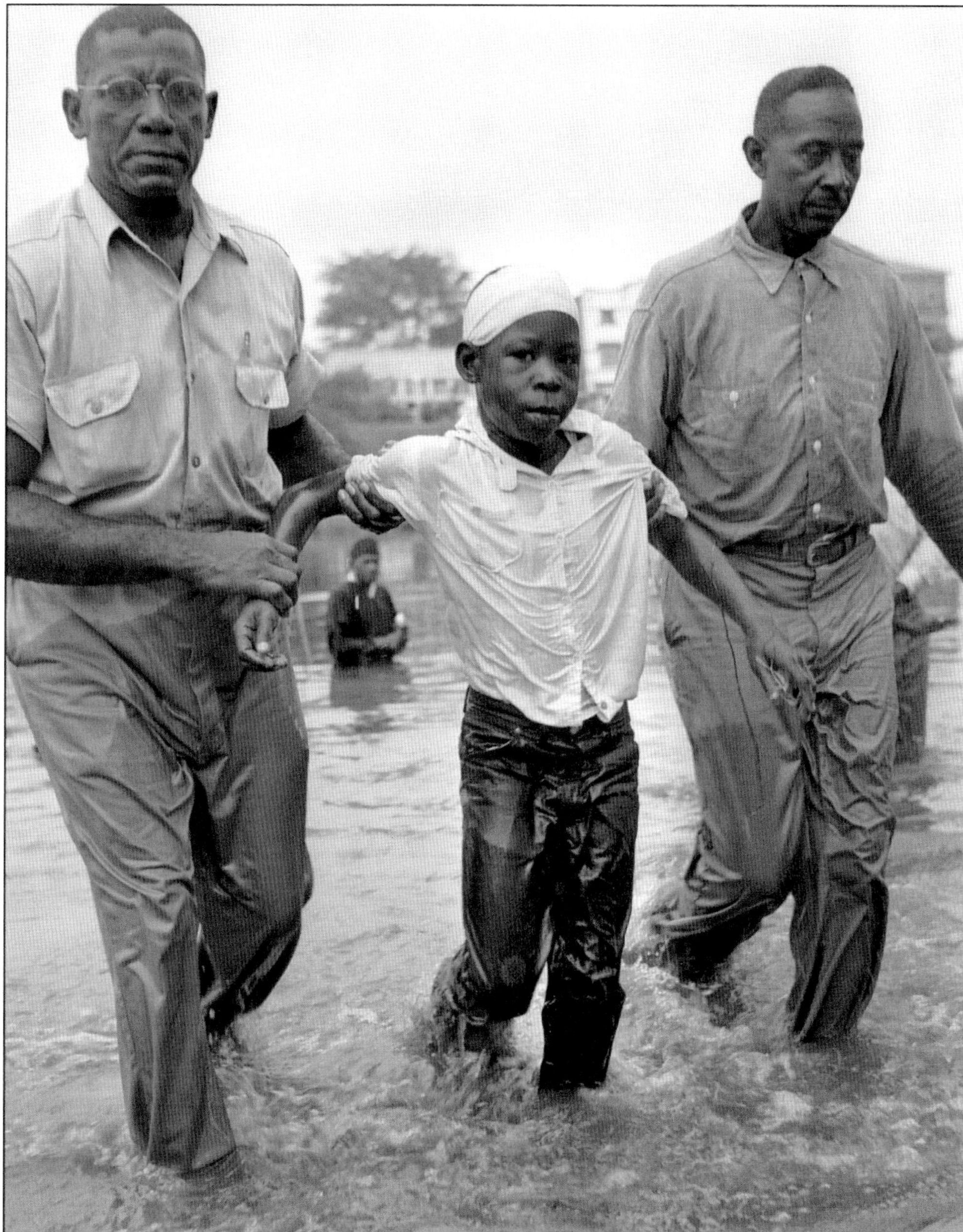

Although candidates were all baptized at the same ceremony, they were often separated by gender during various parts of the ceremony. This young boy probably went in the water with another male candidate. (Courtesy of John Thomas Guillet.)

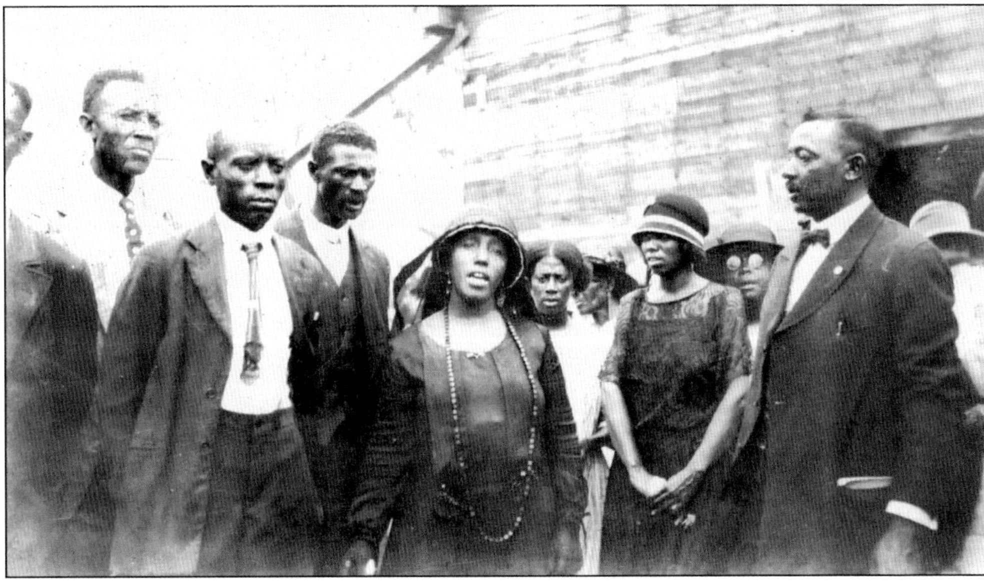

Funerals were another religious activity that brought members of the community together. Harry Jackson commented on the funeral process in his area: "You know what they do if anybody died? That body stayed right there. They would call, and the undertaker would come, and he would embalm you lying there in your house. Then after they embalm you, you got to stay there. They wake [the body] that night, and it wouldn't be moved until that next day when it was carried to the graveyard." (Courtesy of Cammie Henry Research Center, Northwestern State University.)

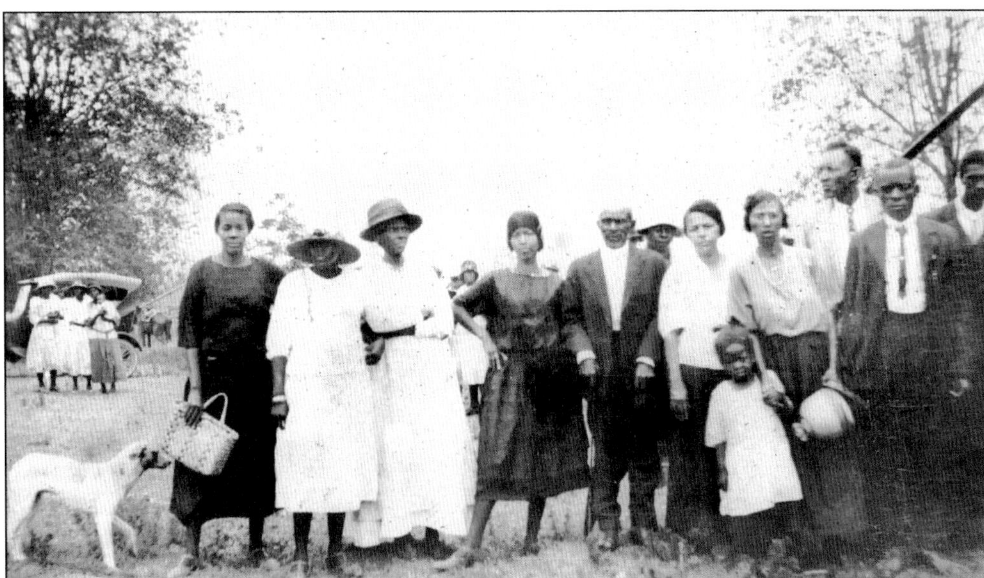

These people have gathered to attend the funeral of a local resident. Izola Bryant recalled that most funeral services were held on Sundays because people were "too busy to have them during the week." It is likely that funerals took place whenever it was possible to gather people together. (Courtesy of Cammie Henry Research Center, Northwestern State University.)

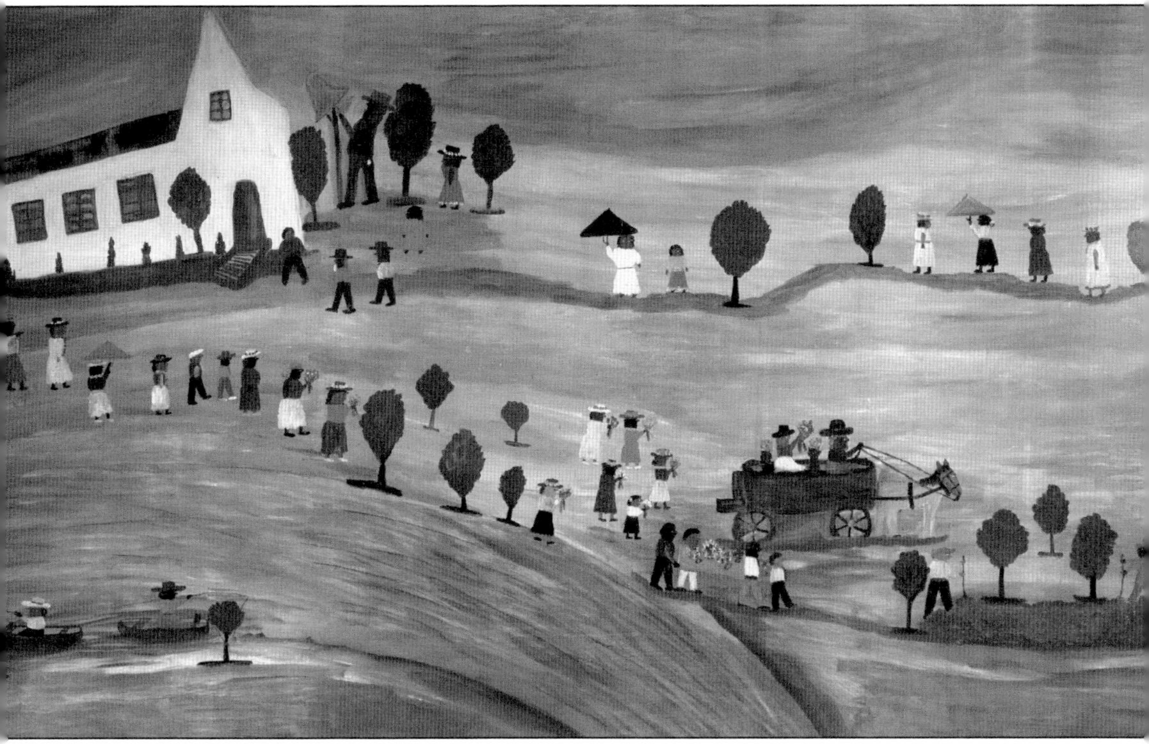

This scene from the African House murals shows a procession with a horse-drawn carriage as it winds its way to the graveside. A common practice in African American communities, people would sing while marching to the grave, chant and shout at the graveside, and sing on the return from the grave. (Courtesy of the Historic American Buildings Survey, photographer James Rosenthal.)

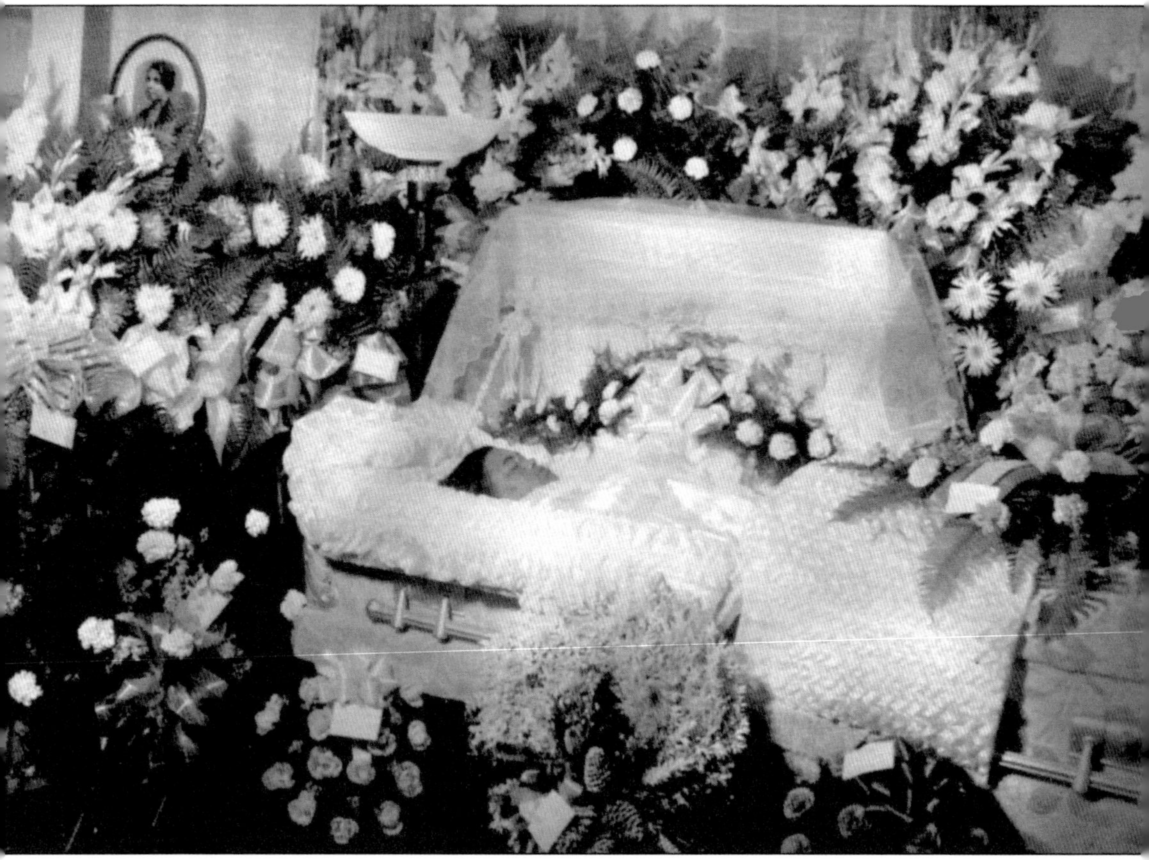

Mattie Burton Burke, a local educator from the southern end of the parish, lies dressed for public viewing before her funeral. The numerous floral arrangements suggest that Mattie was well known and liked. Photographing the dead became part of funerary traditions in the 1950s. (Courtesy of Edward Ward Jr.)

Three

Education Is the Only Way Out

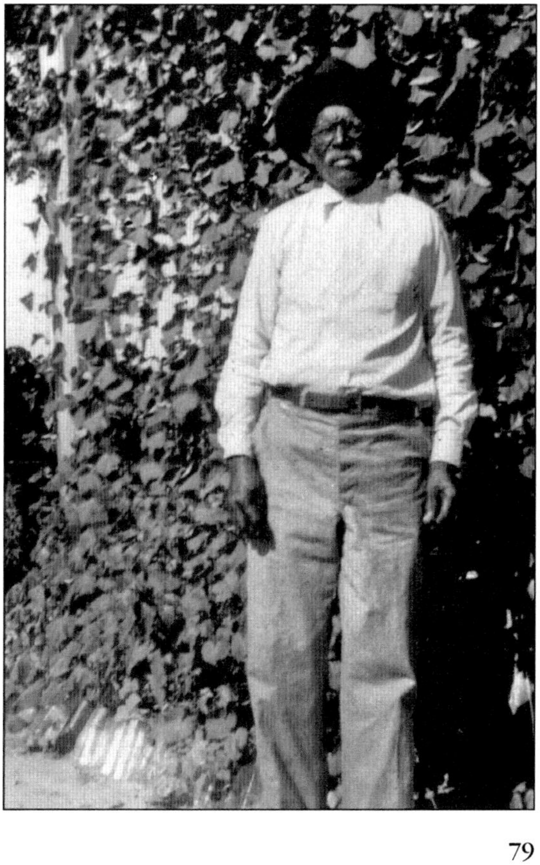

Prof. J. W. Thomas arrived in Natchitoches from Baton Rouge sometime around 1910. It was through his leadership and vision that the Lincoln Institute formed. This school differed from other African American schools in the parish because it was supported entirely by the parents of the students. Dubbed the first private school for blacks in Natchitoches, it later gained financial support through Rosenwald funds. Philanthropist Julius Rosenwald created Rosenwald Schools to help improve the quality of education for African Americans in the early-20th-century South. Shown here is James Blakely, who owned the land on which the Lincoln Institute was built. (Courtesy of Lincoln Natchitoches Parish Training School/ Central High School Archives.)

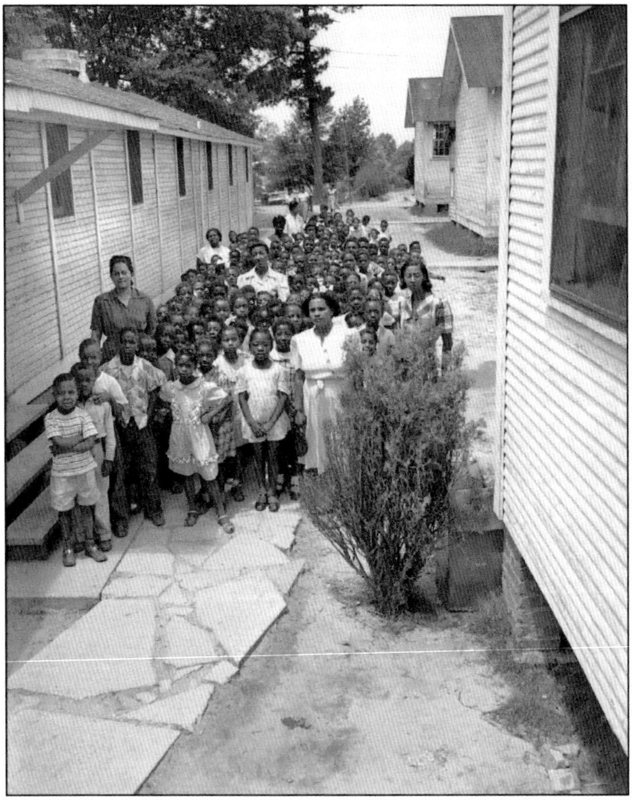

An inability to provide long-term financing to the Lincoln Institute resulted in a change in leadership. The school was deeded to the Natchitoches Parish School Board in 1919. Shown here is a portion of the school campus. The site is currently home to the Ben Johnson Educational Plaza located at 400 Martin Luther King Street. (Courtesy of John Thomas Guillet.)

Children stand in front of the early building of the Natchitoches Parish Training School Trade and Industrial Project. The boys hold a saw or hammer and other tools, which the school taught them how to use. (Courtesy of Lincoln Natchitoches Parish Training School/Central High School Archives.)

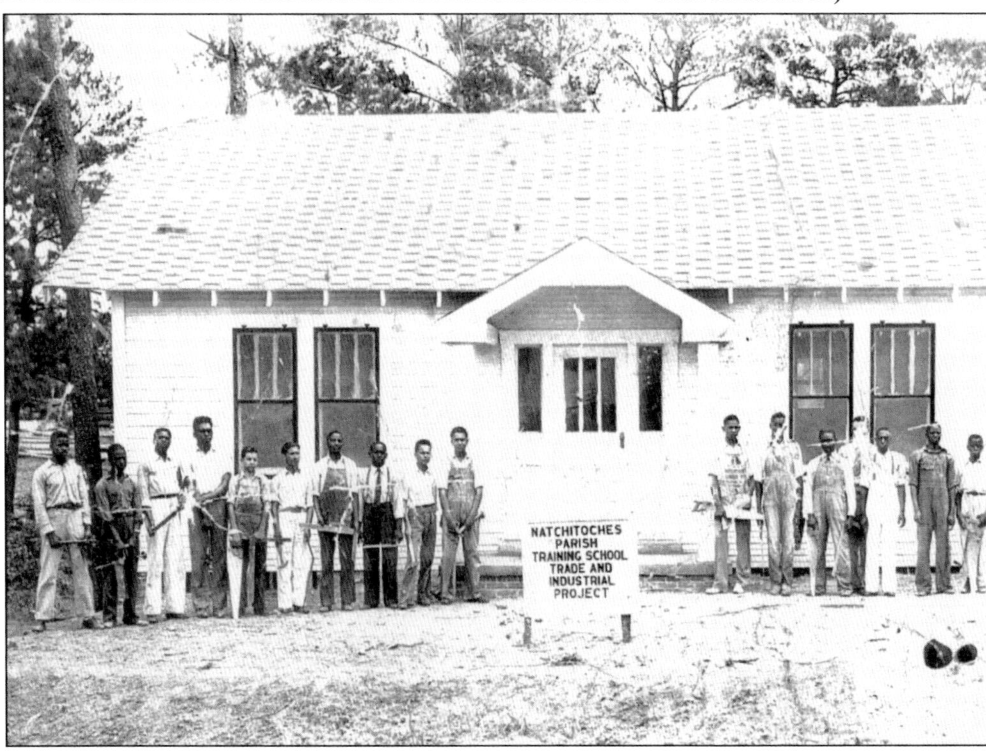

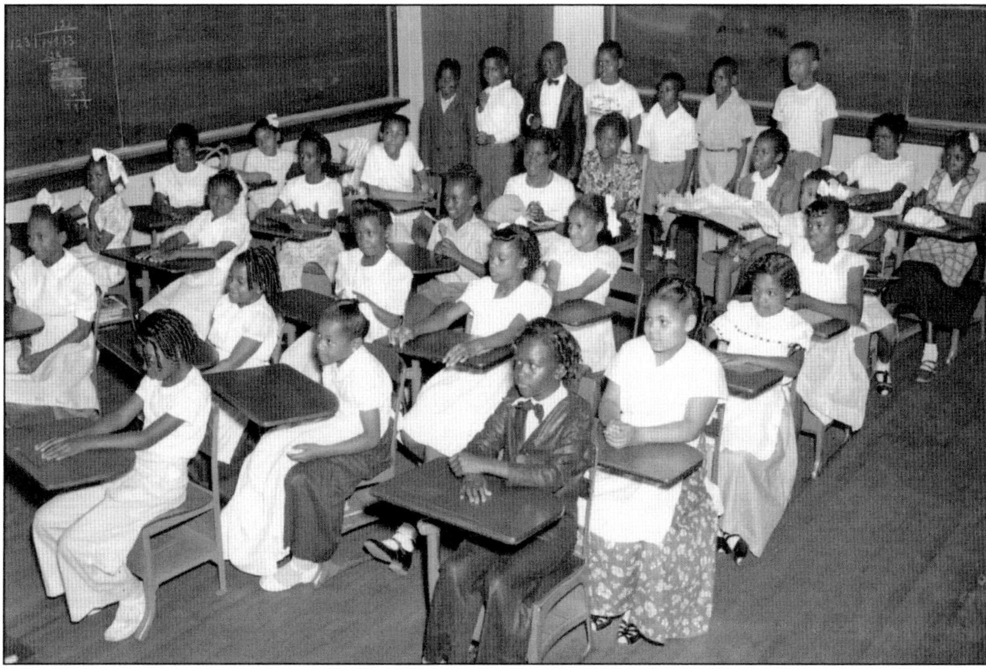

Academic and industrial schools for African Americans operated under a firm Victorian code of ethics. Boys were not allowed to associate with girls unsupervised. Dress, manners, and language were monitored. Black teachers assumed the responsibility of enforcing that code with the belief that children would grow up to be contributors to the greater good of society. (Courtesy of John Thomas Guillet.)

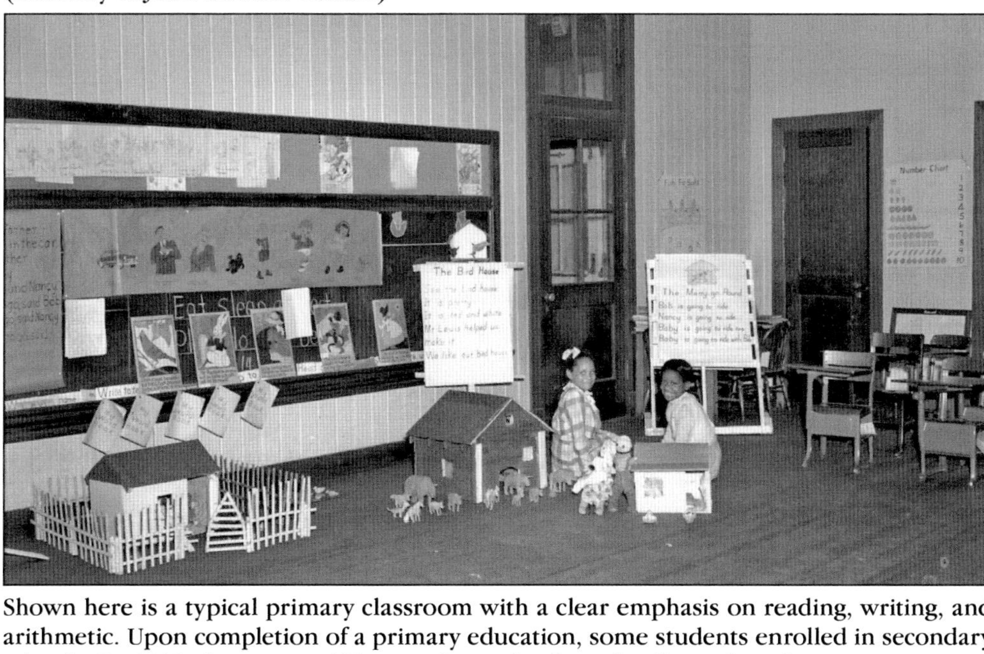

Shown here is a typical primary classroom with a clear emphasis on reading, writing, and arithmetic. Upon completion of a primary education, some students enrolled in secondary schools. By 1915, there were 117 secondary schools and colleges for African Americans in the nation. Of that number, 27 were state-funded agricultural and mechanical colleges. Natchitoches Parish had several secondary schools. (Courtesy of John Thomas Guillet.)

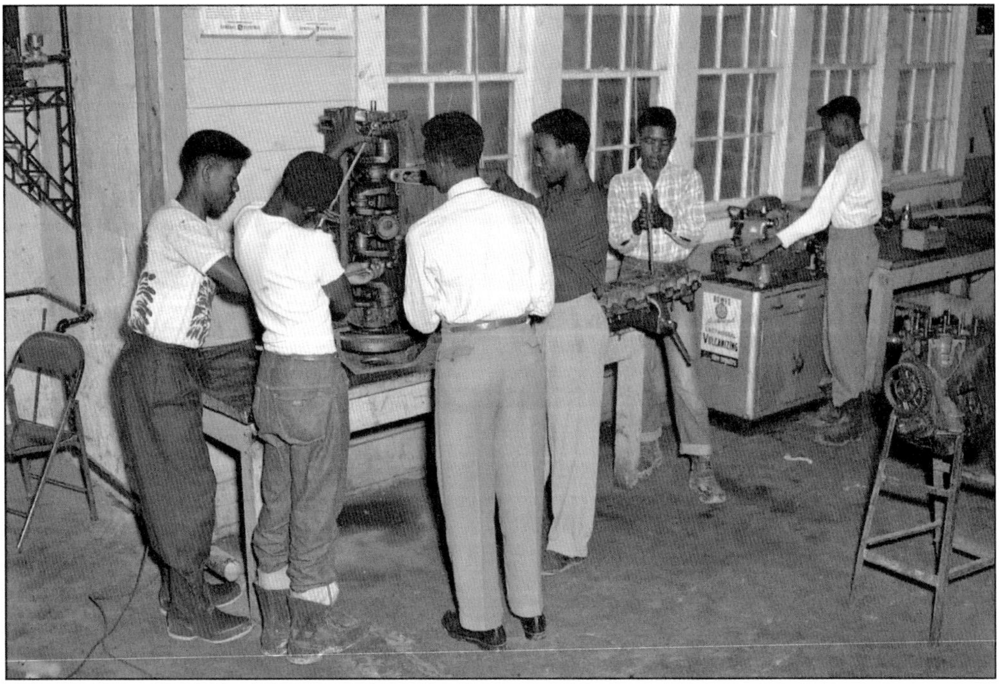

Under the name Natchitoches Parish Training School, students formed various clubs, including the Trade and Industry Club, New Farmers of America, and the Natchitoches Players. By 1935, the students were printing their own school newspaper named *The Tosh*. (Courtesy of John Thomas Guillet.)

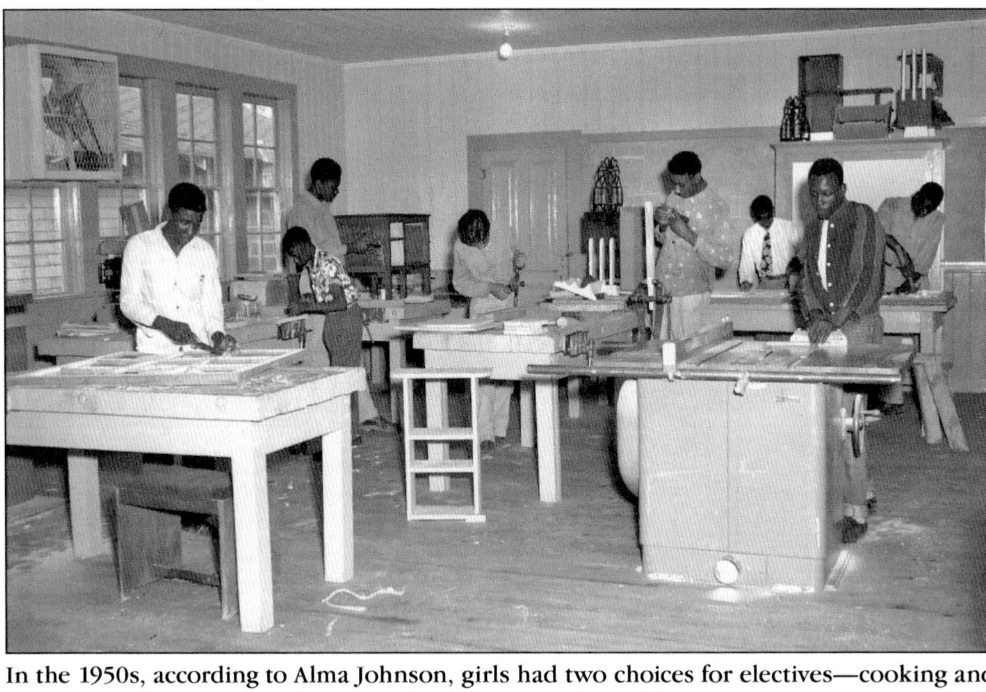

In the 1950s, according to Alma Johnson, girls had two choices for electives—cooking and sewing. Boys could choose between shop and agriculture. These young men are working in the woodshop, where they learned carpentry skills. (Courtesy of John Thomas Guillet.)

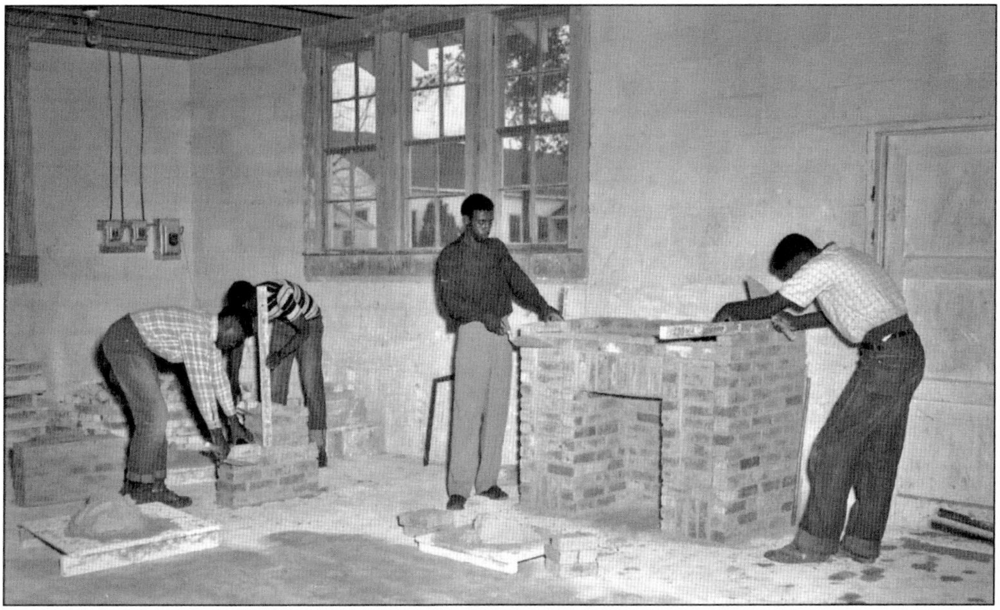

The young men shown in this photograph are learning carpentry skills. The addition of assorted clubs and electives provided students with opportunities to learn skills, take trips, and enter contests that exposed many of them to a world beyond the boundaries of the plantation. Several of the schools battled with one another for first place in science, home economics, and carpentry competitions. (Courtesy of John Thomas Guillet.)

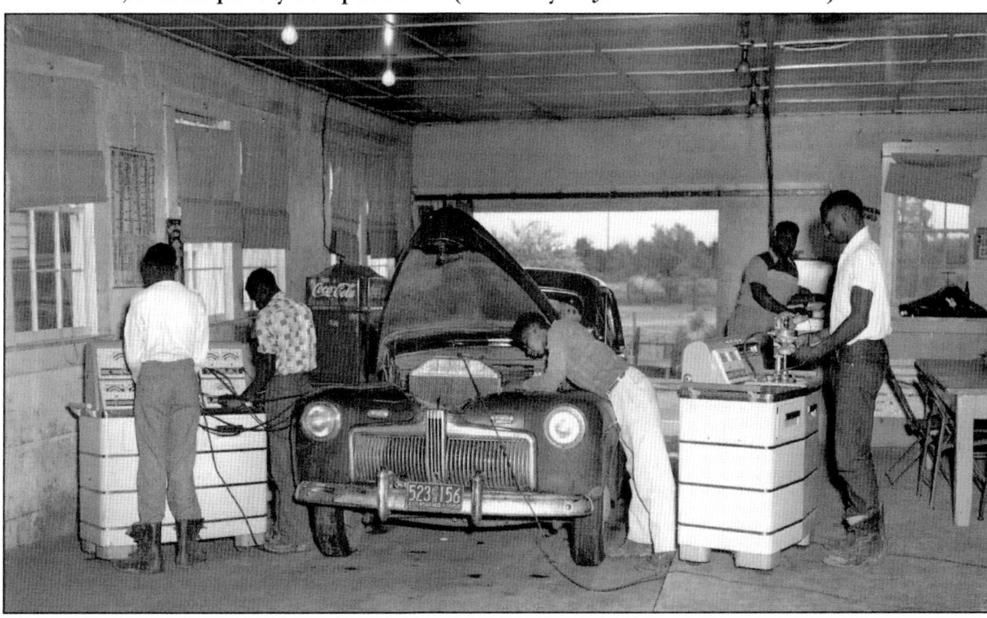

The young men shown here are learning automobile mechanics at Natchitoches Parish Training School. Ophelia Dumars described the change in school names: "The white school was Natchitoches High, and we were Natchitoches Parish Training School. The whites decided that they didn't need two schools named Natchitoches, so therefore in the [1950s], we had to change our school's name from Natchitoches Parish Training School. That's how we got to be Central High School." (Courtesy of John Thomas Guillet.)

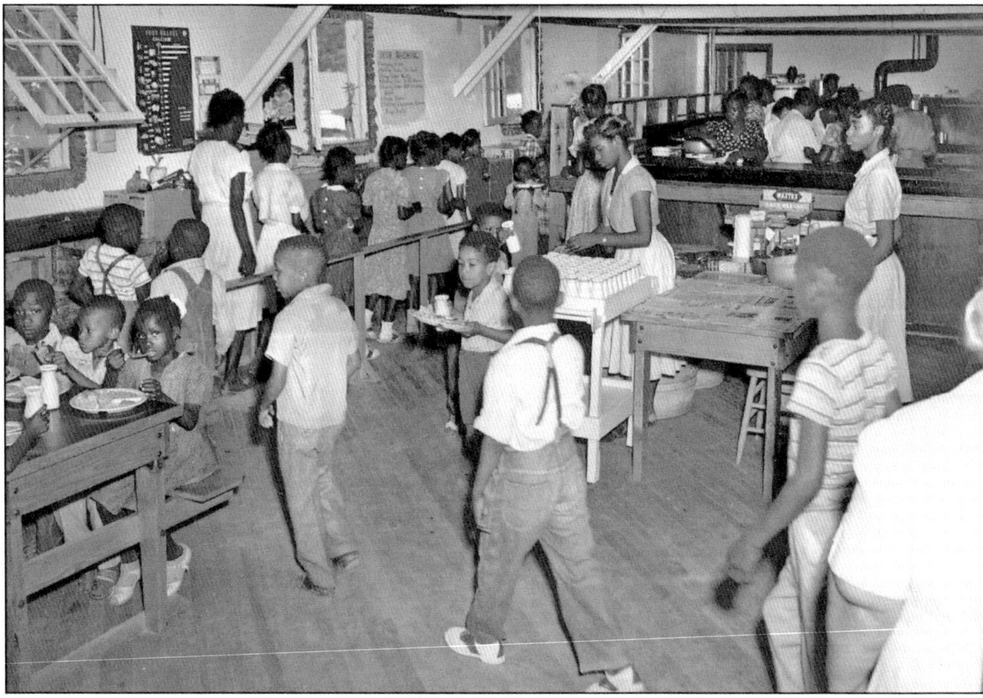

The Free Lunch Program afforded poor students a hot, nutritionally balanced meal. Wesley Johnson recalled that when he started school, he had to bring his own lunch. The lunch program did not come to his area until 1938, when Pres. Franklin Roosevelt authorized that money be sent to state educational agencies. Prior to the introduction of the Free Lunch Program, parents who didn't have money would send a load of wood or eggs to the school and that donation was applied toward the child's food bill. (Courtesy of John Thomas Guillet.)

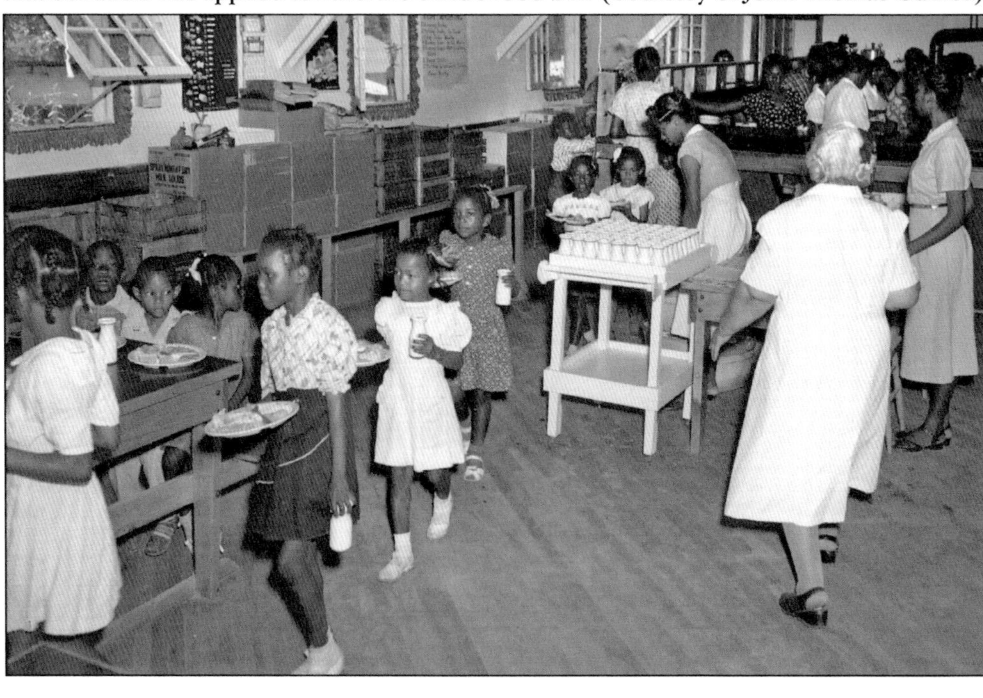

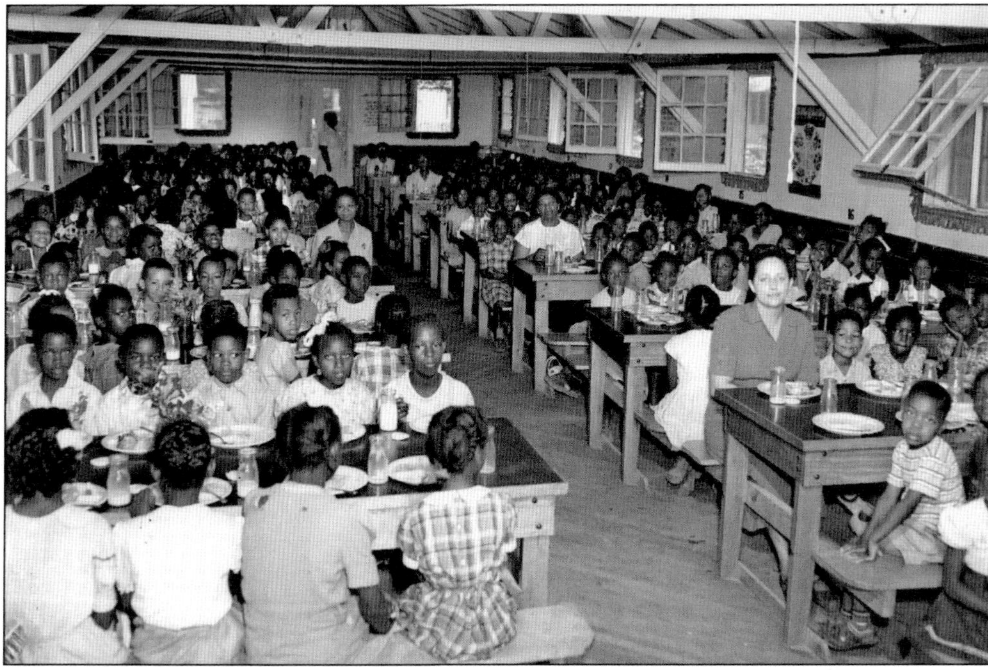

"It was down home cooking, pinto beans and rice, cabbage, greens and cornbread. I can remember those [lunch] menus," recalls Marvin Toussaint. Toussaint attended St. Matthew School, where the weekly menus were basically the same, including servings of fish on Friday and lots of spaghetti. (Courtesy of John Thomas Guillet.)

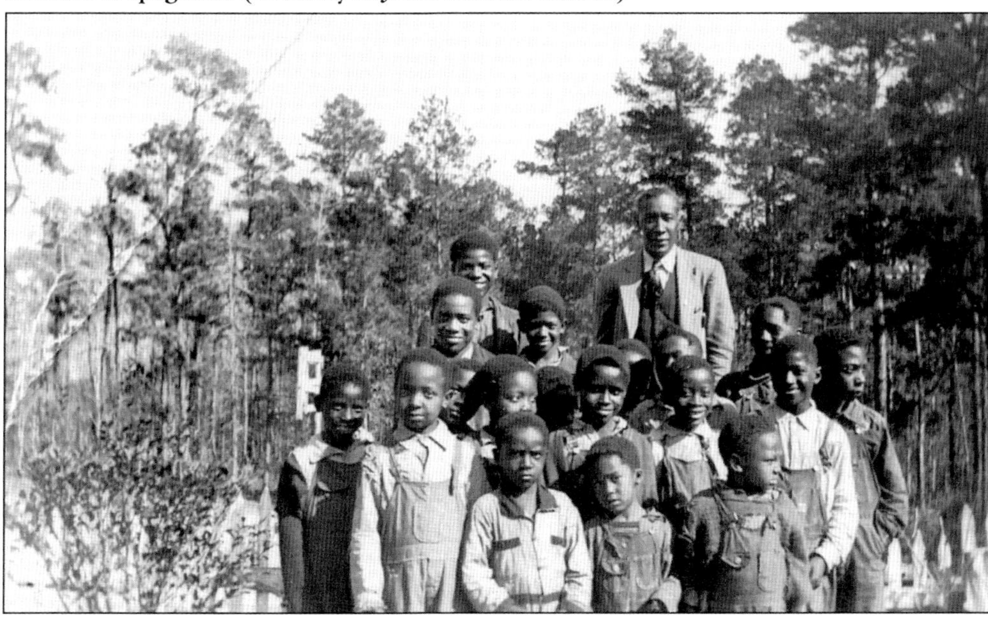

Boys of varying ages stand outside with their teacher in this image. Dorothy Presley recalled the names of some of the teachers in the early years: "There was Miss Girst, Miss Mary Ester, Miss Mary Adams, Mrs. Beatrice Breeder, Professor J. W. Thomas, Mr. Fred Richardson, and there may be others." According to Presley, "Life was good in those days for many of us." (Courtesy of Edward Ward Jr.)

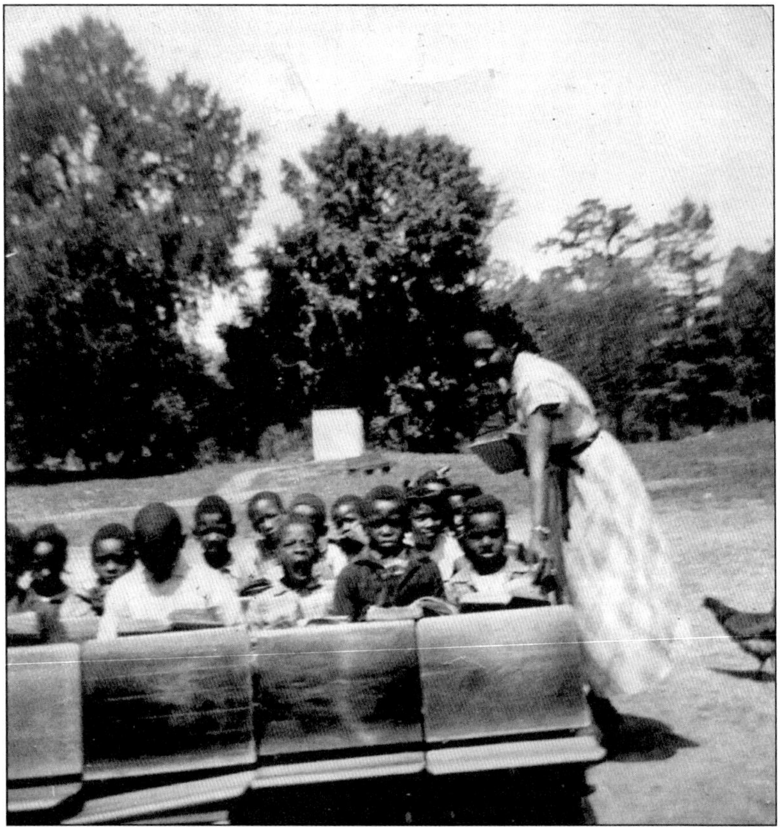

Many of the rural schools were located inside the church. On occasion, students were required to hold class outdoors while the church was being used to conduct a funeral. (Courtesy of Edward Ward Jr.)

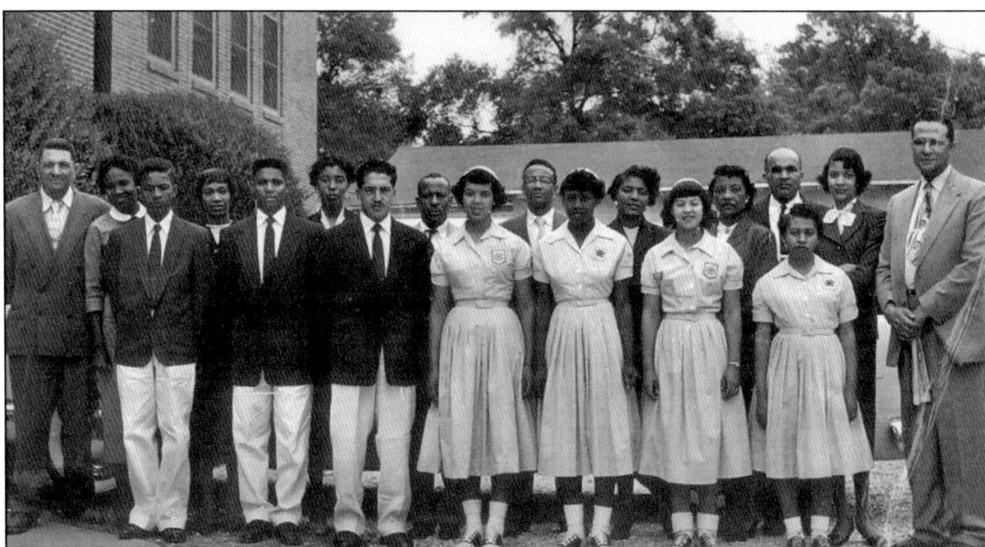

Terrel Delphin, shown third from the left in the first row, is an Isle Breville Creole who joined the 4-H Club while a student at St. Matthew High School. St. Matthew provided education to both African American and Creole students at a time when racially segregated classes were the norm. This photograph was taken while students were on a field trip. (Courtesy of Terrel Delphin.)

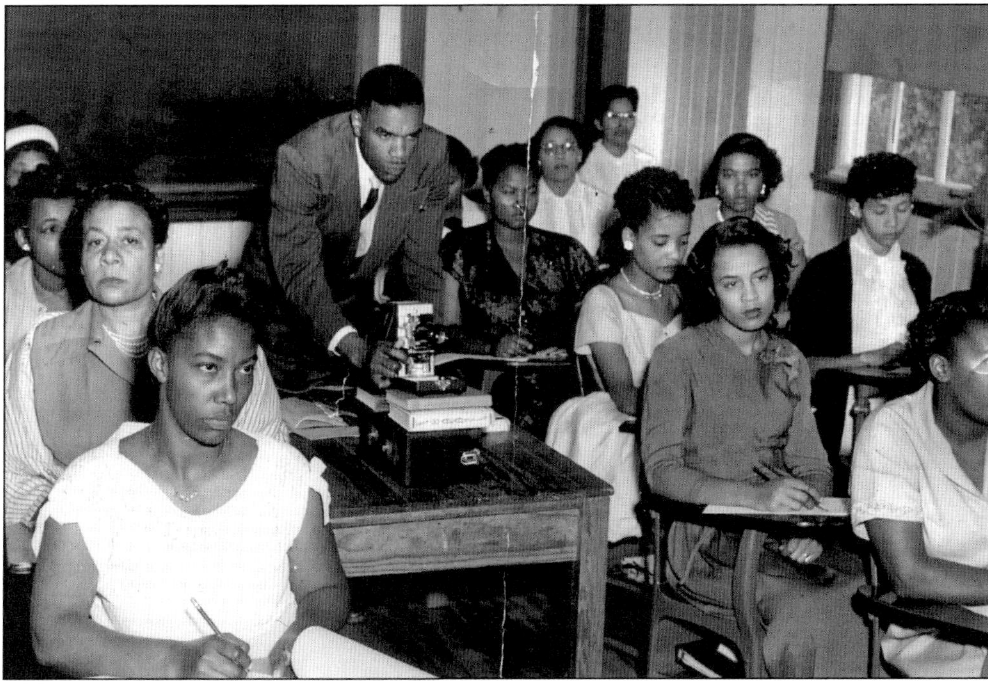

Evelyn Gair Jones arrived in Natchitoches in 1945 and assumed the position of assistant home demonstration agent. Teachers constantly received training on new educational techniques. Much of the instruction received in Natchitoches came from faculty at Southern and Grambling State Universities. (Courtesy of Edward Ward Jr.)

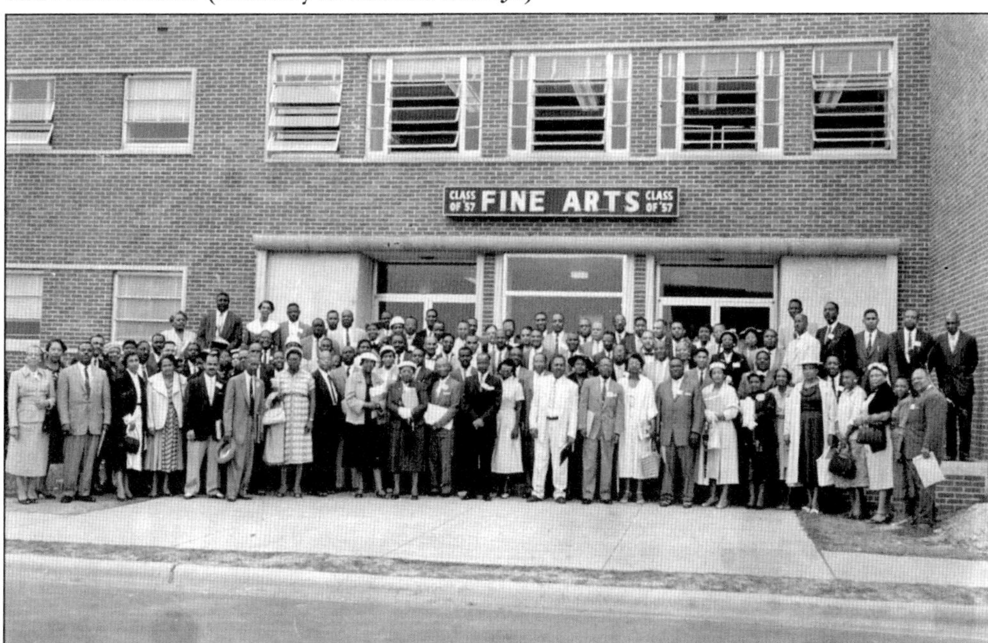

The Grambling State University class of 1957 visits their alma mater for a school reunion. This group of fine arts majors represents some of the first in their family who received a college education. (Courtesy of Edward Ward Jr.)

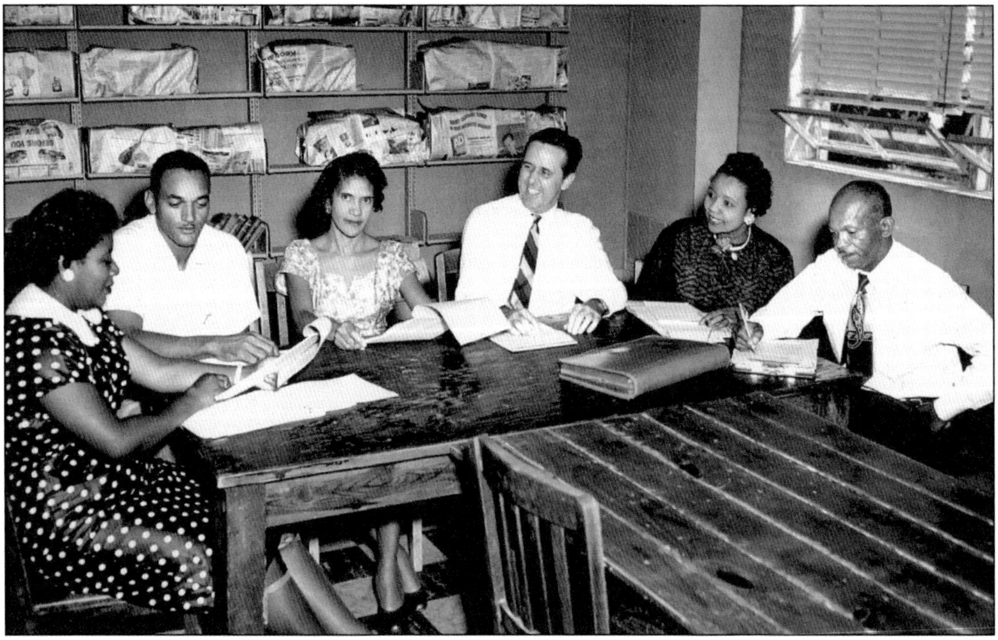

Pictured are, from left to right, Gloria Augustus (piano teacher), Rudolph Davis (band director), Alberta Harrison (Jeanes supervisor), unidentified, Odile Cage-Ward (Jeanes supervisor), and Alcee Vaughn (teacher). The Vaughn family migrated to Natchitoches from Chatawa, Mississippi, and made significant contributions toward the education of African Americans in this region. Alcee's daughter Lynn is a reporter for CNN News. (Courtesy of Edward Ward Jr.)

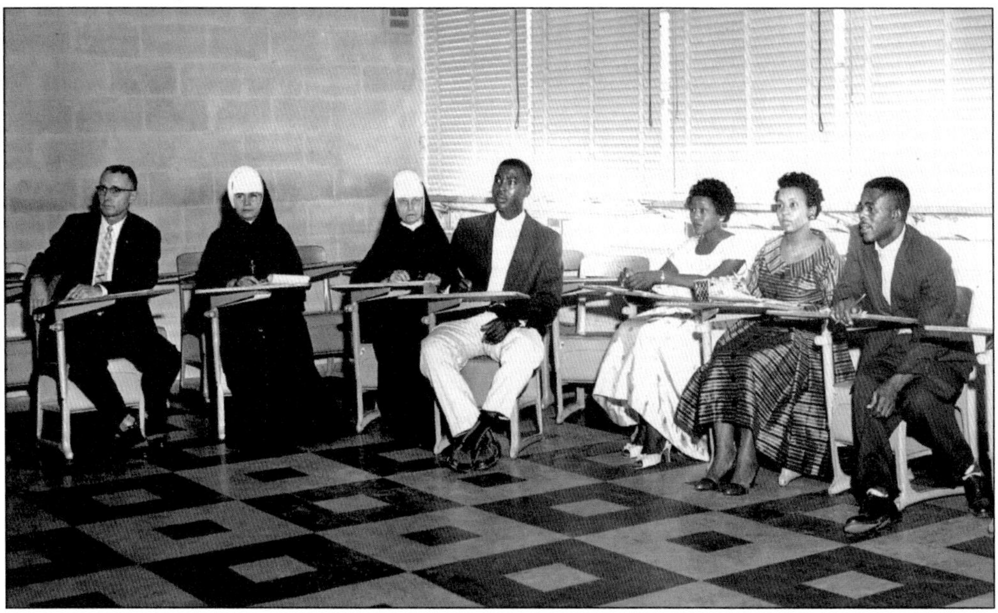

All educators were required to receive the same state standards and training. Pictured from left to right are several teachers from the city of Natchitoches: E. A. Lee (school superintendent), Sister Mary and an unidentified colleague (from the Convent of Divine Providence), Rubin Wafer, Anna Bell Knight, Emma Wilson, and Isaiah Combest. (Courtesy of Edward Ward Jr.)

The integration of school systems and other public facilities allowed for deeper, more meaningful relationships to develop across cultural barriers. Laurel Weaver kneels in front of her friend Marsha Manning. The girls often played together and were virtually inseparable. (Courtesy of the Weaver family.)

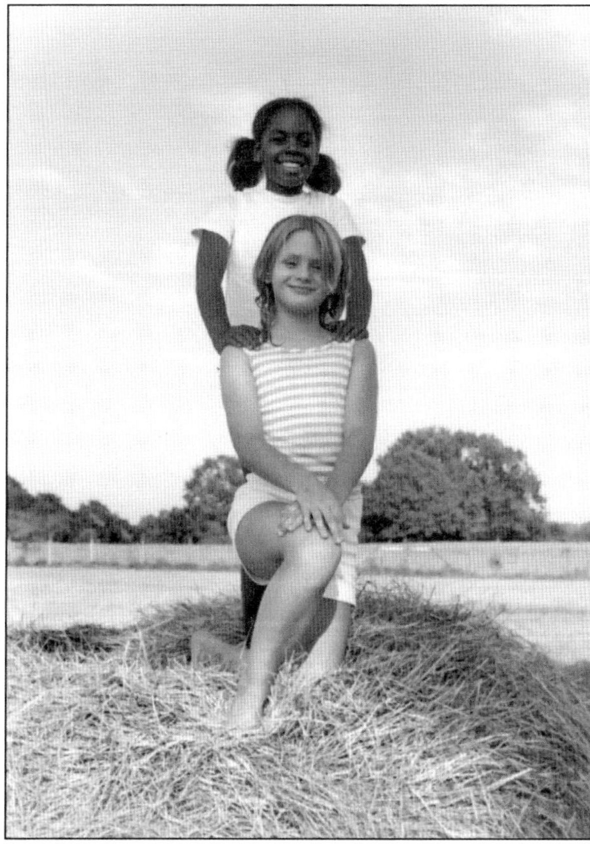

Edward Ward Jr. clenches a Black Power cane while attending his graduation ceremony at Southern State University in 1971. The "Marshall Baton" was usually given to honor students to carry; however, this time a clenched fist with a snake wrapped around the staff was handed to graduates. This symbol is reflective of the social climate of the 1970s. Political activist Vernon Jordan gave the keynote address at this event. (Courtesy of Edward Ward Jr.)

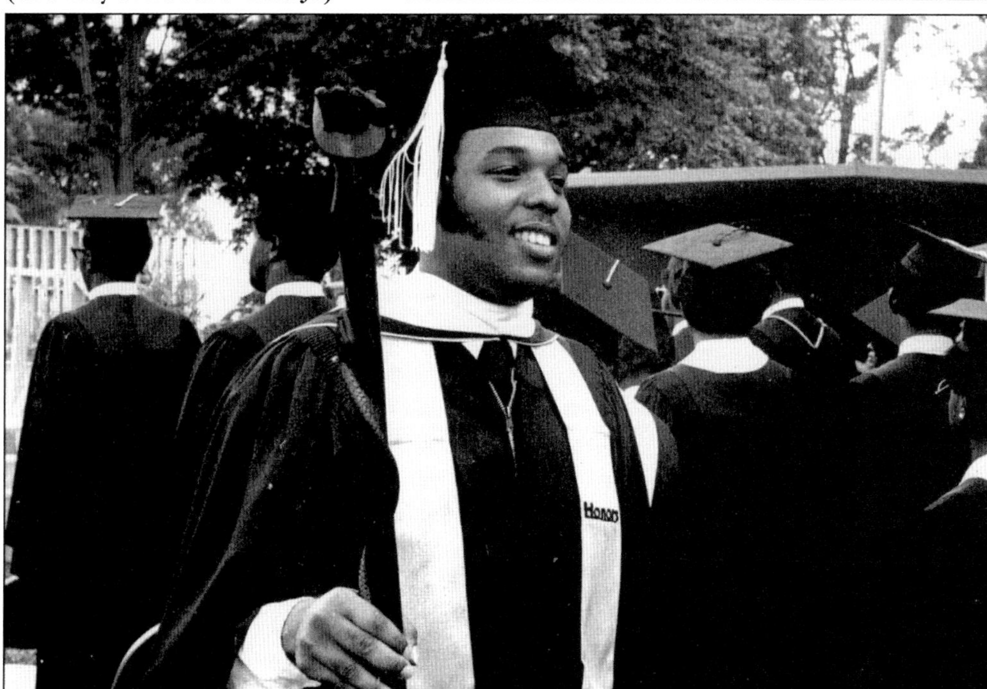

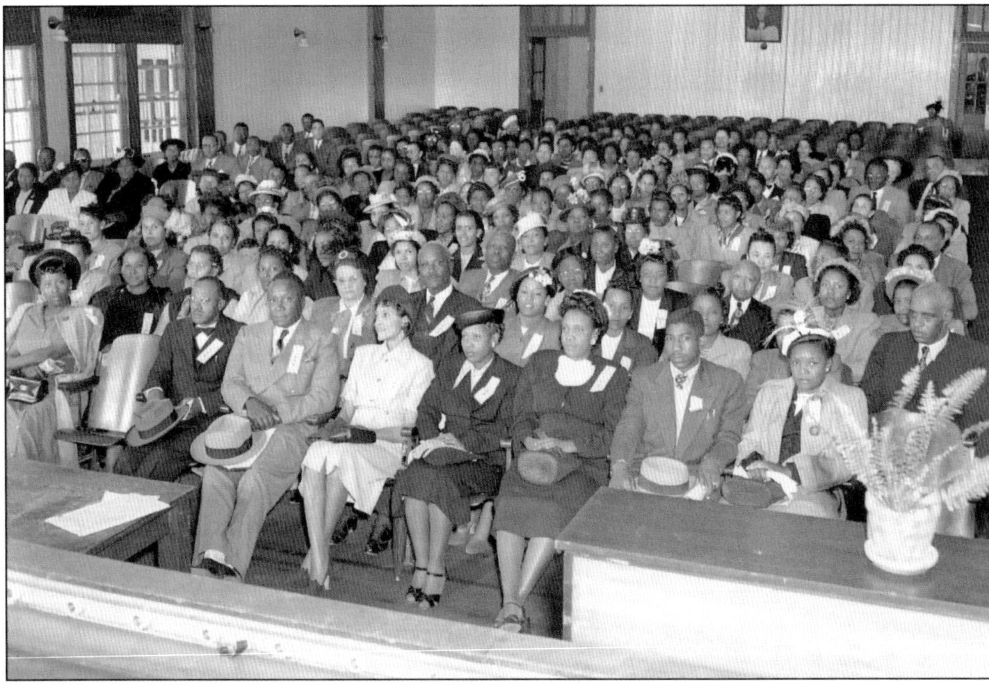

Parents attend a program at Natchitoches Parish Training School. The school produced an annual Christmas performance. Drama students wrote their own plays and held talent competitions. (Courtesy of John Thomas Guillet.)

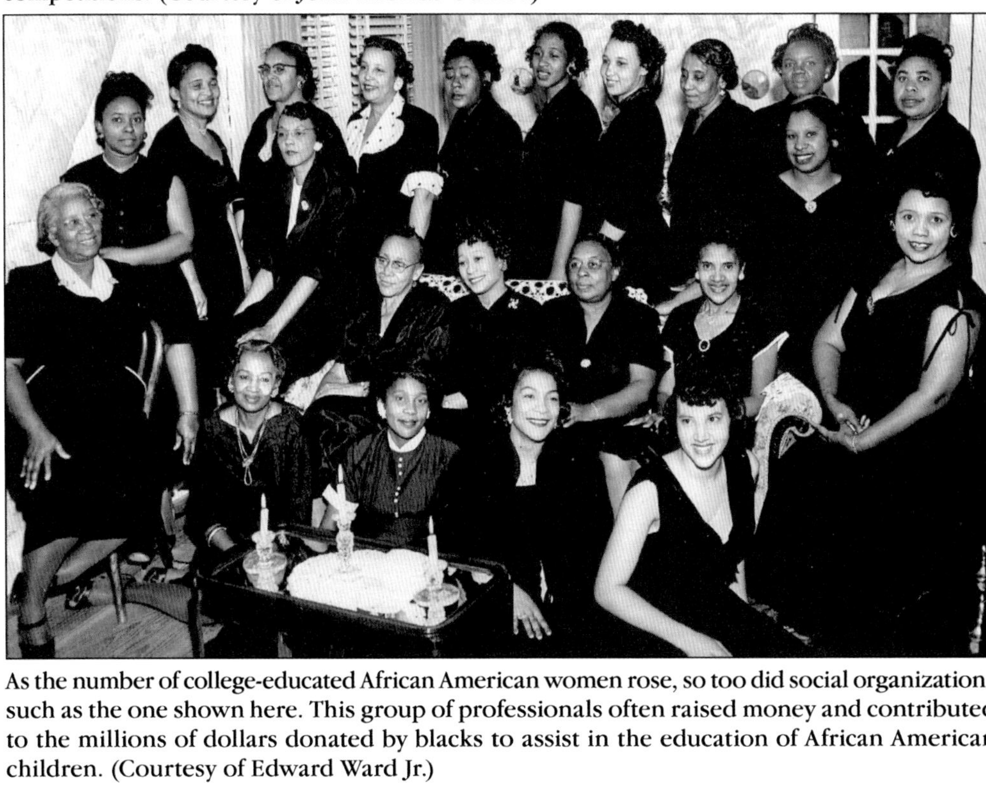

As the number of college-educated African American women rose, so too did social organizations such as the one shown here. This group of professionals often raised money and contributed to the millions of dollars donated by blacks to assist in the education of African American children. (Courtesy of Edward Ward Jr.)

Four

Time Sho' Flies When Ya' Having Fun

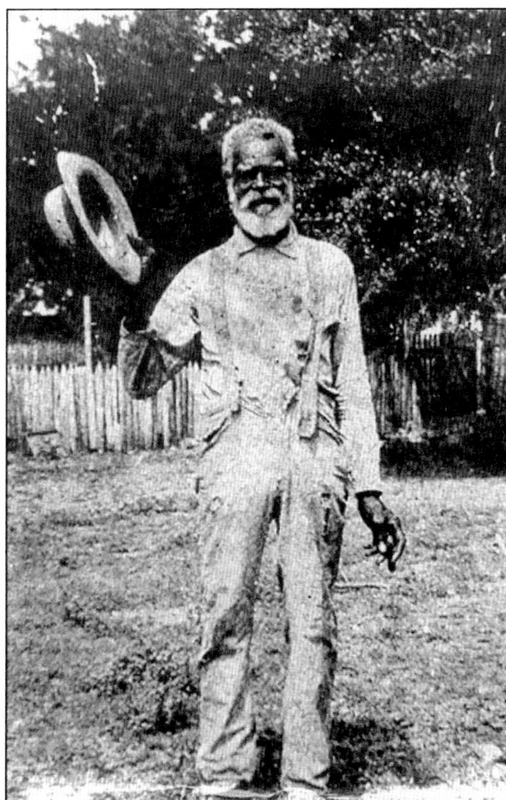

Minique Toussaint, a former slave at Oakland Plantation, is believed to have been the plantation fiddler. As a fiddler, Toussaint likely played at plantation balls, weddings, and Christmas dances. There are many descendants of the Toussaint family who still live in the Natchitoches area. (Courtesy of the Toussaint family.)

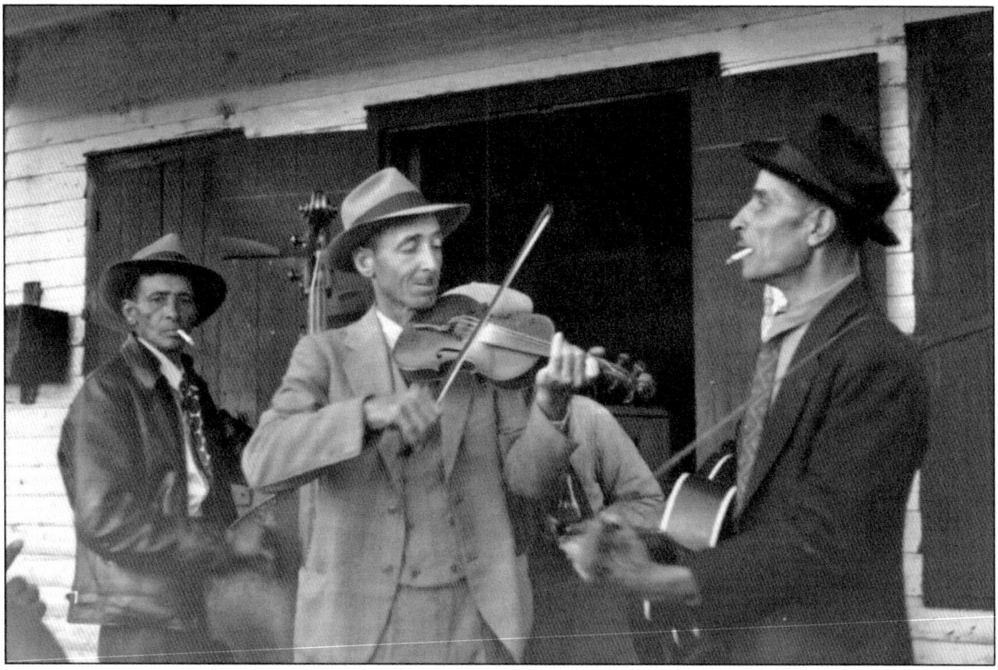

Pictured from left to right, Yuke, Duma, and Shake were members of the Creole of color band Yuke and Duma. In this image, they are seen performing on the steps of the plantation store at Magnolia Plantation. The plantation store became a popular gathering spot for the people who lived there, as well as for surrounding community members. (Courtesy of Ambrose Hertzog Jr.)

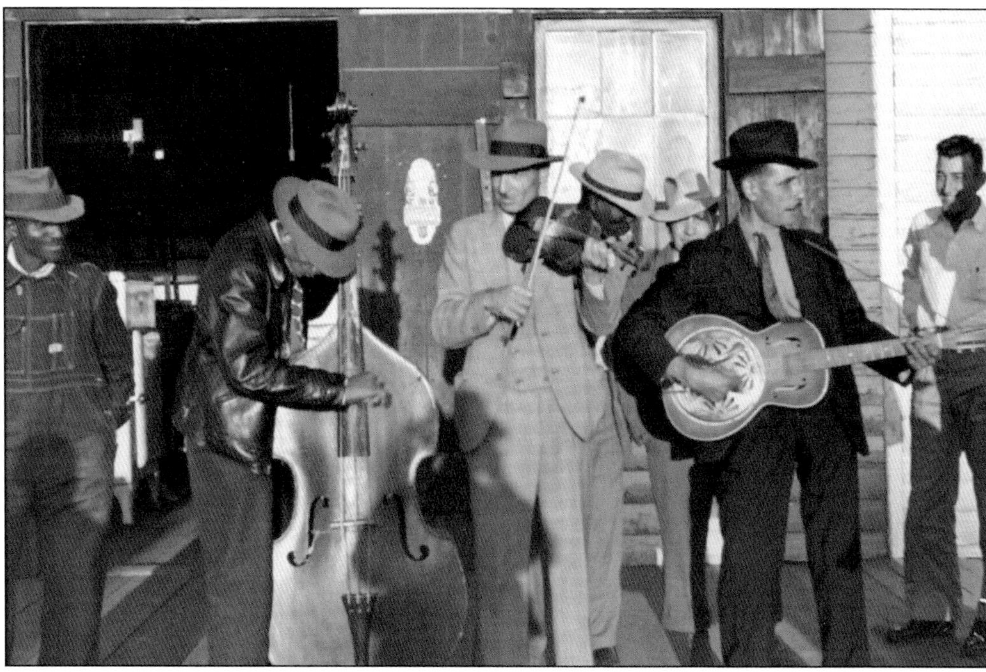

Members of the band play while sharecropper Johnson Dugas (left) looks on. Most socializing took place on Saturday evenings after a week's work. (Courtesy of Ambrose Hertzog Jr.)

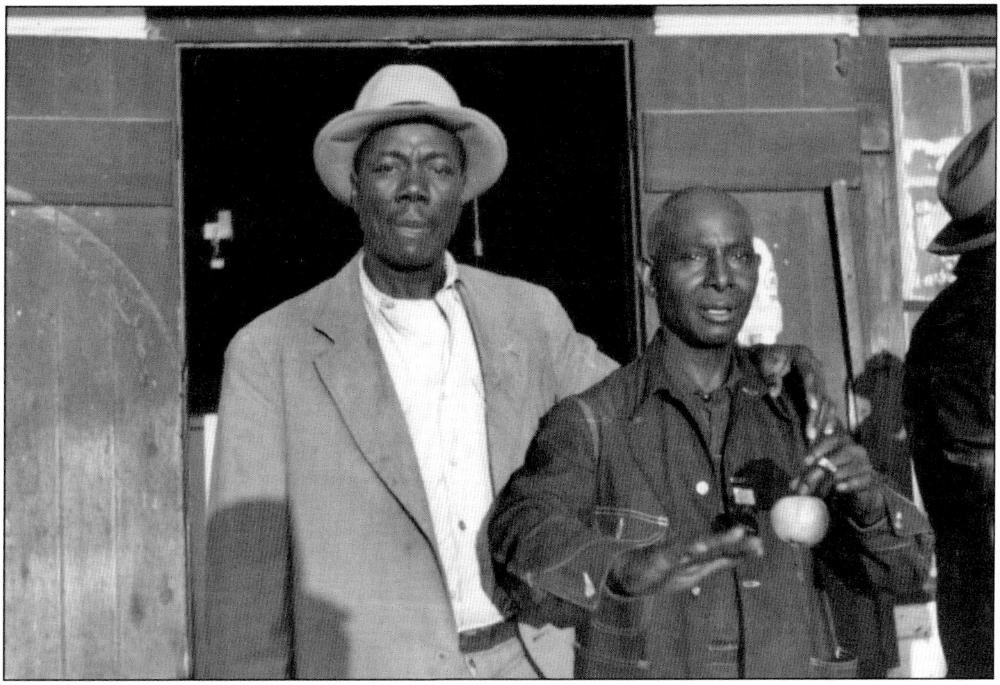

Walter Telphin (left) and John Parker, two sharecroppers from Magnolia Plantation, enjoy the evening festivities. The Magnolia Plantation store lies on property that currently belongs to Cane River Creole National Historical Park. (Courtesy of Ambrose Hertzog Jr.)

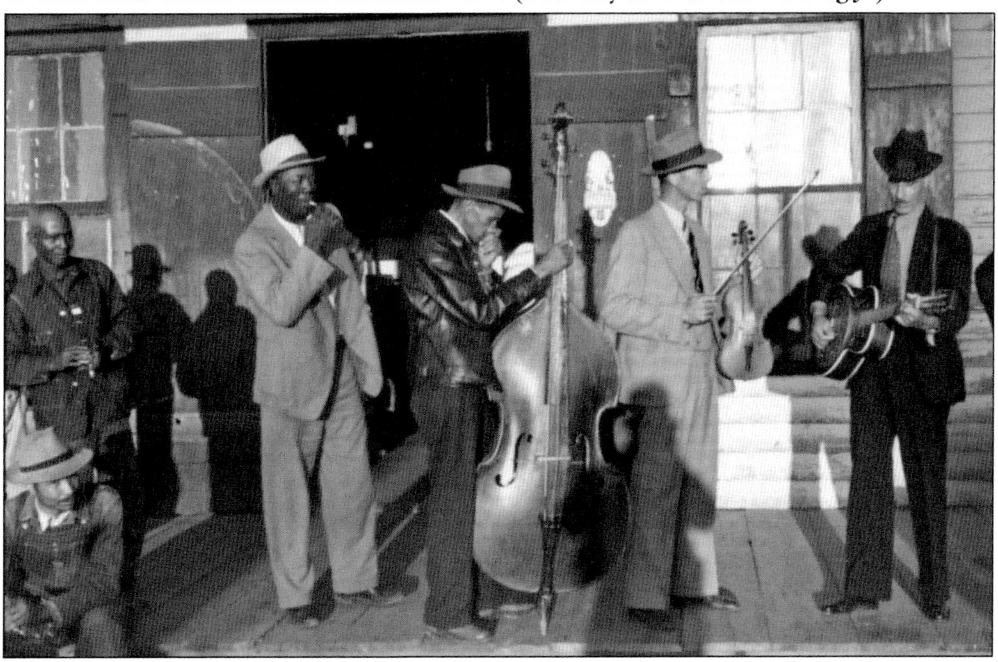

John Parker, standing at left in denim overalls, and Walter Telphin, who is lighting a cigarette, listen to the music. These images seem to suggest the absence of females at this gathering. However, women and girls stood in the road watching all that took place. (Courtesy of Ambrose Hertzog Jr.)

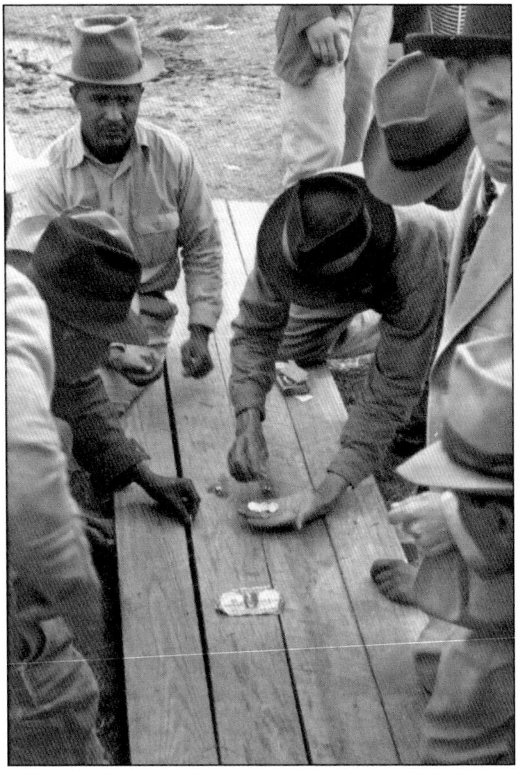

Men assemble around a few wooden planks to play a game of dice. The men who actually rolled the dice could make or lose money, but so, too, could those men kneeling on the sidelines. "Side bets" offered another way to gamble. (Courtesy of Ambrose Hertzog Jr.)

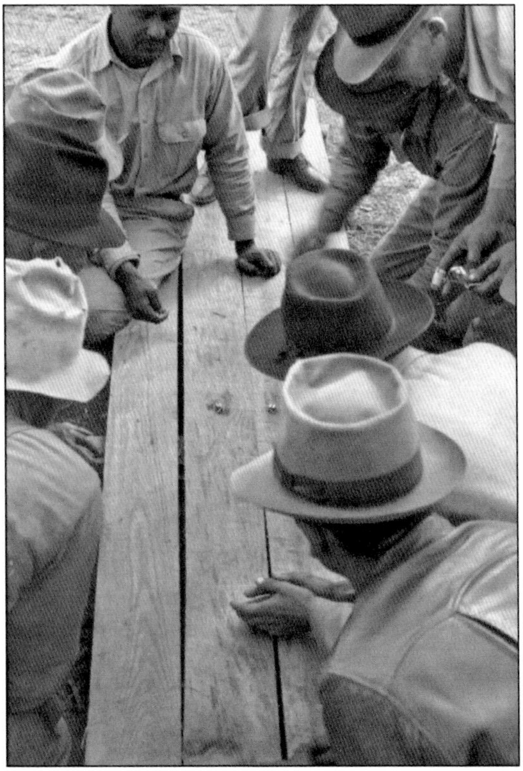

There are many variants to the game of craps; however, generally, the dice are rolled in hopes of hitting the numbers 7 or 11. (Courtesy of Ambrose Hertzog Jr.)

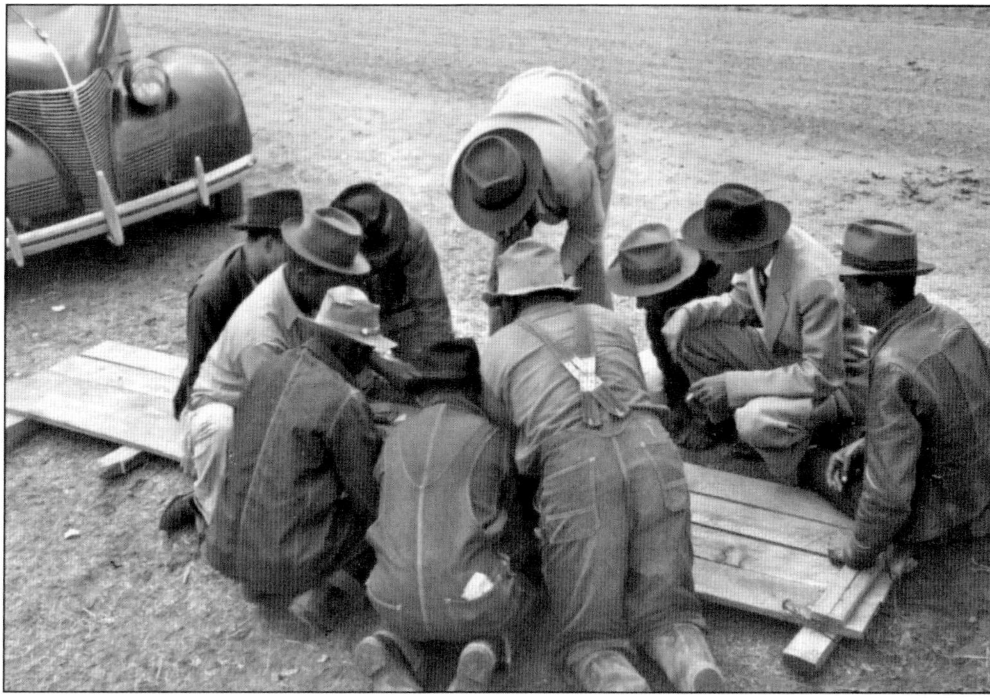

Here is a bird's-eye view of a craps game in progress. Primarily men played this game, although women were known to play on occasion. (Courtesy of Ambrose Hertzog Jr.)

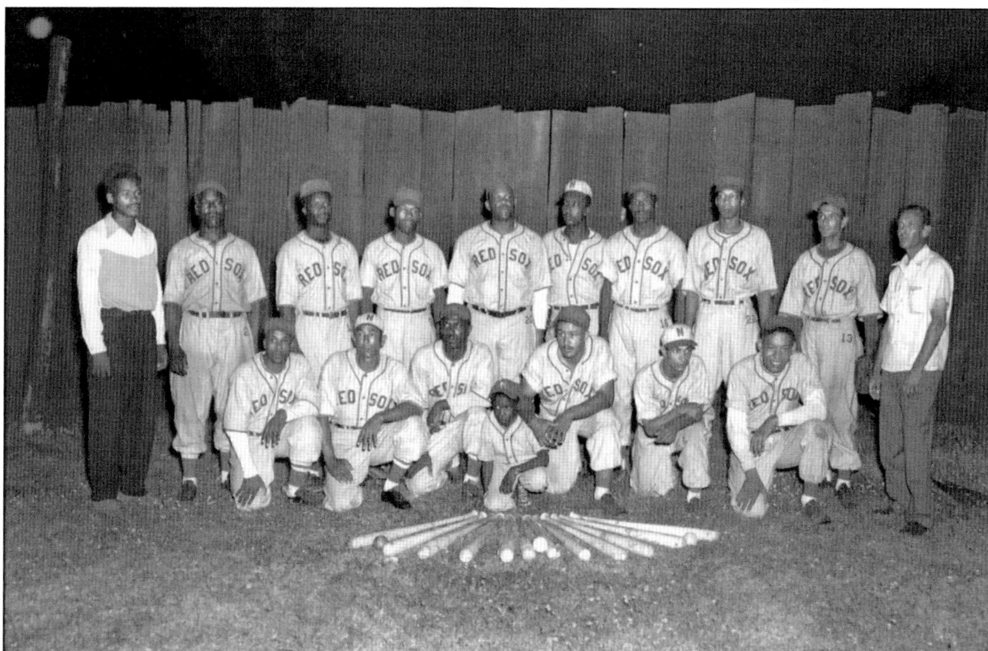

Earnest Luchin recalled that there were several baseball teams in the region representing the towns of Cloutierville, Derry, Little River, and Melrose. Each team competed with the other until a final champion for the area was decided. The team shown here is from the city of Natchitoches. (Courtesy of John Thomas Guillet.)

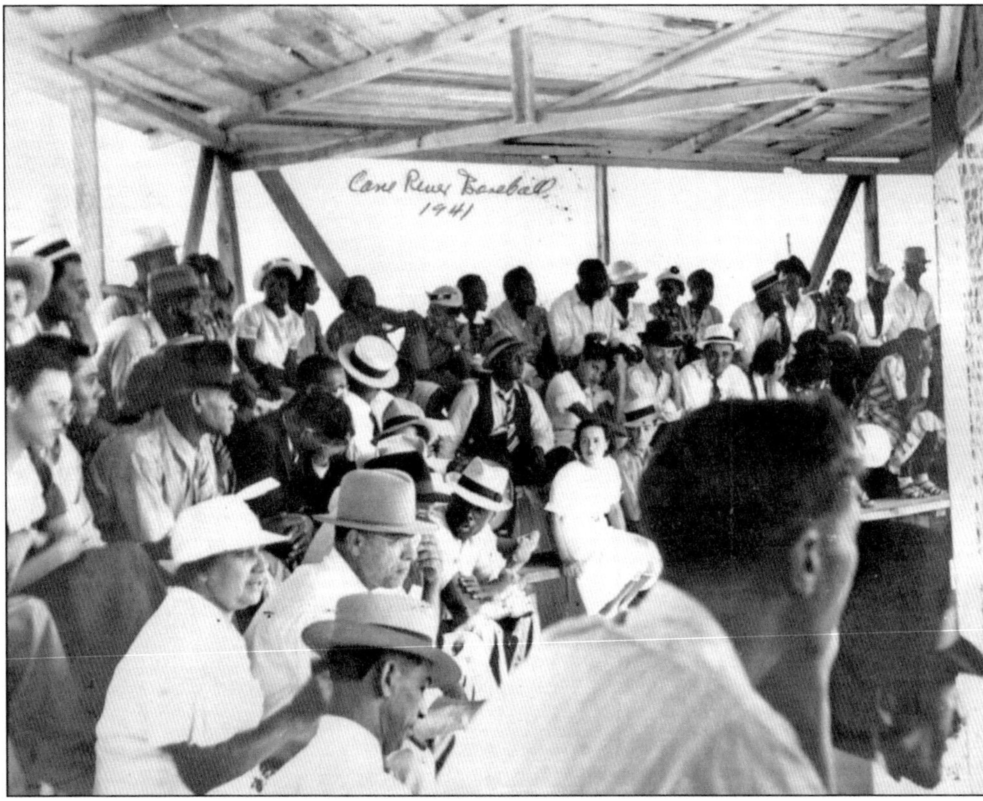

Alfonse Metoyer had the responsibility of building this grandstand, located on Lake View Plantation. People from surrounding plantations such as Melrose and Magnolia often gathered here for tournament games. According to Metoyer, sometimes, "we used to have more people than that grandstand could hold." (Courtesy of Ambrose Hertzog Jr.)

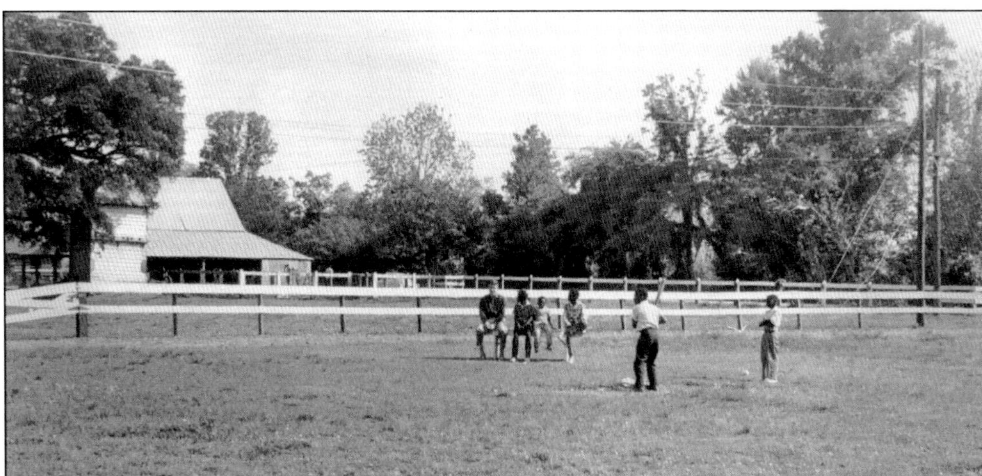

In the absence of a grandstand in which to show off their skills, these young boys practice in the grass area of the horses' riding ring at Magnolia Plantation. This photograph taken in 1961 shows the old blacksmith shop in the background, which is now part of Cane River Creole National Historical Park's complex. (Courtesy of Ambrose Hertzog Jr.)

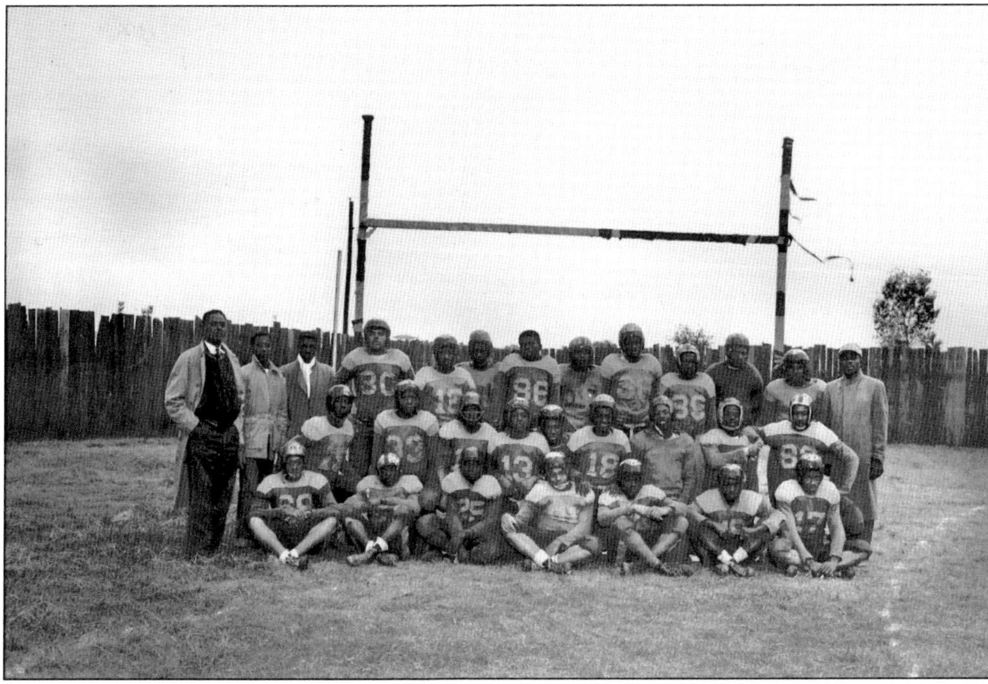

In the 1950s when Natchitoches Parish Training School wanted to start a football team, they received their first uniforms from Northwestern State University. Ophelia Dumars remembered, "We didn't have football uniforms or shoes or balls. We got that from Northwestern; they gave us that old stuff. Lot of time the players couldn't even wear [the uniforms] because they were too big or too small. It was the same with the band uniforms. They would give our school their old band uniforms." (Courtesy of John Thomas Guillet.)

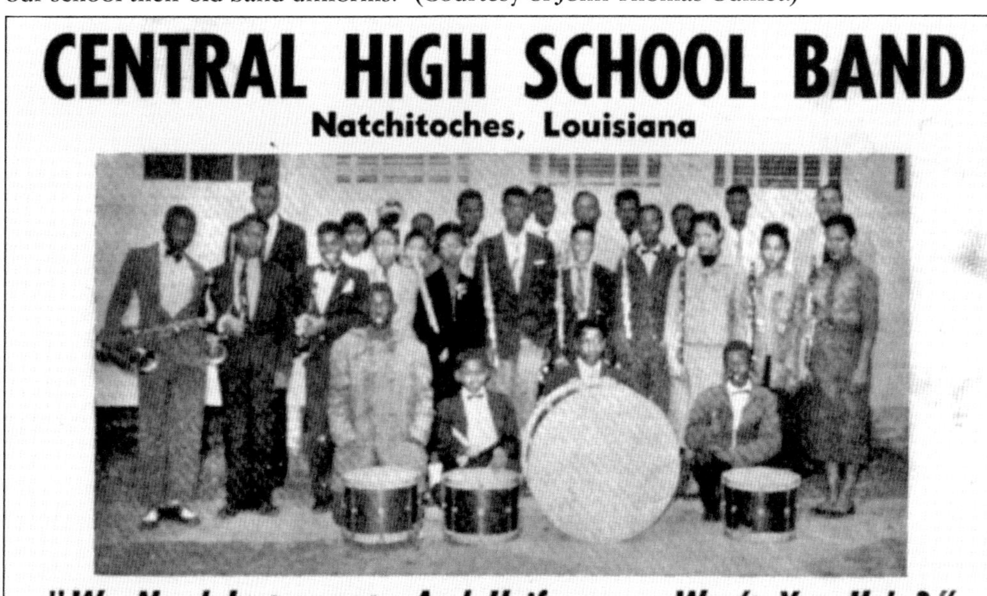

Determined to have their own school uniforms and equipment, parents, students, and teachers sought donations through advertisements and fund-raisers. (Courtesy of Edward Ward Jr.)

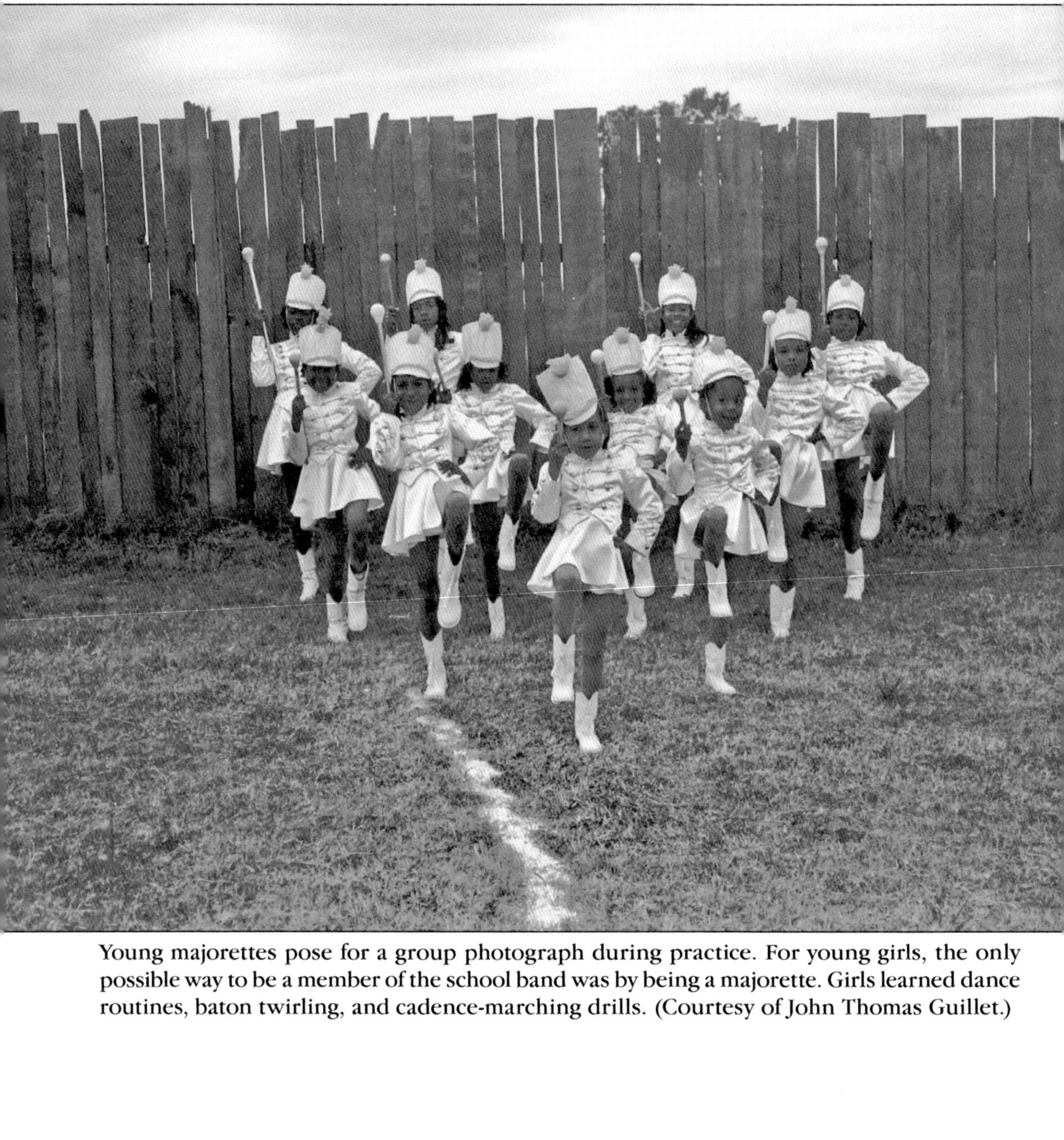

Young majorettes pose for a group photograph during practice. For young girls, the only possible way to be a member of the school band was by being a majorette. Girls learned dance routines, baton twirling, and cadence-marching drills. (Courtesy of John Thomas Guillet.)

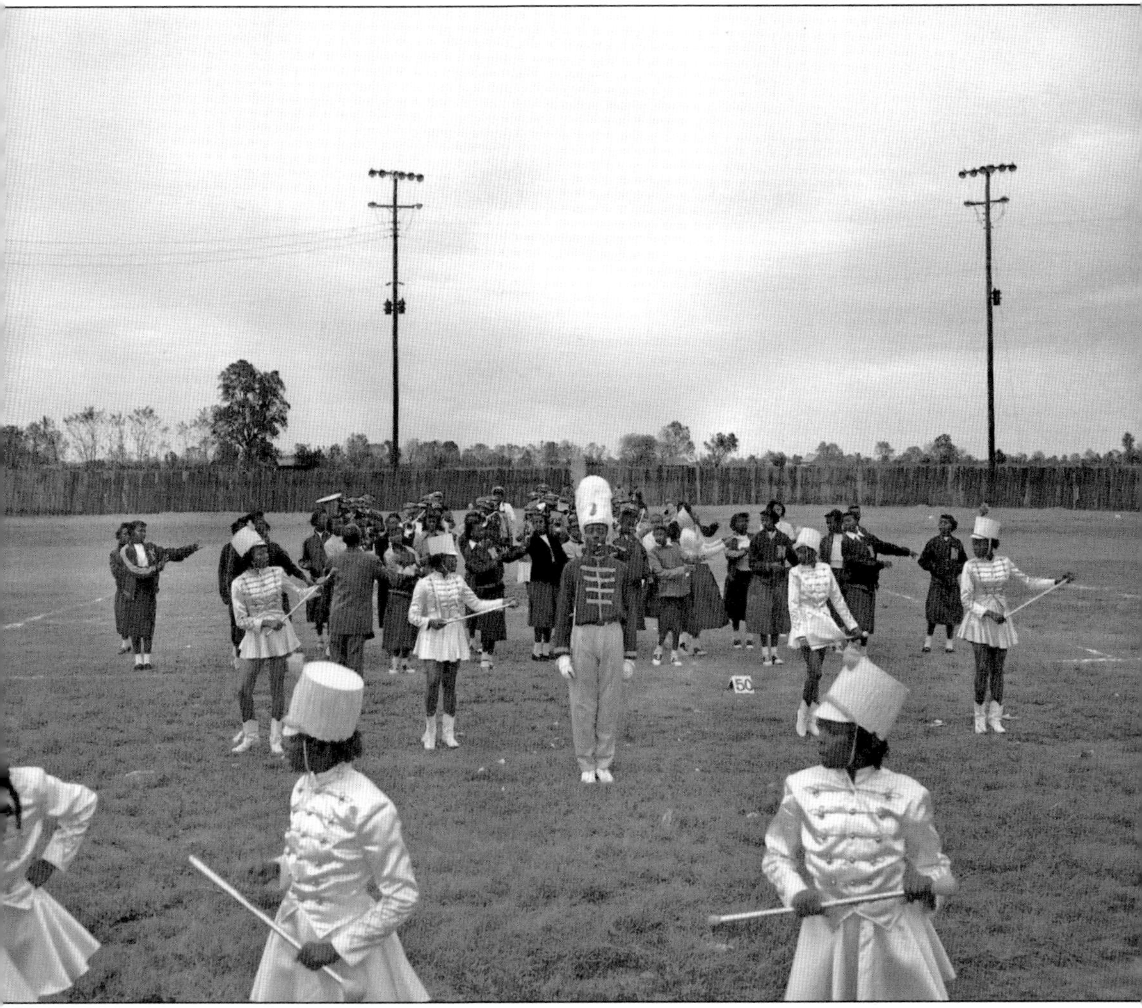

Majorettes and the drum major are shown practicing before a performance. Behind them are the flag girls, whose job it was to wave brightly colored flags and ribbons during band routines. In addition to school performances, majorettes and drum majors also participated in community parades. (Courtesy of John Thomas Guillet.)

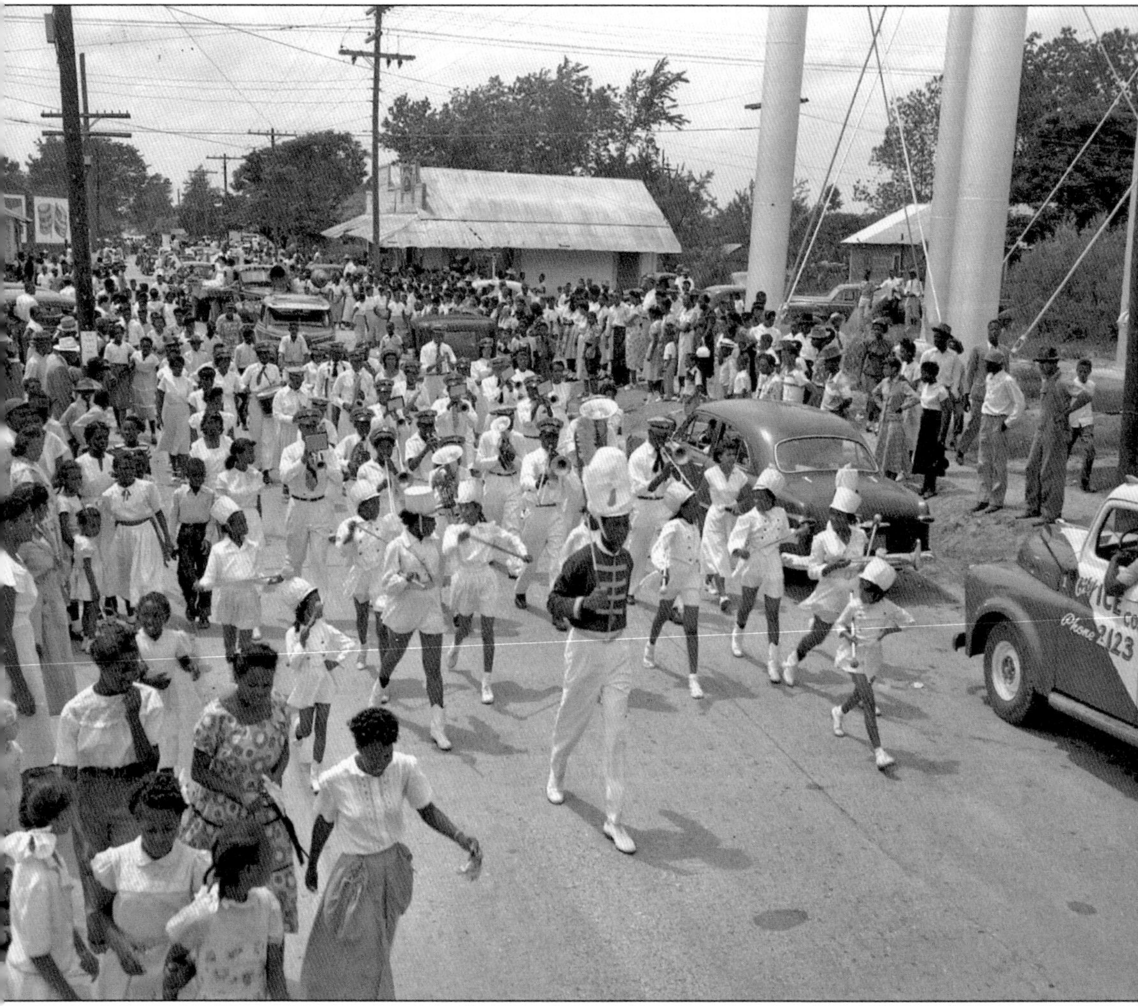

Practice pays off as members of Central High's band walk a parade route that winds down Amulet Street in Jackson Square at the heart of the African American community in the city of Natchitoches. Prior to the 1960s, parades were segregated. The four columns to the right form the base of the city water tower. Also visible in the photograph is a city ice truck and Maggio's Liquor Store. (Courtesy of John Thomas Guillet.)

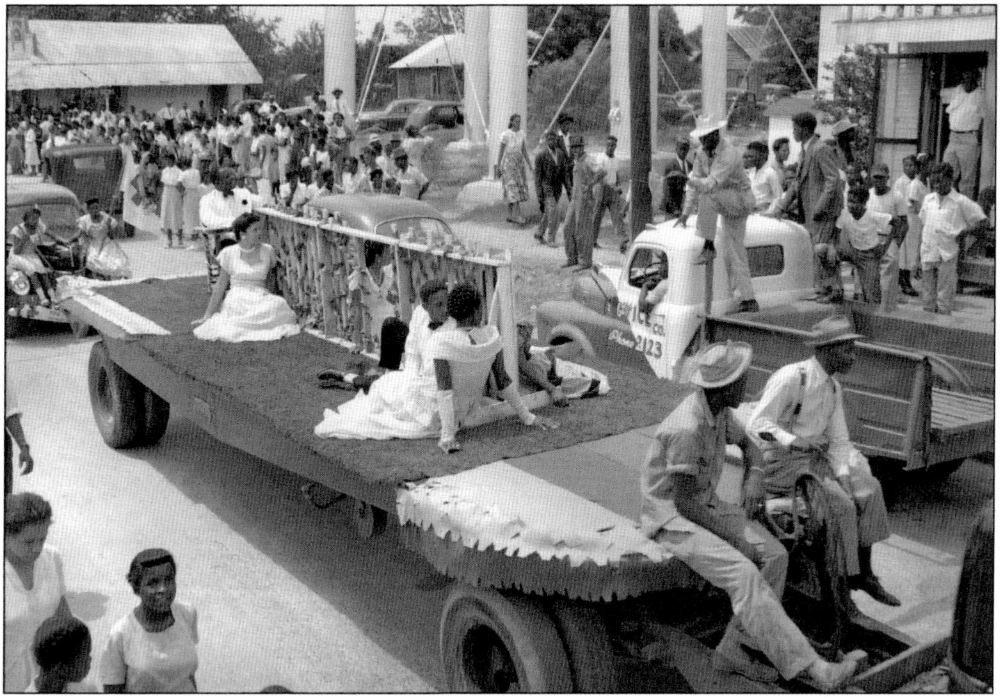

Bessie Blake stated that most of the early parades were connected with the school's homecoming day. These youths are dressed in evening attire and were likely part of the homecoming court. Katherine Johnson recounted how she and Edward Rogers were chosen as queen and king for the elementary component of St. Matthew High in the 1970s. They got to ride on top of the cars and floats during the parade. (Courtesy of John Thomas Guillet.)

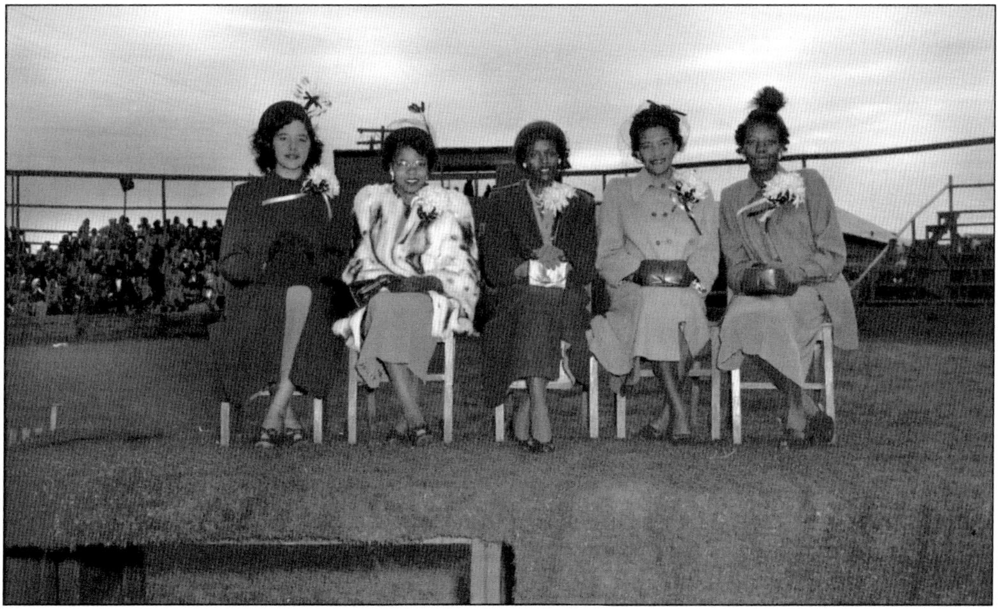

This is the senior homecoming court at Natchitoches Parish Training School. The year is unknown; however, the ladies certainly seem to represent the finest students the school had to offer. (Courtesy of John Thomas Guillet.)

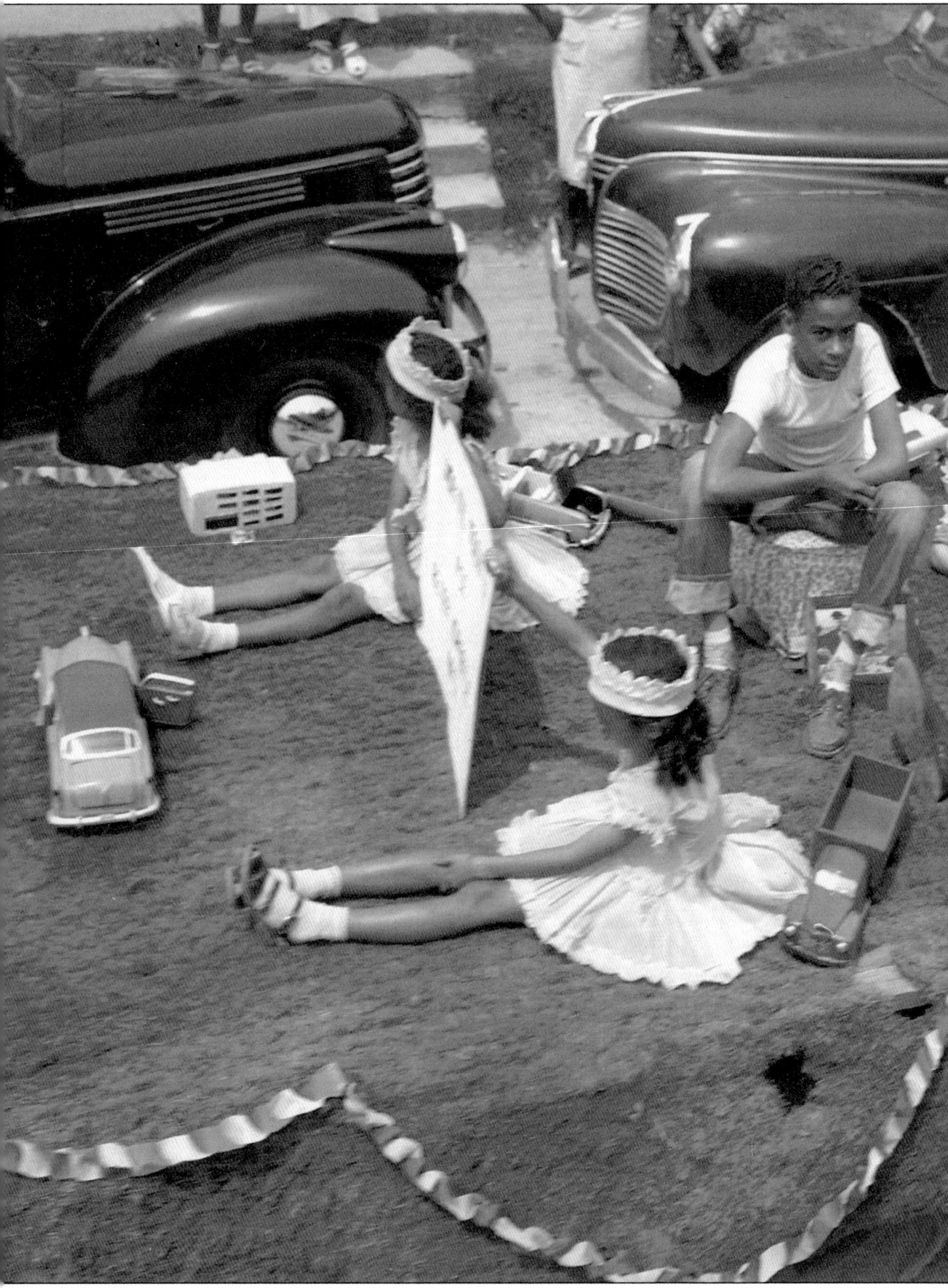

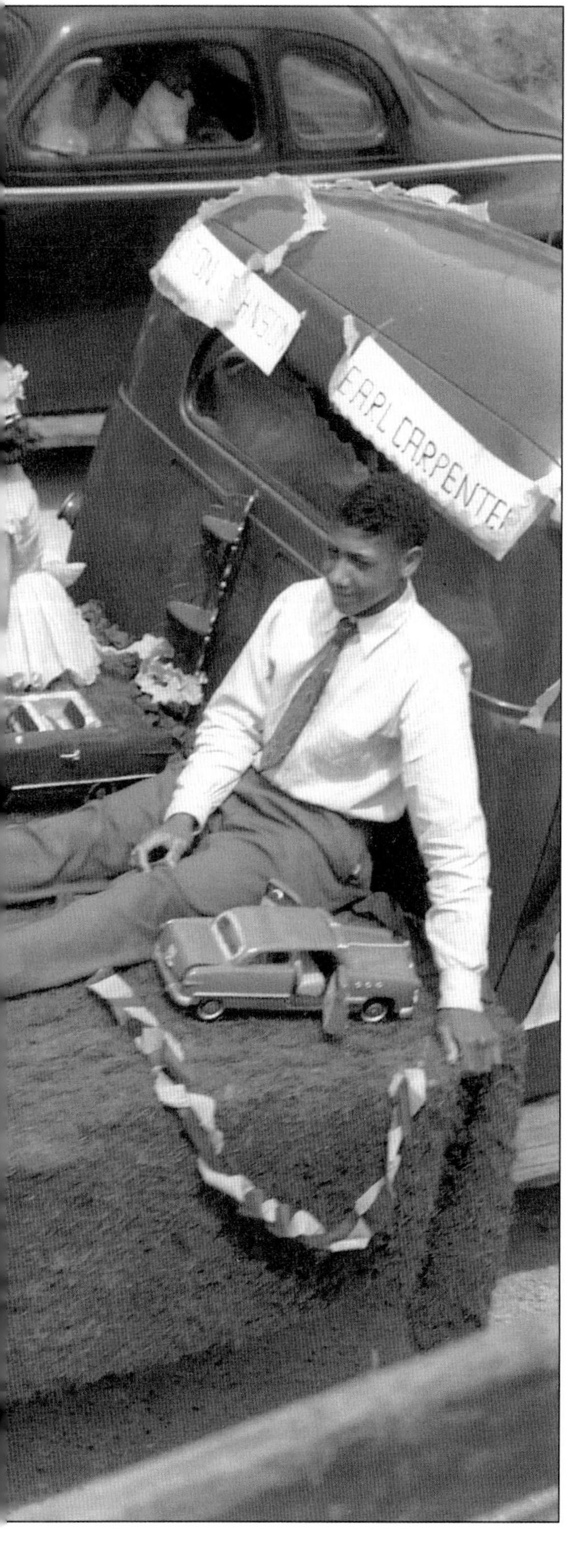

Alton Johnson (left) and Earl Carpenter, students at St. Matthew High, show off model cars designed by the boys. Local lore states that Johnson designed either the 1952 or 1958 Chevrolet Impala. Fisher Motors in Detroit, Michigan, bought the design idea, and Alton moved to California. (Courtesy of John Thomas Guillet.)

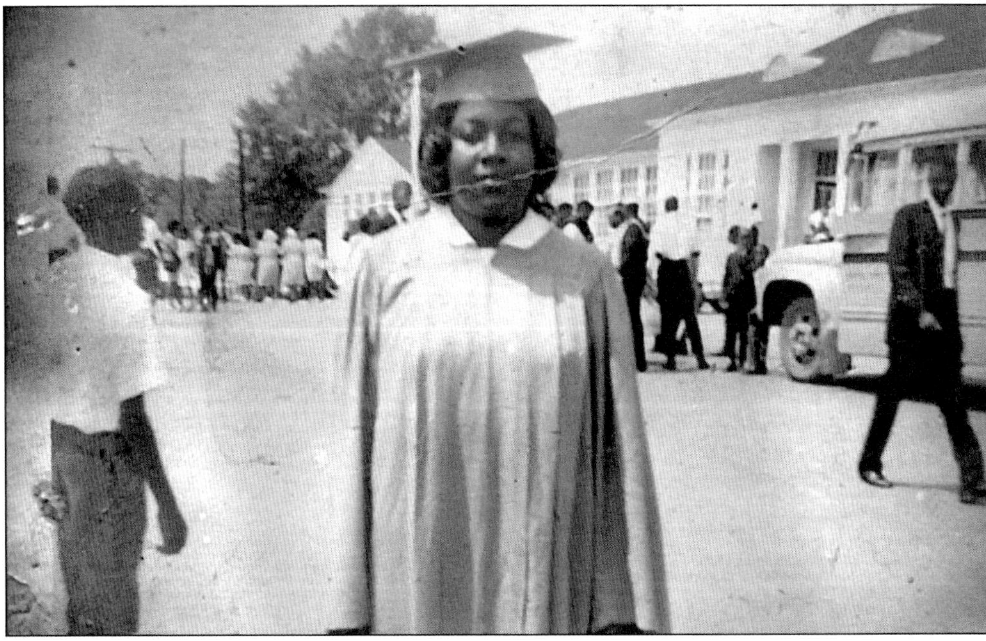

This image shows a graduation day for this young woman. Her future lies before her. She may take a job in one of the local businesses or attend college. If she chose to pursue a college education, then she would likely have attended a black institution of higher learning such as Grambling State University or Southern University. (Courtesy of Erdis Beaudoin.)

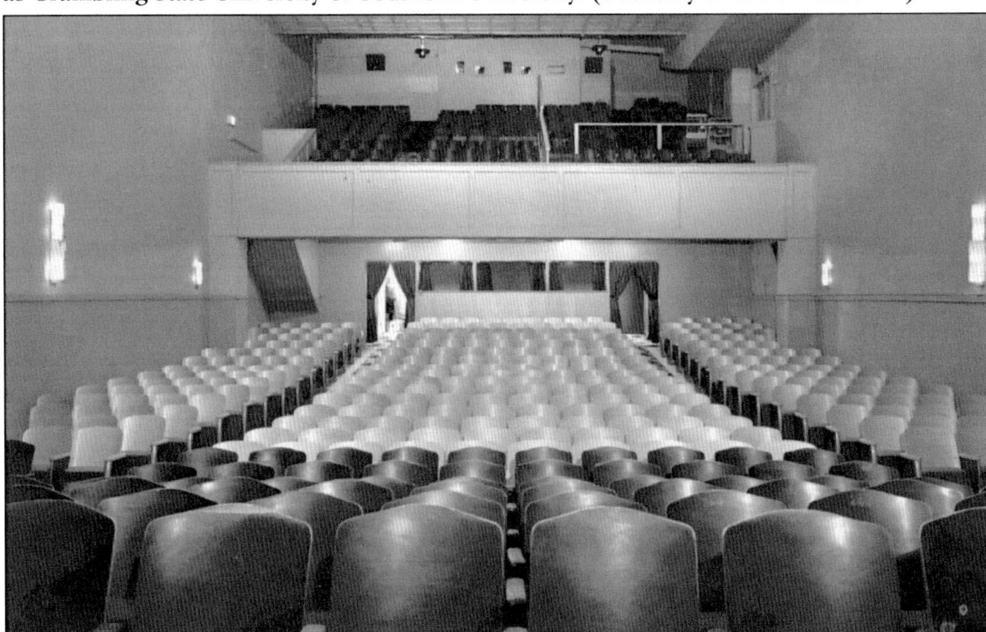

Here is a view of the inside of the Don Theatre, which opened its doors in the early 1960s. Some members of the African American community referred to the top section as the "buzzard roost." Lawrence Vaughn recalled, "You couldn't go on the main floors. Blacks had to go up to the top." The Don Theatre was located on Front Street. (Courtesy of John Thomas Guillet.)

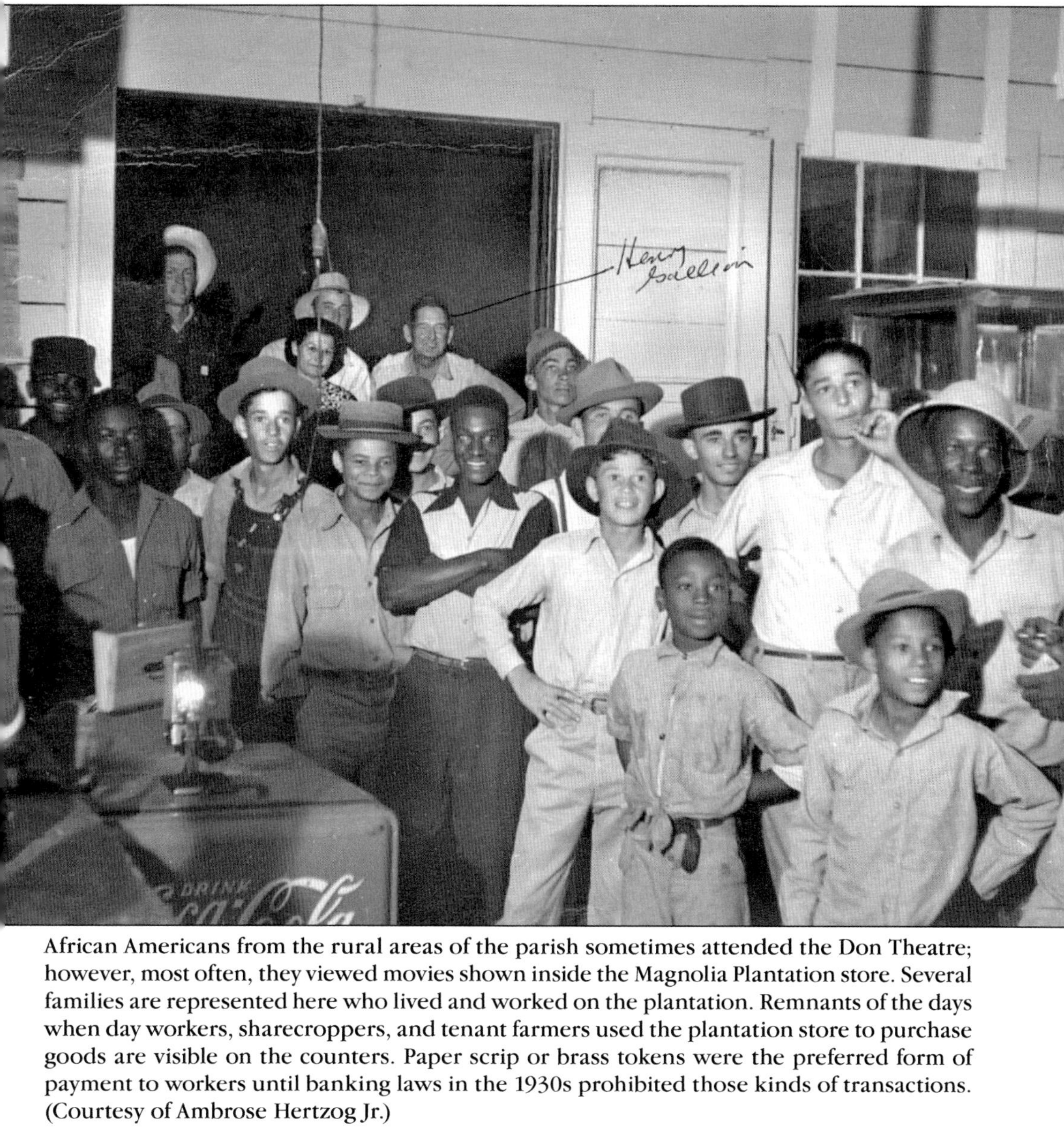

African Americans from the rural areas of the parish sometimes attended the Don Theatre; however, most often, they viewed movies shown inside the Magnolia Plantation store. Several families are represented here who lived and worked on the plantation. Remnants of the days when day workers, sharecroppers, and tenant farmers used the plantation store to purchase goods are visible on the counters. Paper scrip or brass tokens were the preferred form of payment to workers until banking laws in the 1930s prohibited those kinds of transactions. (Courtesy of Ambrose Hertzog Jr.)

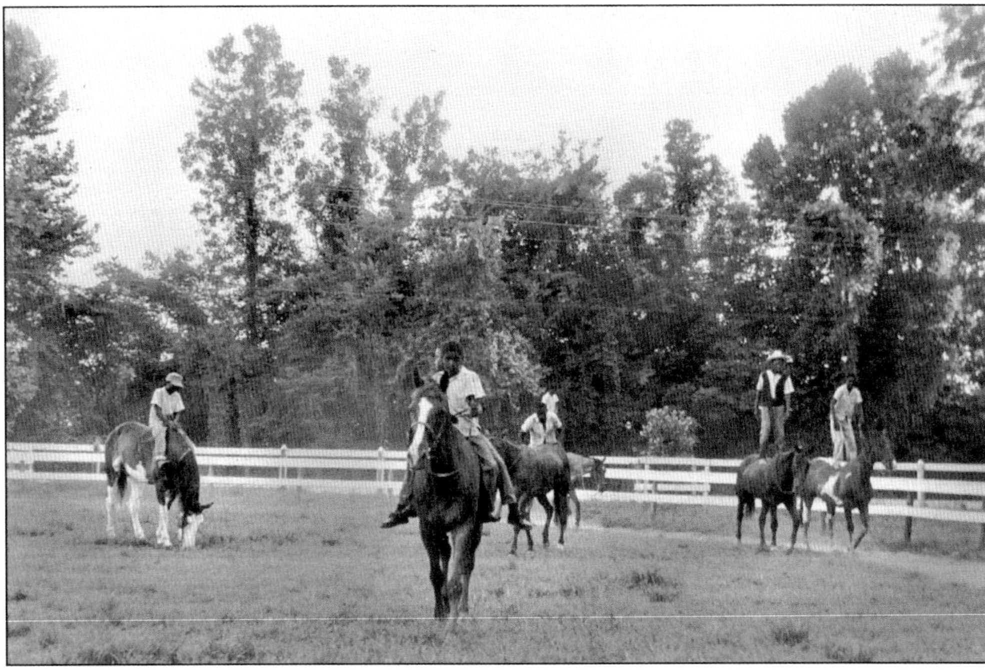

Riding horses has long been important in the African American community in the parish. Several African American riding clubs still exist today. McDuffie Raymond recalled that his father went to Shreveport and bought two young unbroken mules when McDuffie was 17 years old. From that time forward, he became a "professional in breaking in horses and mules." (Courtesy of Ambrose Hertzog Jr.)

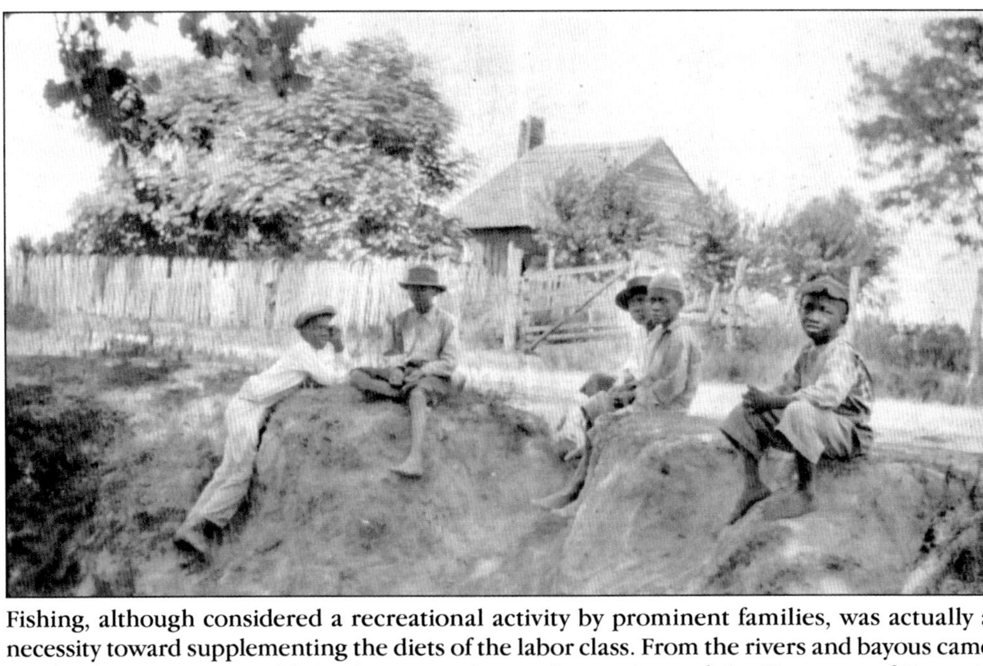

Fishing, although considered a recreational activity by prominent families, was actually a necessity toward supplementing the diets of the labor class. From the rivers and bayous came meals of various types of fish, shrimp, crabs, turtles, and crawfish. (Courtesy of Cammie Henry Research Center, Northwestern State University.)

Emma Lee Page Manning stands with a string of fish caught in the Cane River. Sometimes people fished at night with pine torches or flashlights that were reflected on the water to attract the fish. White perch fish was one of the favorite night catches. (Courtesy of the Weaver family.)

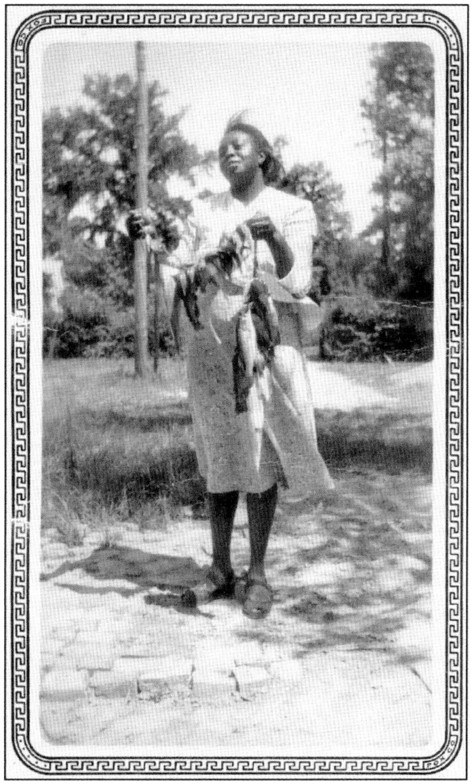

This small child sits and waits as her guardian fishes in the river. Cane poles were commonly used for fishing from riverbanks since they provided the length needed to reach deep water. In addition, cane poles allowed flexibility so that the pole would not break under the weight of a fish. (Courtesy of John Thomas Guillet.)

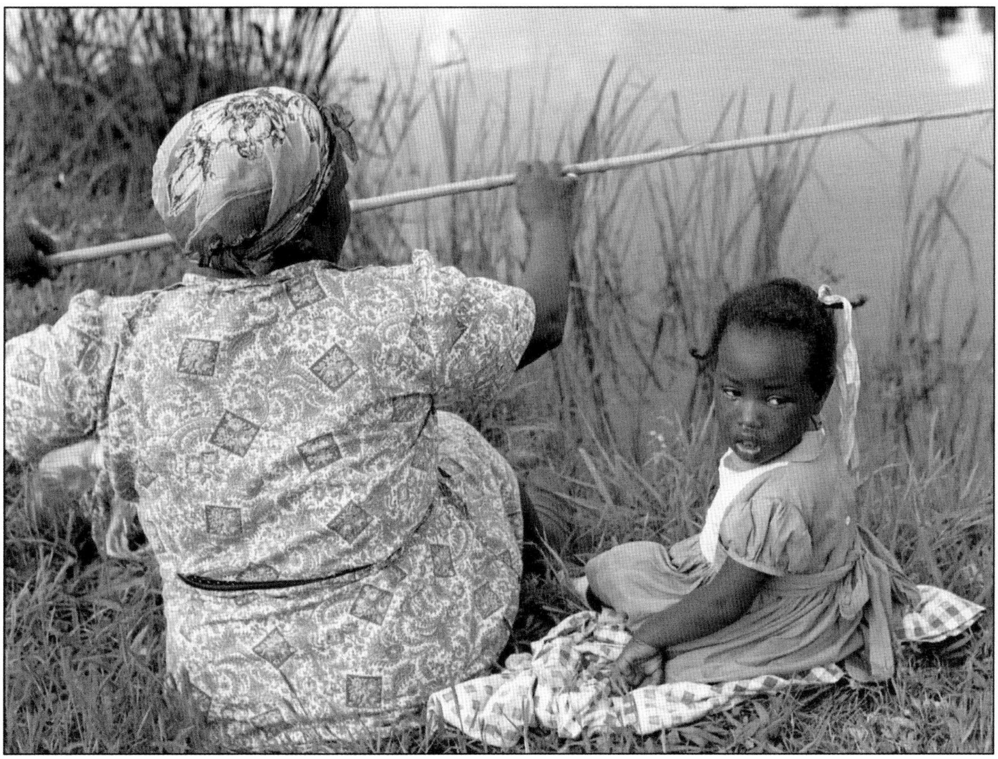

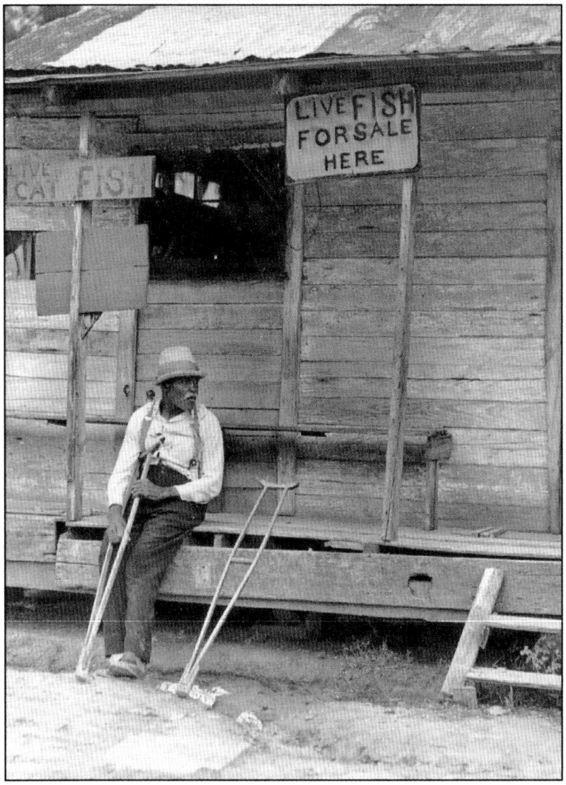

An injured man sits outside a fish market near Black Lake. Fishing, which required minimal labor, allowed a physically challenged person a way to make a living. Black Lake Bayou forms part of the boundary between Natchitoches Parish and Red River Parish. (Courtesy of the Library of Congress.)

A group of Eastern Star members meet in 1954. The Order of the Eastern Star, a fraternal organization, gained popularity among African Americans because of its principle of brotherhood. Herbert Baptiste described it in this manner: "If somebody needed help in the community, these brethrens would get together and help them because they had pledged fraternal loyalty." (Courtesy of John Thomas Guillet.)

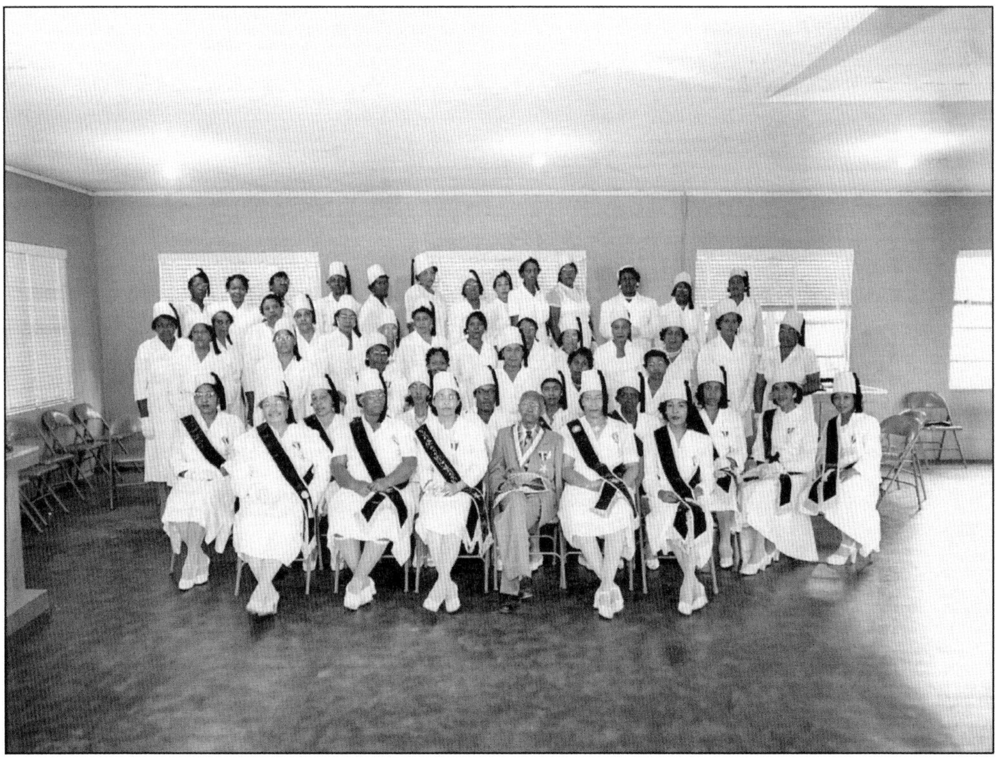

Five

People, Places, and Things

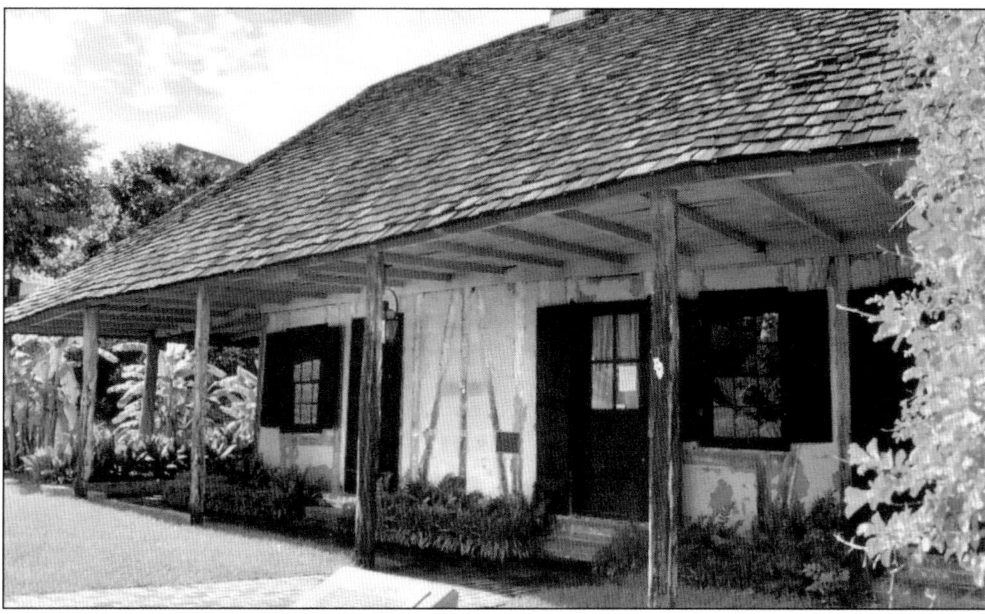

Hyves Pacalé was about 60 years old when his owner, the widow Marie Leclair D'herbanne died. D'herbanne's succession papers placed Pacalé's value at $100, and it is believed his skills as a carpenter allowed him to earn the money to buy his freedom. In time, he also manumitted his wife and daughter. Pacalé is credited with constructing the building in this image, which is listed in the National Register of Historic Places as the Roque House. The Natchitoches Historic Foundation moved this building from down river to its current location in the 1970s. (Courtesy of Candice Pauley, Cane River National Heritage Area.)

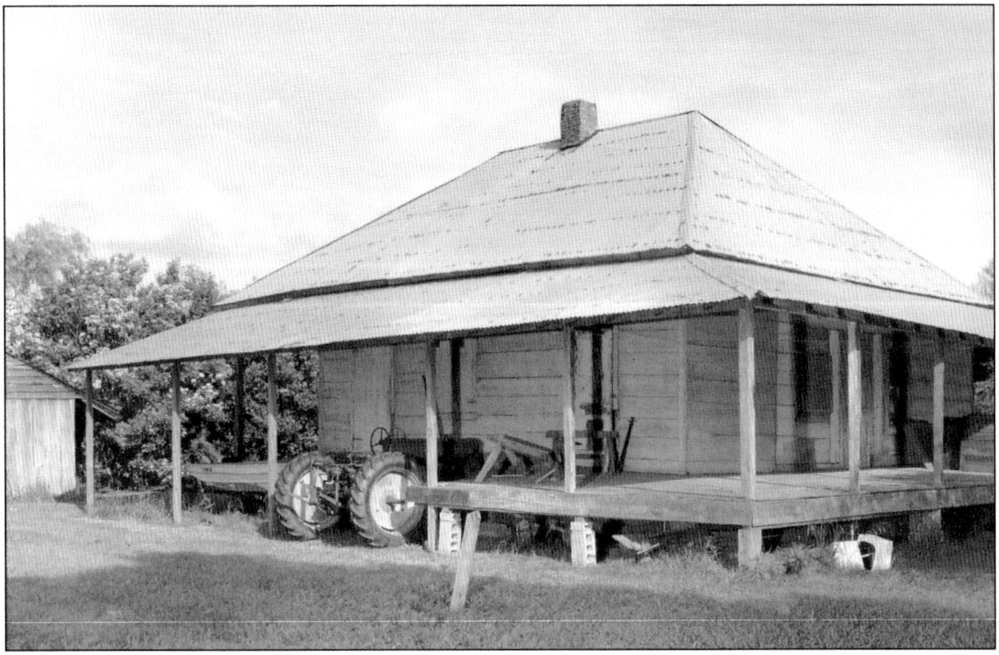

Marie Thérèse Coincoin, believed to be an African-born slave, is credited with being the matriarch of the community of Creoles who inhabit Isle Breville. Purchased in the late 1770s by French planter Pierre Metoyer, Coincoin and Metoyer joined in a relationship that produced 10 children and lasted for several years. Metoyer later freed Coincoin, and she and some of their descendants became some of the most prosperous slave-owning families in the region. Archaeologists Kevin McDonald and David Morgan are currently studying this home, which was once thought to belong to Coincoin. (Courtesy of the Historic American Buildings Survey, photographer James Rosenthal.)

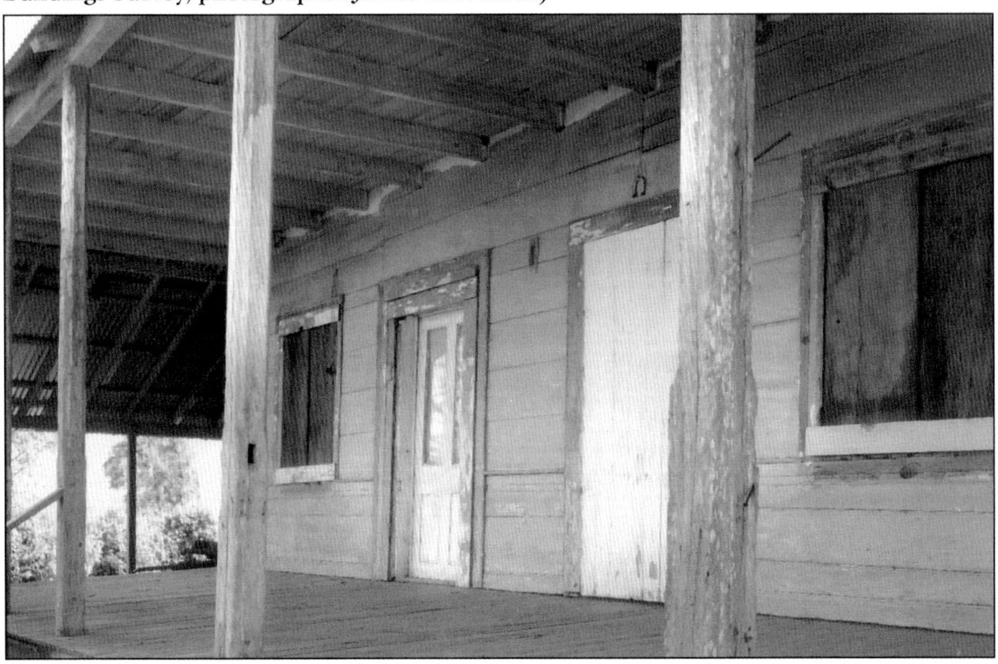

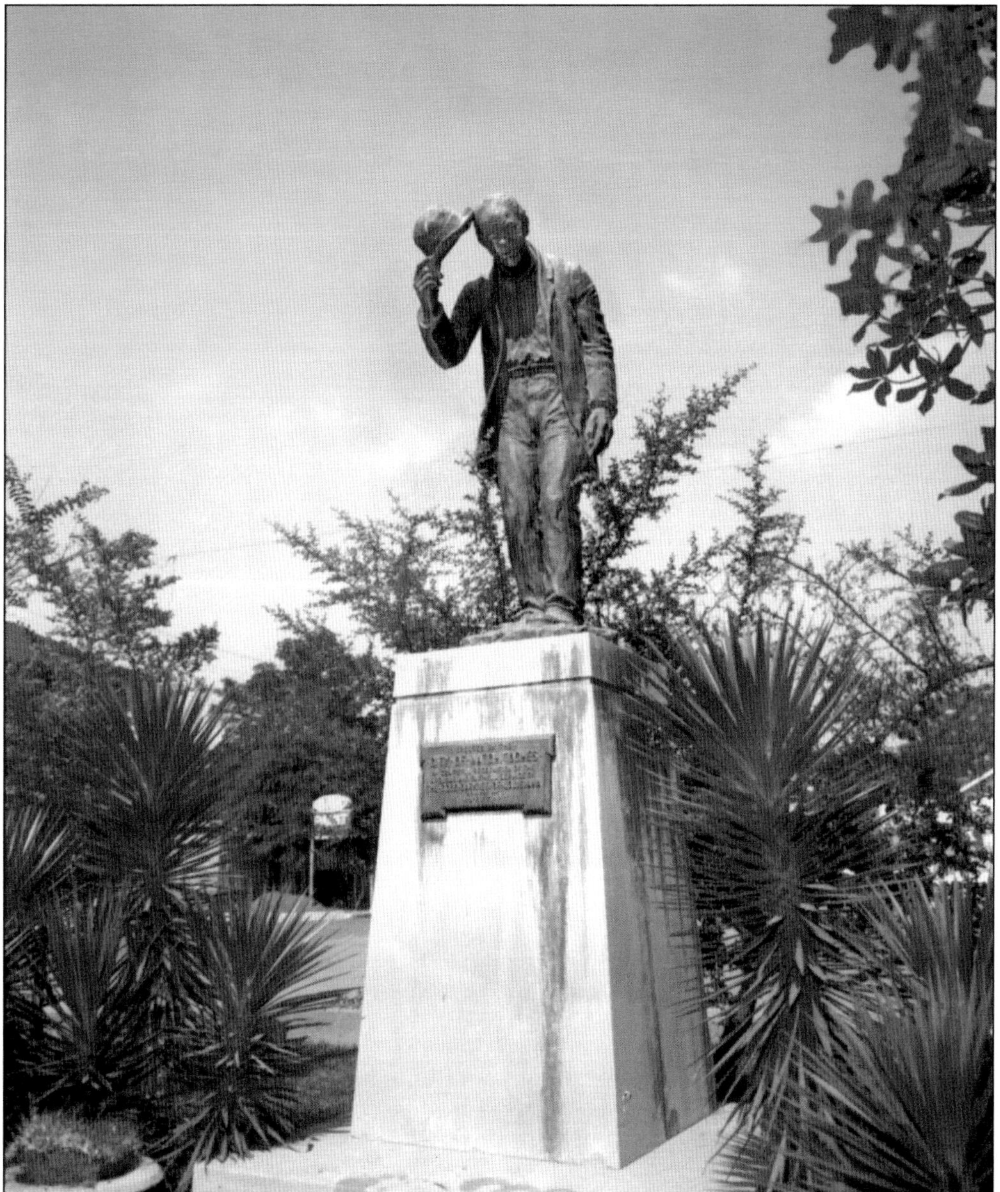

"The Good Darkey" statue, also known as "Uncle Jack," was displayed for 41 years at the corner of Washington and Lafayette Streets in the city of Natchitoches. The statue depicted an elderly black man with head and shoulders bent downward while holding a hat in his hand. Jackson Bryan, a prominent member of Natchitoches' social and political leadership, conceived the idea for the statue and convinced city officials to erect the statue in 1927. This controversial sculpture created a rift between some citizens of Natchitoches' black and white communities at the height of the civil rights movement. The plaque on the base of the statue reads: "Erected by the City of Natchitoches in grateful recognition of the arduous and faithful service of the good darkies of Louisiana. Donor J. L. Bryan, 1927." (Courtesy of Cammie Henry Research Center, Northwestern State University.)

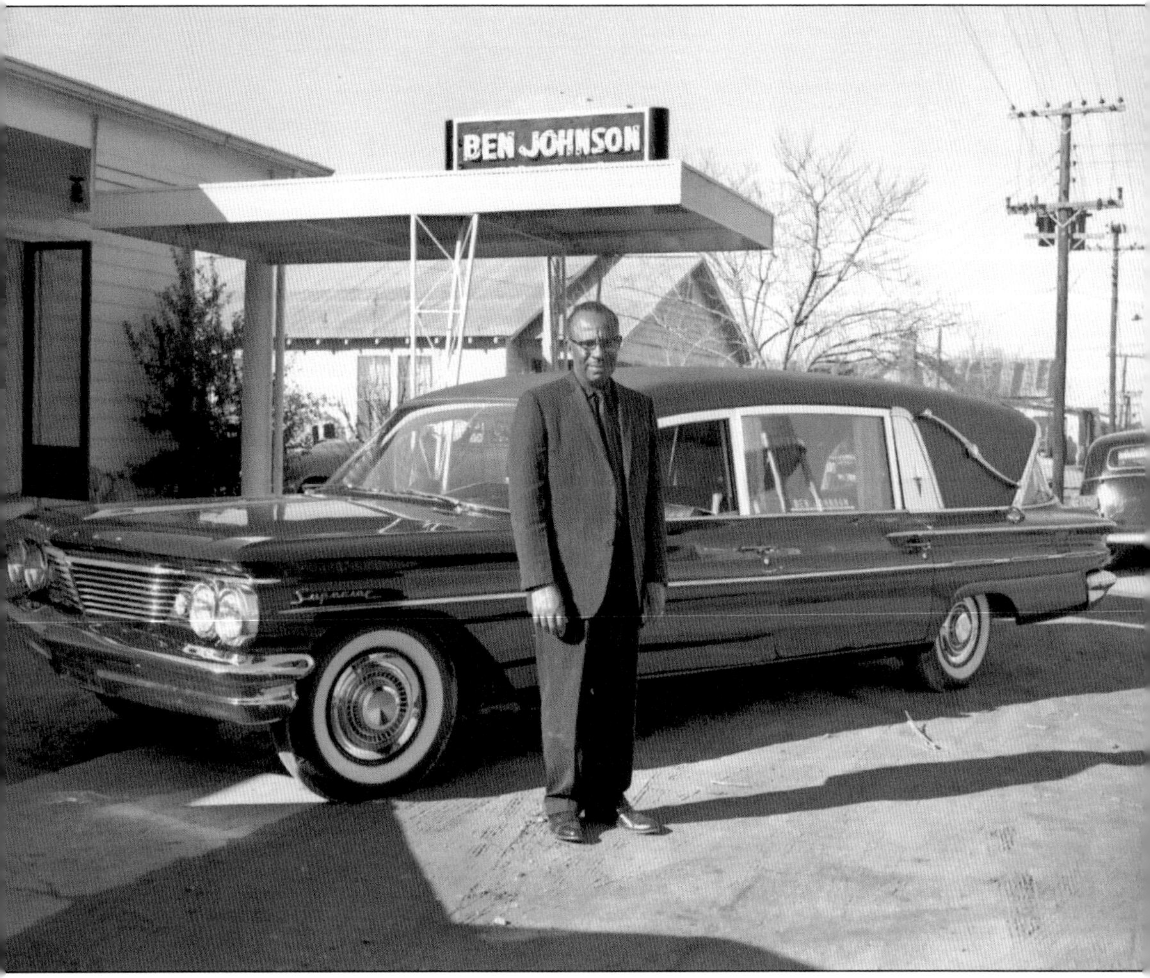

Ben D. Johnson, born in Campti, Louisiana, in 1910, was one of the most influential men in Natchitoches. Johnson's career began with the establishment of Winnfield Funeral Home in the town of Winnfield, Louisiana, in 1932. Later he joined forces with local ministers and created the Winnfield Colored Burial Association, which provided financial assistance to help bury poor African Americans. This business endeavor was shortly followed by the creation of the Winnfield Casket Company. Johnson received the Man-of-the-Year award from the Natchitoches Chamber of Commerce for helping to stop a potential race riot in the city in 1974. Johnson passed away at the age of 93 in 2005. The simple words of his epitaph perhaps best describe him. They read, "I Tried." (Courtesy of Cammie Henry Research Center, Northwestern State University.)

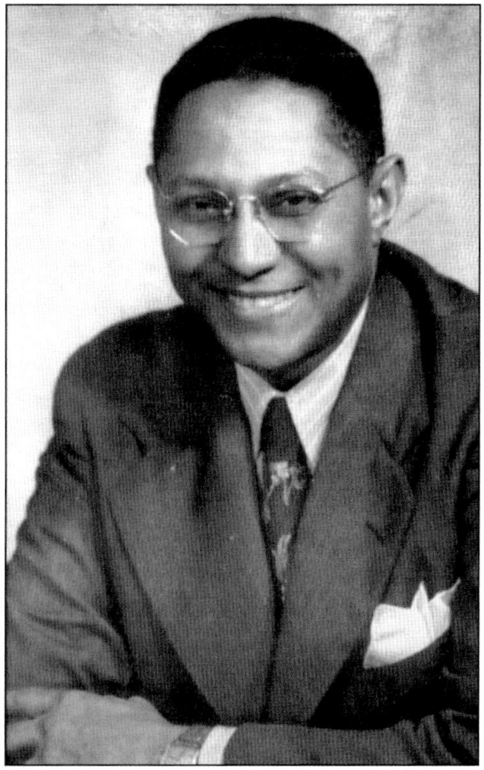

Dr. Edward Johnson and his wife, Crittie, were influential leaders in Natchitoches' African American community. Edward attended McHarry Medical School in Tennessee, and Crittie became one of the first black female morticians in the state. Their home, located at 822 Fifth Street, often provided a haven for visiting guests, which local legend states included the Honorable Thurgood Marshall. When Dr. Johnson suffered a stroke in the 1960s, his home was renovated to include a doctor's office for him and a mortuary for his wife's business. (Courtesy of Billye Sue Johnson.)

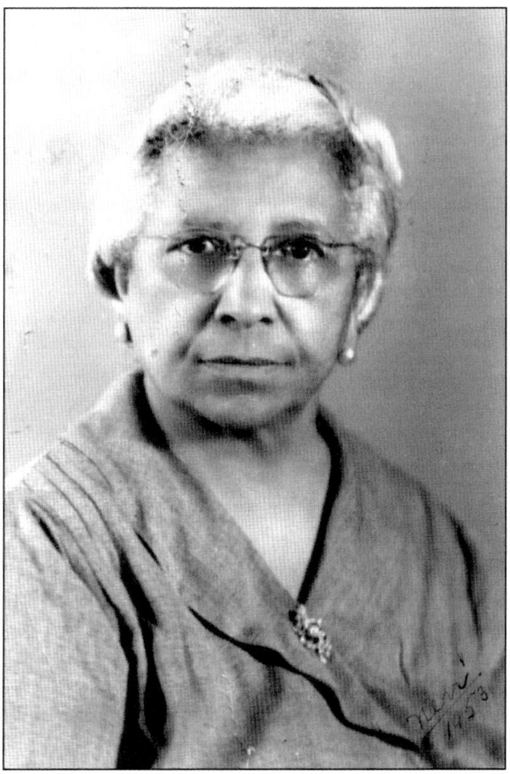

Shown here is Beatrice Cecelia Lewis Breda, the eldest daughter of John Gideon Lewis Sr. Breda was a home economics teacher and the unofficial dean of female teachers at Central High School. After retirement, she became a parish librarian at the Carver Branch Library located on Jackson Square in town. (Courtesy of Edward Ward Jr.)

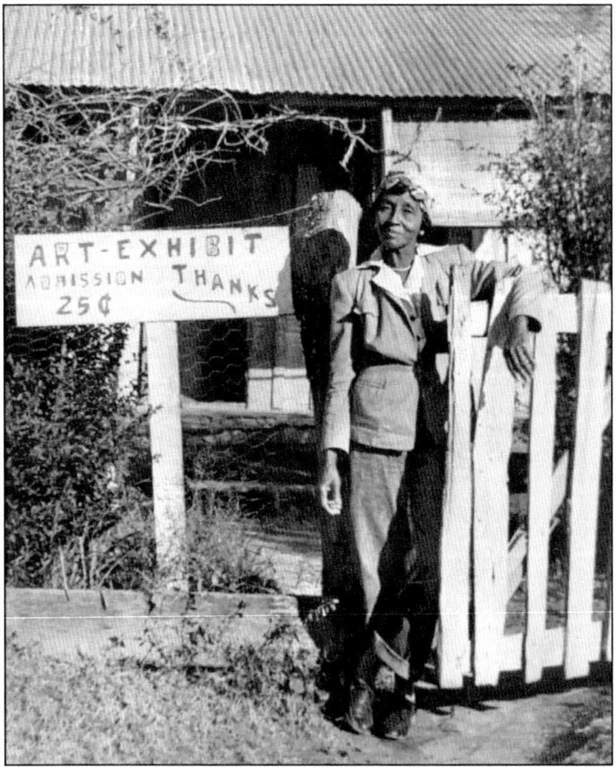

Clementine Hunter stands at the gate outside her home to greet arriving guests at an exhibit held on the grounds of Melrose Plantation. Some of her earliest paintings were traded to neighbors and collectors for butter and eggs. Today a Clementine Hunter painting may be valued at several thousand dollars. (Courtesy of Cammie Henry Research Center, Northwestern State University.)

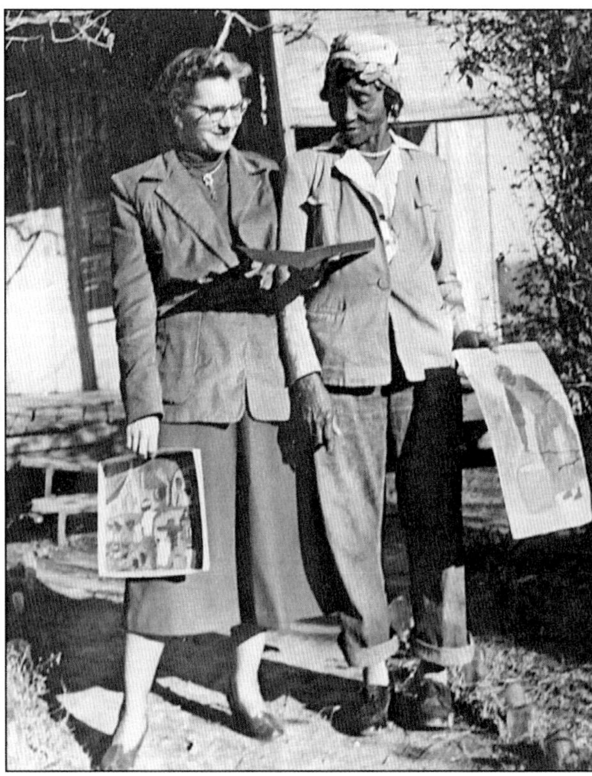

Clementine Hunter and her friend, Carolyn Ramsey, a documentary filmmaker, stand together at Hunter's exhibit opening. Hunter's images are some of the best examples of agricultural practices in the region prior to the mechanization of farming techniques. Hunter was the first African American to host her own exhibit at the New Orleans Museum of Art. (Courtesy of Cammie Henry Research Center, Northwestern State University.)

Edward Ward Jr. sits in his father's arms outside an air force barrack in Texas. Edward Albert Johnson Jr., son of Dr. Edward and Crittie Johnson, stands next to them. The families maintained a friendship for more than 20 years. (Courtesy of Edward Ward Jr.)

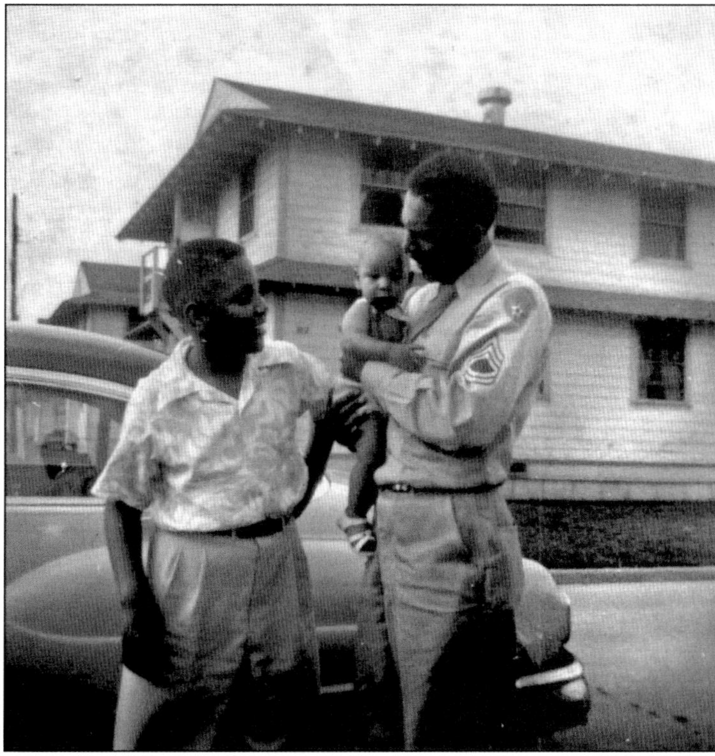

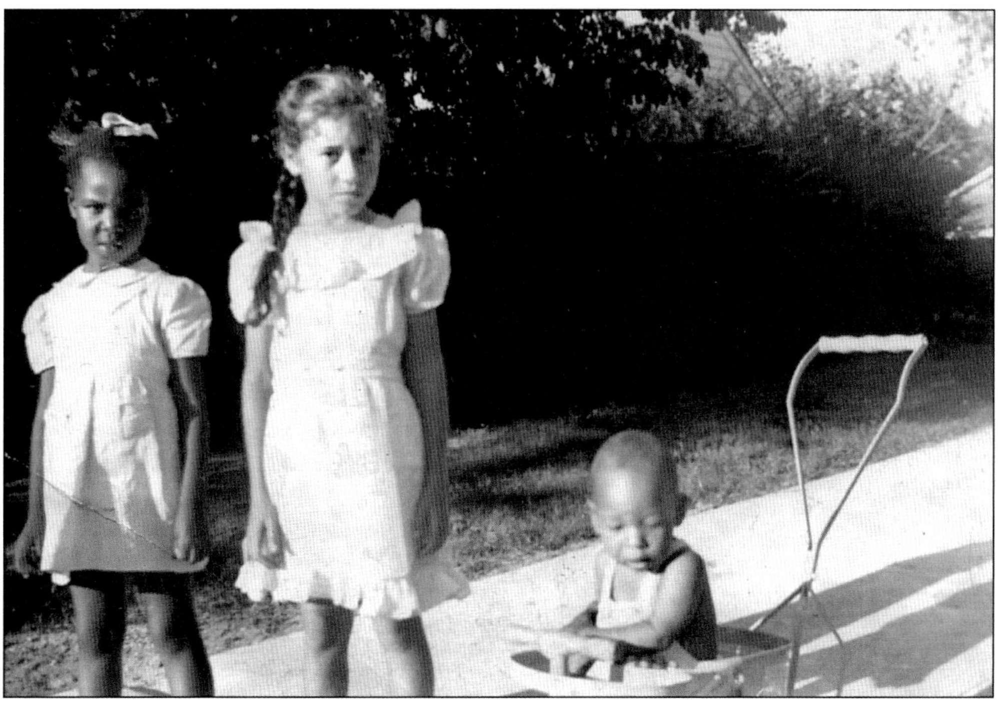

Barbara Jo Mitchell-Johnson (left) and Mary Catherine LaCour-Llorence (center) stand next to Edward Ward Jr. Barbara is the wife of Rev. Leo Walker Sr. of St. Paul Baptist Church. Mary was Edward's next-door neighbor for many years. (Courtesy of Edward Ward Jr.)

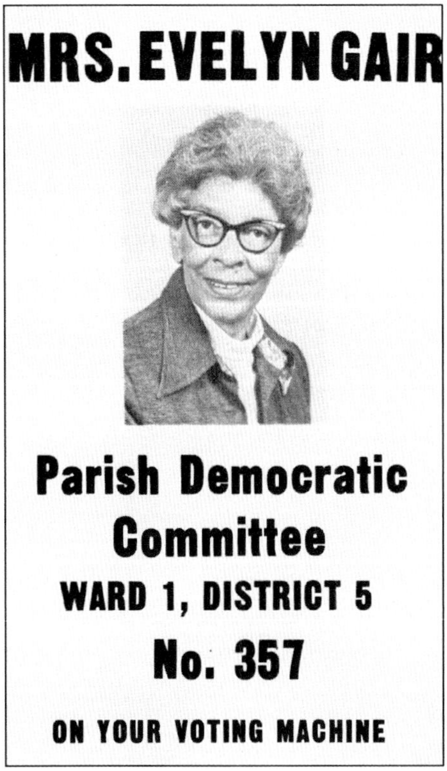
MRS. EVELYN GAIR

Parish Democratic Committee

WARD 1, DISTRICT 5

No. 357

ON YOUR VOTING MACHINE

Evelyn Tucker Gair Jones came to Natchitoches in 1945 and assumed the position of assistant home demonstration agent for work with blacks. "That was my title then. I worked with that for four years, and then I was a little bit tired of running up and down the road, so I sought a job in the schools," she said. Unfortunately, she did not win this election. (Courtesy of Edward Ward Jr.)

Johnson Dugas Jr. (left), Abraham Randolph Jr. (center), and Willie Dugas play a game of marbles. These boys were residents at Magnolia Plantation. (Courtesy of John Thomas Guillet.)

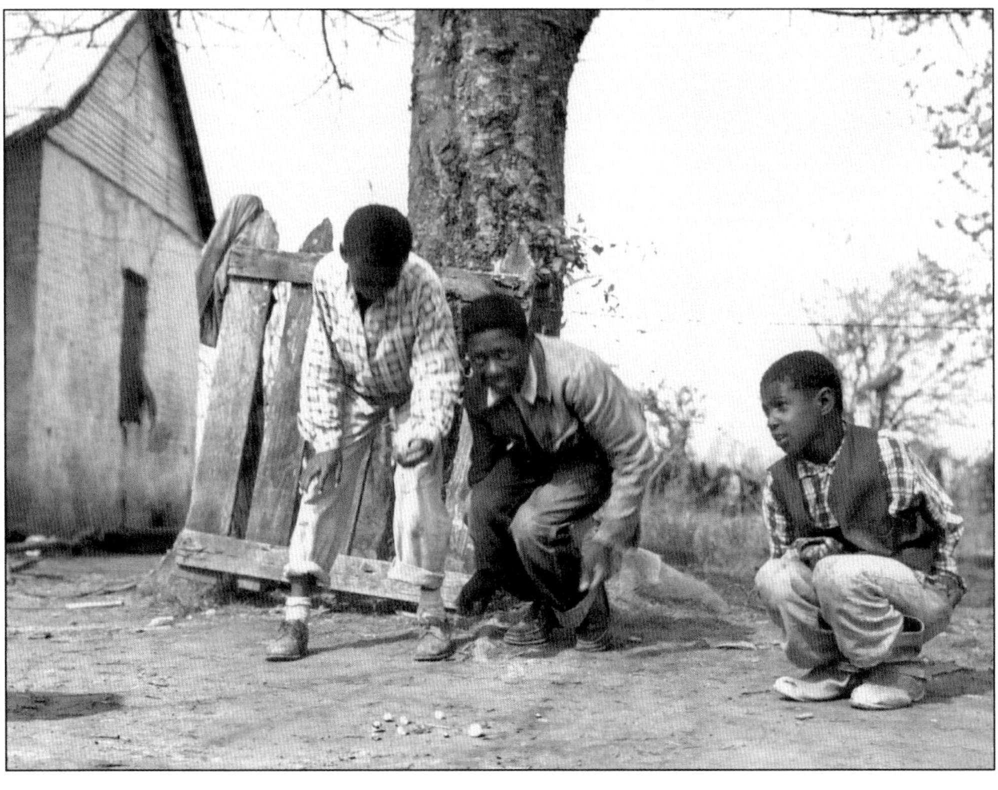

Ocie Lee Smith, father of singer O. C. Smith, lived and taught in Natchitoches for several years. Ocie Jr. changed the spelling of his name to O. C. a few years after joining the Count Basie Orchestra as its lead singer. O. C. is perhaps best known for his 1968 Grammy Award–winning hit "God Didn't Make Little Green Apples." (Courtesy of Edward Ward Jr.)

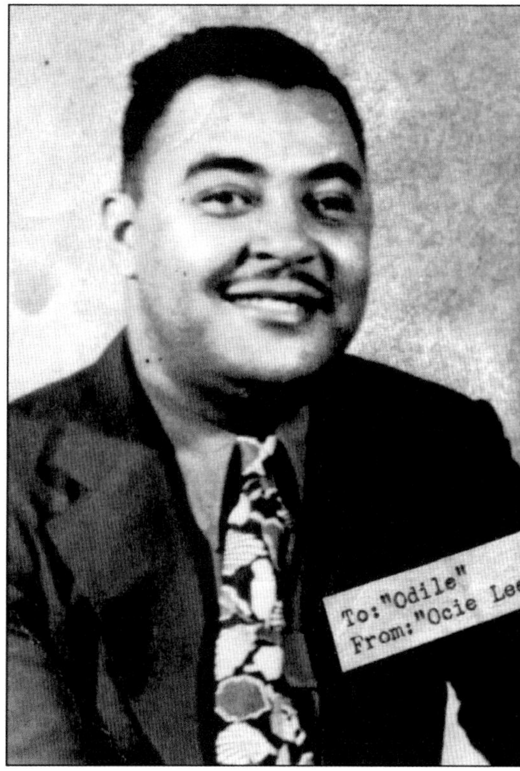

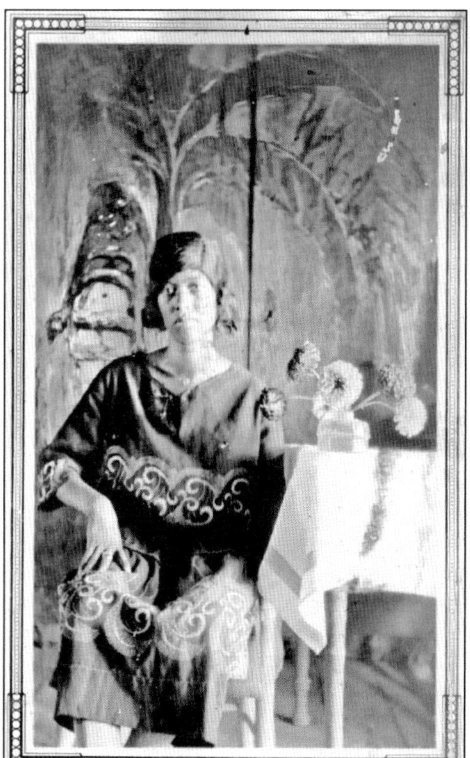

It is unclear where, or if, this photograph was taken in Natchitoches; however, it speaks to the attractiveness professional photography held for the emerging African American middle class. In the painted background is an image of Eve in the Garden of Eden. (Courtesy of Cammie Henry Research Center, Northwestern State University.)

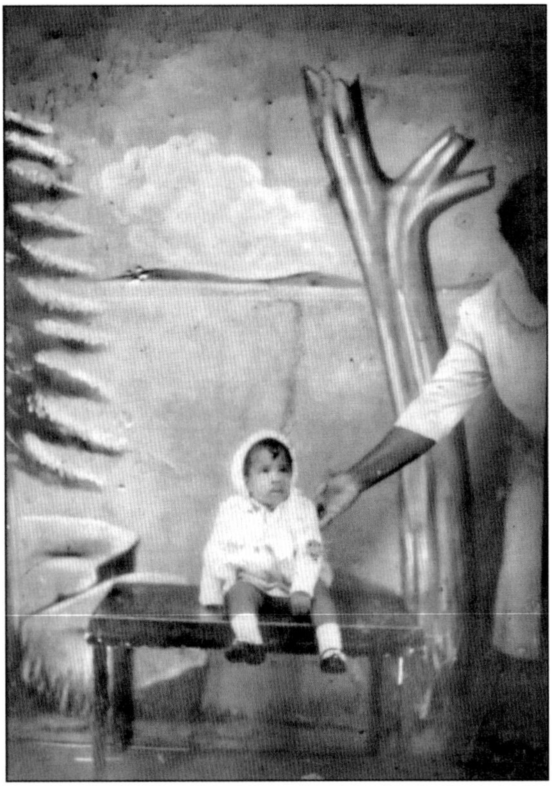

Here is another professional photography session with an uncooperative baby. Notice that the background image is more suited for a child. (Courtesy of Ida Ruth Mitchell-Hamilton.)

Catherine Law Jenkins assists her daughter, Lillian, who is celebrating her first birthday. Catherine at one time lived in the home of Dr. and Mrs. Edward Johnson in order to finish high school in Natchitoches. Her hometown of Powhatan did not have a local high school. The 1950s-era radio and television, factory-made high chair, sheer curtains, and decorated tablecloth all attest to an emerging black middle class in Natchitoches. (Courtesy of Edward Ward Jr.)

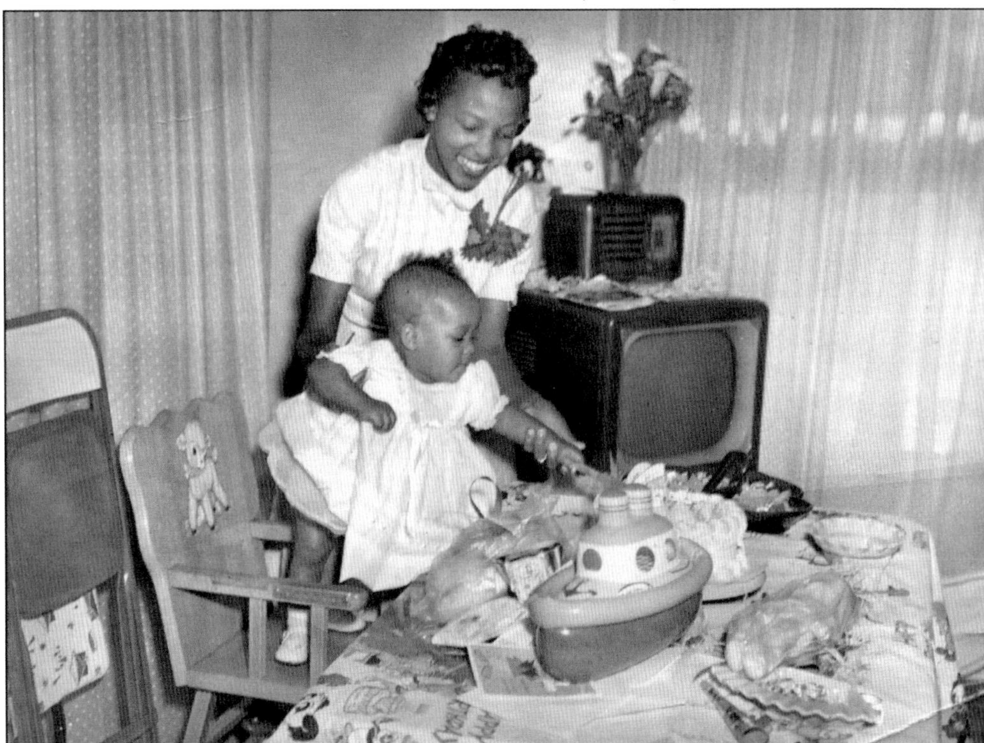

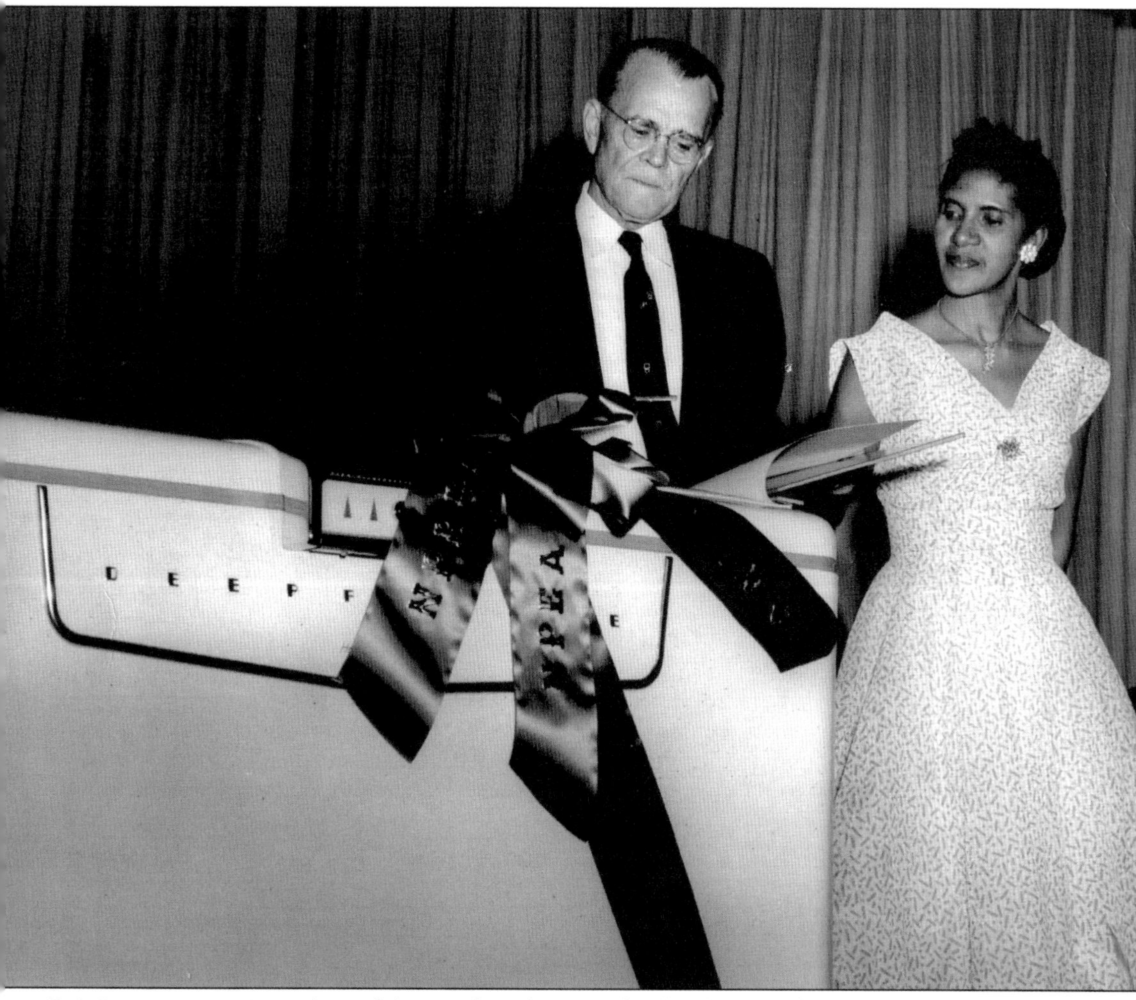

E. A. Lee was superintendent of the Natchitoches Parish school system for more than 20 years. During his tenure, many of the modern school buildings were built on African American campuses. At this retirement party, Lee received a new freezer from the Natchitoches Parish Education Association, which was comprised of multi-cultured teachers. Alberta Harrison (right) presents the gift on behalf of the Jeanes supervisors. (Courtesy of Edward Ward Jr.)

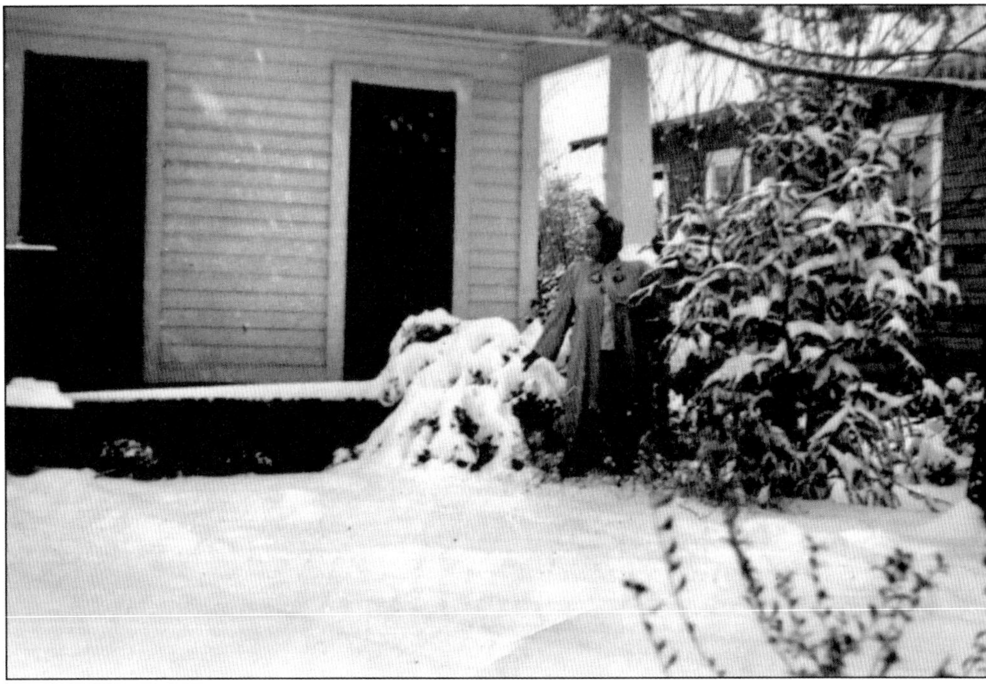

Odile Cage Ward stands above outside her home at 831 Fifth Street. This structure was built on what was once a fishing pond. It is located directly across the street from the former residence of Dr. Edward Johnson at 822 Fifth Street. (Courtesy of Edward Ward Jr.)

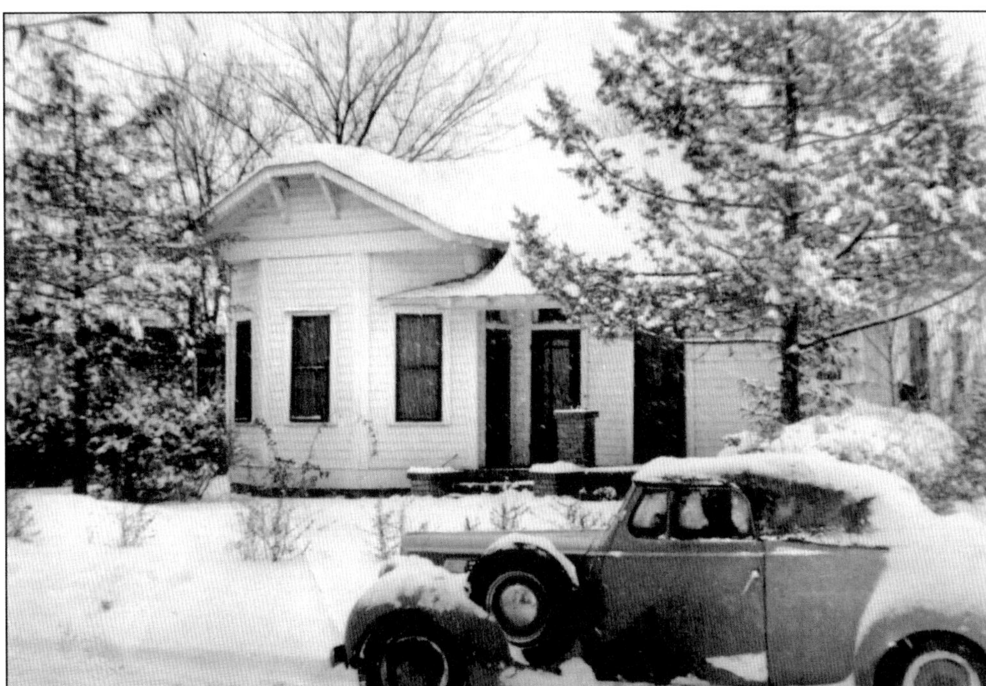

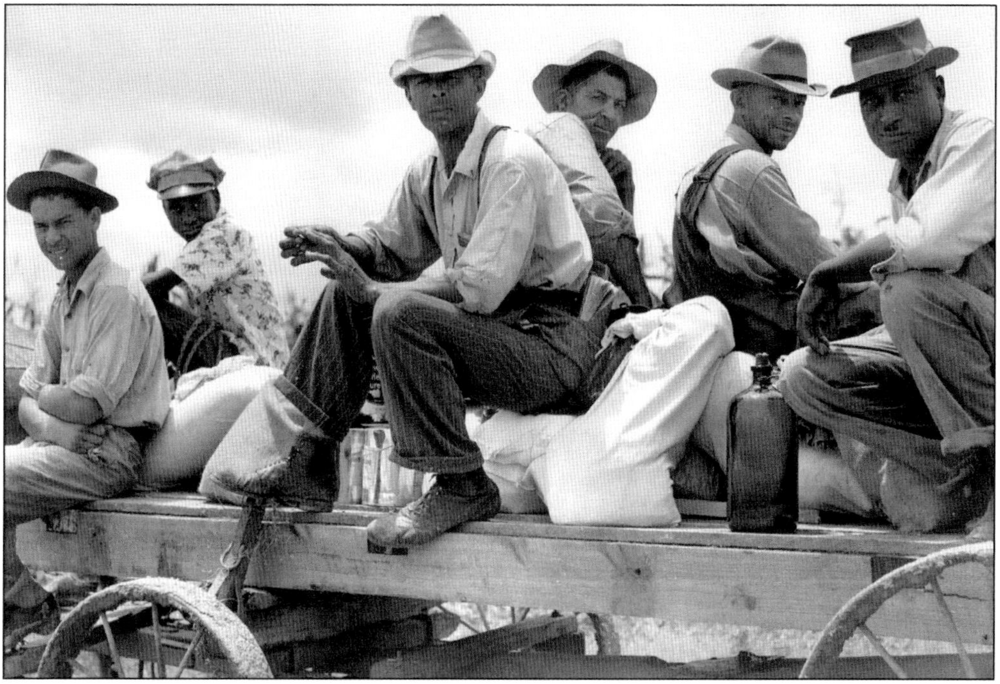

Creoles and African Americans ride together after purchasing commodities for their homes near Melrose Plantation. Plantation stores often supplied rural folks with items they could not provide for themselves, like flour, rice, liquor, and certain medicines. (Courtesy of the Library of Congress.)

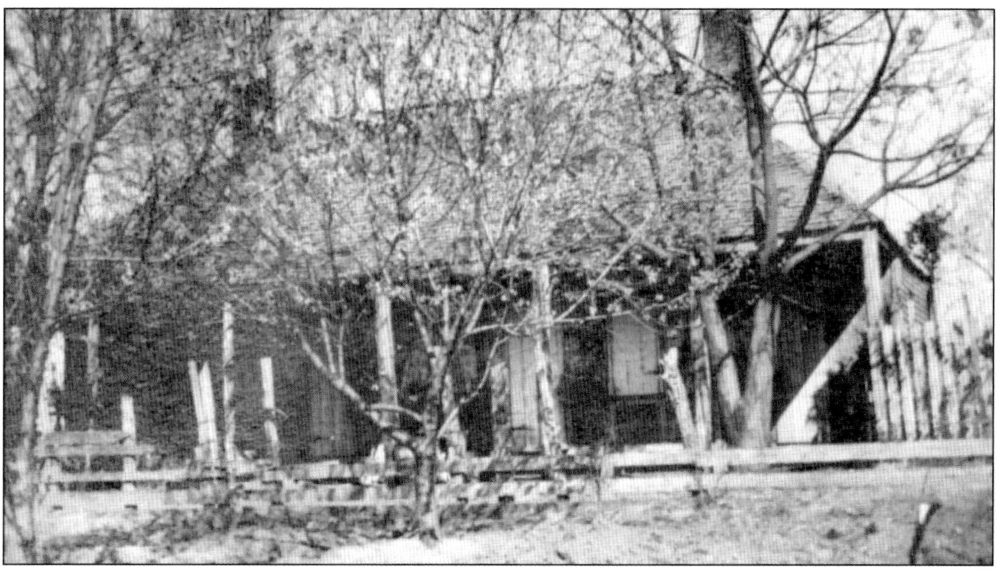

Louis Metoyer, son of Marie Thérèse Coincoin and Pierre Metoyer, built and managed a plantation until 1847 when it was sold. Perhaps the oldest structure on the plantation, the Yucca House, was built between 1796 and 1814 and provides an excellent example of French Creole architecture. This modest-looking structure was the first big house on the plantation, which later became known as Melrose Plantation. (Courtesy of Cammie Henry Research Center, Northwestern State University.)

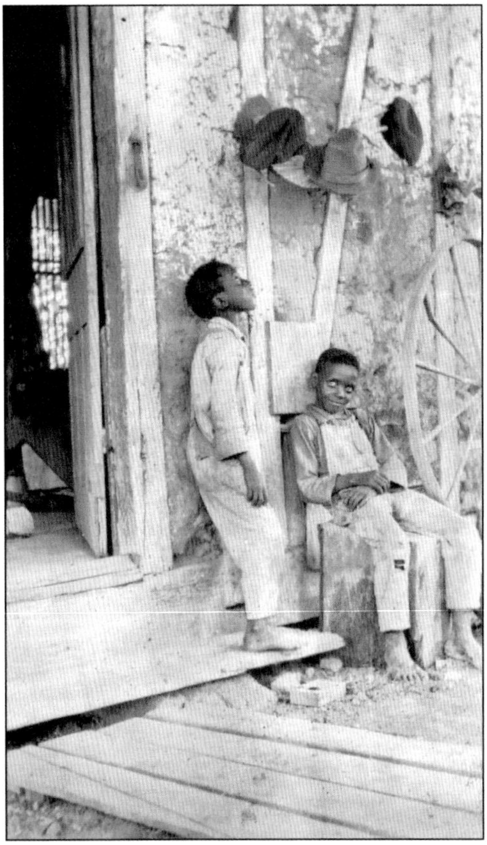

Two young boys sit outside the Yucca House on Melrose Plantation. This building is constructed with a technique called bousillage; a mixture of clay, animal hair, and Spanish moss is placed between the boards to form the walls. (Courtesy of Cammie Henry Research Center, Northwestern State University.)

Discarded spinning wheels, a toy car, furniture, and bottles suggest that this room served as a storage space. It is thought to have been a room located on Melrose Plantation. (Courtesy of Cammie Henry Research Center, Northwestern State University.)

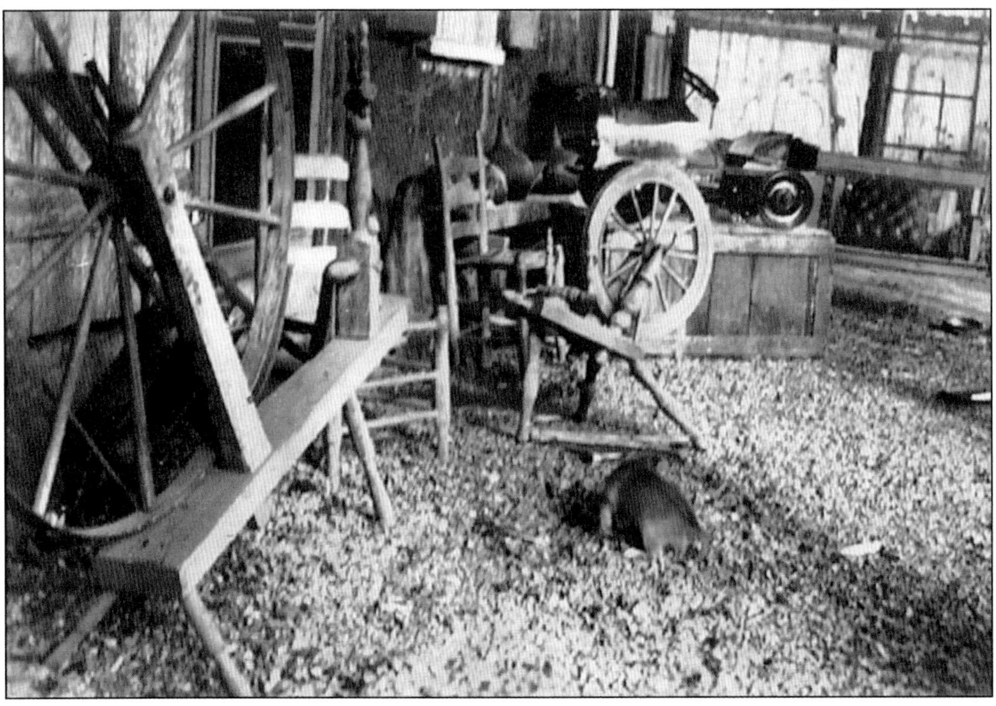

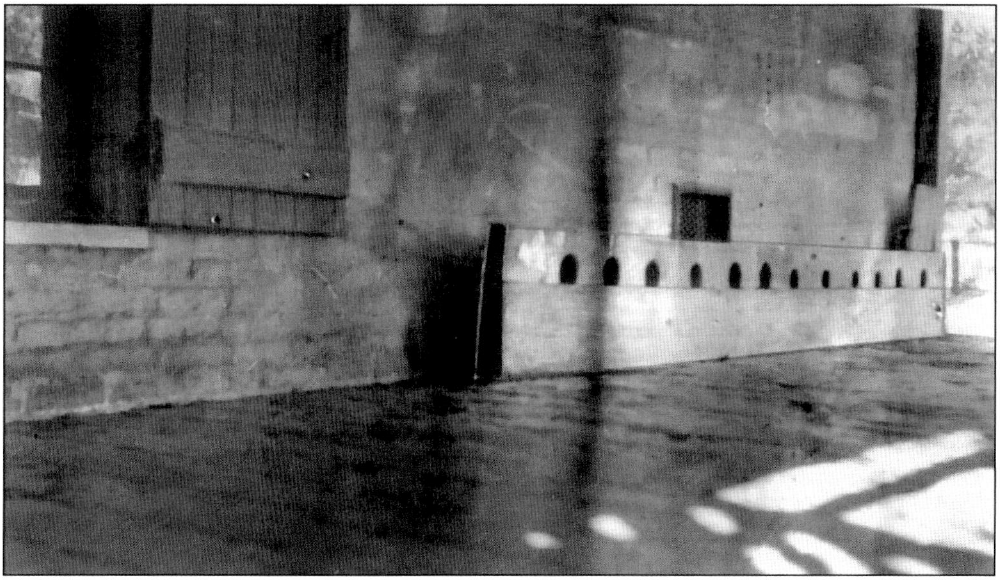

This slave stock now sits abandoned at the main house at Magnolia Plantation. This device was used to punish enslaved laborers by making them lie on their backs with ankles in the holes. The stocks were exhibited at the grand opening of Cane River Creole National Historical Park in May 2005. (Courtesy of Cammie Henry Research Center, Northwestern State University.)

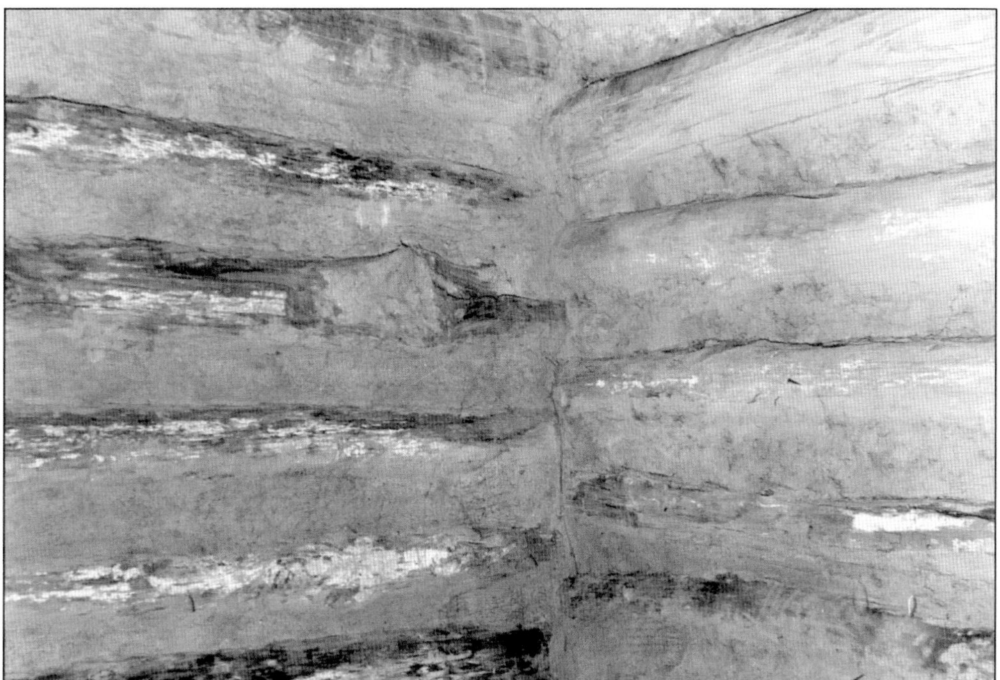

Pictured here is a portion of a wall made with a process known as chinking. This photograph was taken at Melrose Plantation, and the building is thought to have stored cottonseeds, corn, or hay. The Works Progress Administration program took this image in the 1940s. (Courtesy of the Library of Congress.)

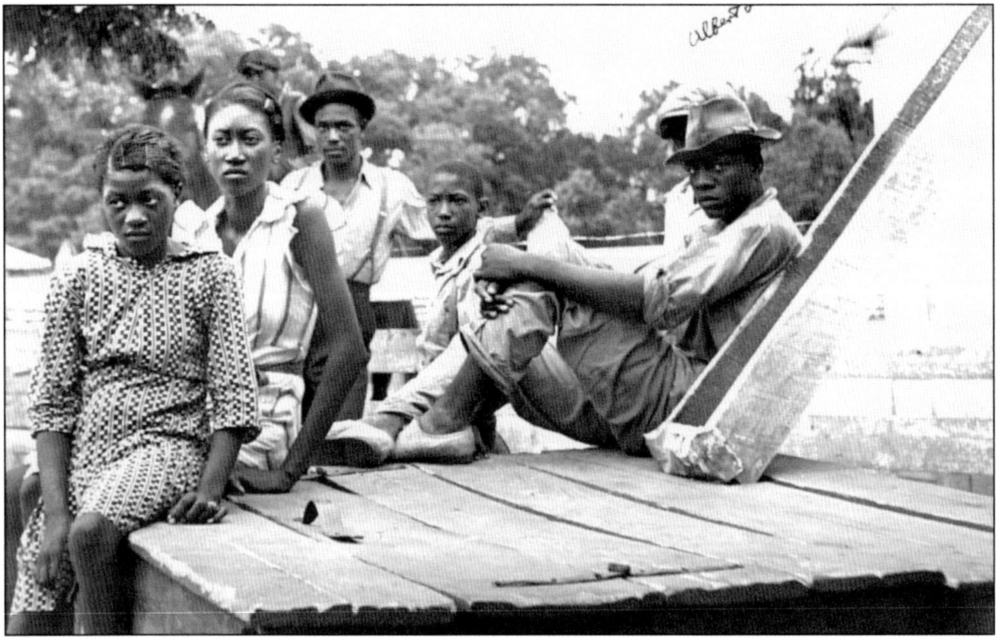

A group of young people sits on the cistern outside the Magnolia Plantation store. Leo Metoyer recalled going to the store at Oakland Plantation as a child to buy candy or make purchases for adults. Jacques A. Prud'homme established the store about 1874. (Courtesy of Ambrose Hertzog Jr.)

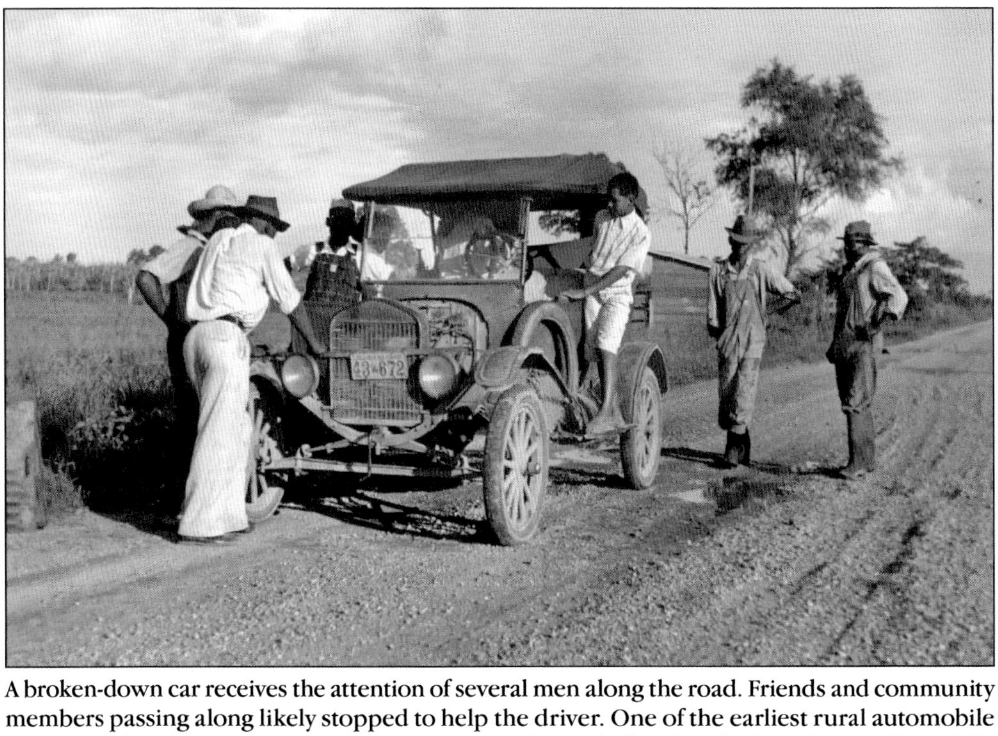

A broken-down car receives the attention of several men along the road. Friends and community members passing along likely stopped to help the driver. One of the earliest rural automobile owners in the African American community was the Wade family, who bought a Ford Model T for $65 in the mid-1940s. (Courtesy of the Library of Congress.)

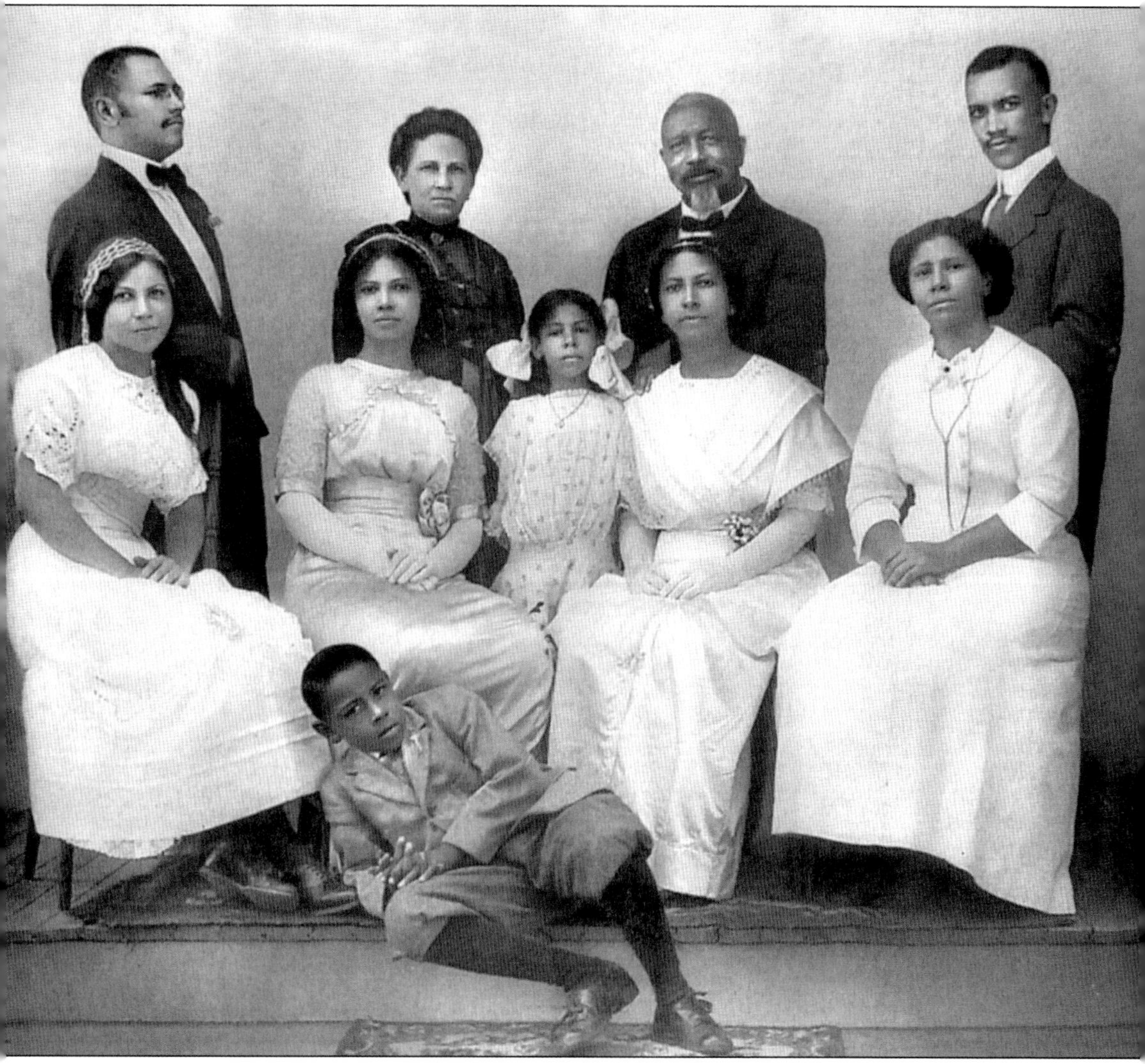

The Corinthian Lodge and the Dawn of Light Lodge No. 22 formed in Natchitoches in the late 19th century under the leadership of John Gideon Lewis Sr. (second from left), who arrived in the area from Canada. The Prince Hall Masons under Lewis's direction became an integral part of Natchitoches' African American community. The first black printing company in Natchitoches formed in 1910 and published a Masonic journal known as *The Plum Line*. After Lewis's death in 1931, his son, John Jr., became the next leader of the organization. The Corinthian Lodge no longer exists; however, the Dawn of Light Lodge is still located at 920 Fifth Street. (Courtesy of the Lewis family.)

Bibliography

Anderson, Eric and Alfred Moss Jr. *Dangerous Donations: Northern Philanthropy and Southern Black Education, 1902–1930*. Columbia, MO: The University of Missouri Press, 1999.

Breedlove, Caroline. "Bermuda/Oakland Plantation, 1830–1880." Natchitoches, LA: unpublished master's thesis, 1999.

Cunningham, Floyd. "Wandering in the Wilderness: Black Baptist Thought After Emancipation." D. Nieman, ed. *African American Life, 1861–1900: Church and Community Among Black Southerners, 1865–1900*. 1994: 186–199.

docsouth.unc.edu/fpn/washeducation/washing.html

Dollar, Susan. *The Freedmen's Bureau Schools of Natchitoches Parish, Louisiana, 1865–1868*. Natchitoches, LA: Northwestern State University Press, 1998.

Fry, Gladys Marie. *Stitched from the Soul: Slave Quilts from the Antebellum South*. Chapel Hill, NC: University of North Carolina, 2002.

Genovese, Eugene. *Roll, Jordan, Roll: The World the Slaves Made*. New York: Vintage Books, 1976.

Grim, Valarie. "African American Rural Culture, 1900–1950." R. Douglas Hurt, ed. *African American Life: In the Rural South, 1900–1950*. 2003: 108–128.

Haynie, Sandra Prud'homme. *Legends of Oakland Plantation: The Prud'hommes of Natchitoches Parish*. Shreveport, LA: LA Press Company, 2001.

Keel, Bennie C. with Christina Miller and Marc Tiemann. *A Comprehensive Subsurface Investigation at Magnolia Plantation*. Tallahassee, FL: Southeast Archaeological Center, National Park Service, 1999.

Malone, Ann. *Sweet Chariot: Slave Family and Household Structure in Nineteenth-Century Louisiana*. Chapel Hill, NC: University of North Carolina Press, 1996.

MacDonald, Kelvin, David Morgan, and Fiona Handley. "Cane River: The Archaeology of 'Free People of Color' in Colonial Louisiana." *Archaeology International* 6. 2002–2003: 52–55.

Mills, Gary. *The Forgotten People: Cane River's Creoles of Color*. Baton Rouge, LA: Louisiana State University Press, 1977.

Prud'homme Family Papers. Southern Historical Collection, Wilson Library. University of North Carolina at Chapel Hill.

Shiver, Art and Tom Whitehead. *Clementine Hunter: The African House Murals*. Natchitoches, LA: Northwestern State University Press, 2005.

Wilson, Carter A. *Racism: From Slavery to Advanced Capitalism*. Thousand Oaks, CA: Sage Publications, 1996.

www.cr.nps.gov/archeology/pubs/studies/study04P.htm

INDEX